Q&A
Equity
Trusts

Routledge Questions & Answers Series

Each Routledge Q&A contains questions on topics commonly found on exam papers, with comprehensive suggested answers. The titles are written by lecturers who are also examiners, so the student gains an important insight into exactly what examiners are looking for in an answer. This makes them excellent revision and practice guides.

Titles in the series:

Q&A Company Law
Q&A Commercial Law
Q&A Contract Law
Q&A Criminal Law
Q&A Employment Law
Q&A English Legal System
Q&A Equity and Trusts
Q&A European Union Law
Q&A Evidence
Q&A Family Law
Q&A Intellectual Property Law
Q&A Jurisprudence
Q&A Land Law
Q&A Medical Law
Q&A Public Law
Q&A Torts

For a full listing, visit www.routledge.com/cw/revision

Q&A
Equity and
Trusts

Mohamed Ramjohn

Routledge
Taylor & Francis Group

LONDON AND NEW YORK

Ninth edition published 2015
by Routledge
2 Park Square, Milton Park, Abingdon, Oxon OX14 4RN

and by Routledge
711 Third Avenue, New York, NY 10017

Routledge is an imprint of the Taylor & Francis Group, an informa business

First edition published by Cavendish Publishing 1995
Eighth edition published by Routledge 2013

British Library Cataloguing in Publication Data
A catalogue record for this book is available from the British Library

Library of Congress Cataloging in Publication Data
A catalog record for this book has been requested

ISBN: 978-1-138-78007-1 (pbk)
ISBN: 978-1-315-77092-5 (ebk)

Typeset in TheSans
by Wearset Ltd, Boldon, Tyne and Wear

Printed and bound in Great Britain by
TJ International Ltd, Padstow, Cornwall

Contents

Table of Cases

Table of Legislation

■ European Legislation

Guide to the Companion Website

www.routledge.com/cw/revision

Visit the Law Revision website to discover a comprehensive range of resources designed to enhance your learning experience.

The Good, The Fair, & The Ugly

Good essays are the gateway to top marks. This interactive tutorial provides sample essays together with voice-over commentary and tips for successful exam essays, written by our Q&A authors themselves.

Multiple Choice Questions

Knowledge is the foundation of every good essay. Focusing on key examination themes, these MCQs have been written to test your knowledge and understanding of each subject in the book.

Bonus Q&As

Having studied our exam advice, put your revision into practice and test your essay writing skills with our additional online questions and answers.

Introduction

The trust concept has been heralded as a unique development of English law over the centuries and its principles are enshrined essentially in case law that has occasionally been tempered by statutory intervention. The principles of trusts law were initially created out of necessity to achieve fairness or justice to litigants who were aggrieved by the harshness of the common law. Today, as the principles of trusts law have become settled, some of its rules are still regarded as relatively flexible and adaptable enough to meet the changing needs of modern society. Such developments are best understood by considering the exposition of judges and the precise words used in statutes.

Many students are initially filled with trepidation in reading this module at undergraduate level (or its equivalent). This may be due to the inherently complex nature of property law concepts, its overlap with many other subject heads, such as contract law, commercial law, revenue law, land law, succession law, company law, bankruptcy law, etc., or the fine distinctions that judges sometimes make in an effort to resist undesirable precedents. That aside, the study of trusts law is stimulating, challenging and dynamic.

Students sometimes confess to being unclear about how to present answers to examination questions in trusts law. The aims of writing a book on questions and answers on trusts law are to assist the student in analysing a variety of standard examination questions and demonstrating some of the techniques involved in writing examination answers. Although this book is not intended to be a substitute for the reading of textbooks, cases, statutes and articles, it is a book full of questions and answers and could be an important acquisition that you, as a student, make in preparation for your examination. Having experienced similar questions on subjects covered in the syllabus will give you a tremendous advantage and greater confidence before sitting down to write the examination. Having actually answered, say, 50 questions on the same topics as those on which you are to be examined must give you a good chance of meeting the complexities and peculiarities that arise in an examination paper on trusts law.

The book is laid out by dividing the subject into 12 chapters. Each chapter commences with an introduction to the topic by summarising the salient points within the chapter. This is followed by a variety of essay and problem questions that are engineered within the confines of the issues raised in each chapter. Each question is analysed with an answer plan for quick reference and each chapter contains questions with 'aim higher' and 'common pitfalls' comments for the benefit of students.

ADVICE ON REVISION AND EXAMINATION TECHNIQUE

1. Revision Strategy

There is no substitute for hard work. During this time (revision) it is of the utmost importance that you concentrate on a full and structured revision of the subject. Listed below are some guidelines to assist you in your revision.

(i) Draft a revision plan that will give you sufficient time to revise each topic in full.

(ii) It is necessary to find the right balance in distributing your time to the various topics so that you do not concentrate on your weak topics at the expense of your strong ones.

(iii) Working from memory, devote some time (say 30 minutes) to jot down in your notebook what you consider to be the key points of any topic you have selected for your revision. Re-read the topic from the textbook and add any further points to the list in your notebook. This technique has the advantage of giving you an overview of the topic. This process will sharpen your ability to recognise topics (including relevant details) in dealing with examination questions.

(iv) Always work towards the examination. That is the object of revision. Obtain a generous selection of past examination papers and analyse examination questions on topics you have revised. Structure skeleton answers to these questions. In addition, if you have a friendly tutor, perhaps he or she may be persuaded to mark full examination answers with constructive comments. These answers should be written under simulated examination conditions. Note, however, that drafting full examination answers is fairly time-consuming. Your decision to undertake such a task would depend on the time that is available and, indeed, the enormous effort that is needed to compile full answers.

(v) Keep up to date with new articles and important cases. Examiners tend to be impressed by candidates who demonstrate knowledge of innovations in the law. Adopt the habit of reading one or more of the recent law journals. There is a wide selection of these available, such as *New Law Journal, Modern Law Review, Journal of Business Law, Conveyancing and Property Lawyer, Law Quarterly Review* and *Trust Law International*.

2. Examination Technique

The essence of a good answer to an examination question is one which has a sound structure with sub-headings, and which addresses the issues posed in the question. What follow are useful tips in presenting good examination answers under examination conditions.

(a) Take some time to read all the questions in the examination paper and select the ones with which you are most comfortable. If you are required to answer four questions from eight, then it is prudent to select the four questions that you wish to answer before you start writing. This process has the advantage of avoiding a late change of heart and consequent time wasting. You should bear in mind that the period spent in the examination hall is the most valuable time you may spend on the law of trusts. For these purposes your knowledge of the law is measured by the content of your examination script.

(b) Having selected the questions, it is most important that you are fully conversant with the facts of the problem or the focus of the essay. If necessary, re-read the question and underline or highlight key words or phrases.

(c) Plan your answers as quickly as possible by jotting down notes (cases, phrases and sections of statutes).

(d) Assemble the points in a logical order. This involves the structure of your answer. With a sound structure it is possible to build on it, and the structure itself ought to take top priority.

(e) Get stuck into the issues posed by the question. Avoid writing vague introductions or preambles to your answers. This is distinct from identifying the issues in the first paragraph. Identifying the issues goes some way in structuring your answer. It indicates to the examiner that you appreciate what he or she is asking you to deal with.

(f) Avoid rewriting the question. Many students believe (mistakenly) that they can, in effect, alter the emphasis of a question or even change it completely. Answer the specific question set.

(g) You should not assume that the examiner knows everything pertaining to the question. He or she probably does, but it is up to the examinee to prove to him or her that you do. If you neglect to deal with relevant issues you run the risk of losing marks.

(h) Apportion the time to be spent on each question carefully and try to stick to this plan. If, perchance, you miscalculate your time and feel that you are likely to run short, then, as a last resort, present your answer in note form. This is better than nothing. In any event, you are more likely to be rewarded with five marks for a new question than the last five marks of an earlier one.

(i) One of the skills that the examiner is looking for is your ability to analyse the issues posed by the question, and the application of the relevant principles of law. Accordingly, it is advisable that you present your arguments as clearly as possible, in neat and legible handwriting. It is good practice to use sub-headings and present your answer in short paragraphs, each of which involves a distinct point.

(j) In your concluding paragraph you should try to address the issues raised by the question. It is advisable to relate back to the instructions set out in the question, such as: 'In the light of the arguments set out above, my advice to A is as follows …'

Common Pitfalls

The most common mistake made when using Questions & Answers books for revision is to memorise the model answers provided and try to reproduce them in exams. This approach is a sure-fire pitfall, likely to result in a poor overall mark because your answer will not be specific enough to the particular question on your exam paper, and there is also a danger that reproducing an answer in this way would be treated as plagiarism. You must instead be sure to read the question carefully, to identify the issues and problems it is asking you to address and to answer it directly in your exam. If you take our examiners' advice and use your Q&A to focus on your question-answering skills and understanding of the law applied, you will be ready for whatever your exam paper has to offer!

1

The Creation of Trusts

INTRODUCTION

It might be thought prudent at the start of any book on the law of trusts to attempt to define exactly what a 'trust' is. Unfortunately, that is not as easy as we might hope. Of course, the essential ingredients of a trust are well known: there is a 'trustee', who is the holder of the legal (or 'paper') title to property, and this person holds the trust property 'on trust' for the 'beneficiary' (or *cestui que trust*). The beneficiary is the equitable owner of the property and this is the person (or persons) to whom the real or 'beneficial' advantages of ownership will accrue. The interest enjoyed by the beneficiary is proprietary, or '*in rem*'. Thus, he is able to trace his property and recover it from any intermeddler with the exception of the bona fide transferee of the legal estate for value without notice. Further, although, as just indicated, the trustee usually holds the 'legal' title and the beneficiary holds the 'equitable' title, it is perfectly possible for an equitable owner to create a trust of *that* interest. In such cases, the first equitable owner is the trustee (as well as the beneficiary under the first trust!), holding an equitable interest on trust for a beneficiary. Sometimes this is known as a 'sub-trust'. However, whatever the precise configuration of legal and equitable ownership, necessarily there is a relationship between the trustee and the beneficiary – sometimes referred to as a 'fiduciary relationship' – and it is clear that the former has certain responsibilities and duties to the latter. Furthermore, sometimes the property which is the subject matter of the trust – and this can be any property, tangible or intangible, real or personal – will have been provided by a 'settlor' or a 'testator' and it is they who have set up the trust either during his or her lifetime (settlor) or on death (testator). Indeed, in the case of a trust established by *inter vivos* gift (that is, not by will), the settlor and the trustee may be the same person and, in such cases, the settlor is said to have declared himself or herself trustee of the trust property. Finally, it should be noted that a trustee may also be a beneficiary under a trust. This quite often happens with trusts of cohabited property where the man may hold the property on trust for himself and his lover in some defined shares.

This, then, is a very simple picture of a trust and beyond this it is not easy to make general statements about the nature of a trust without also explaining the one or more exceptions that exist to nearly every rule. The law of trusts is not something that can be neatly dissected, nor can its principles be safely pigeonholed. Perhaps the best way to understand it is through an analysis of the substantive law without recourse to *a priori* definitions and assumptions that may prove wholly inadequate in explaining how the unique legal concept of the trust actually works in practice. With that in mind, the first topics to consider are the requirements imposed by general statute law and general principles of common law for the creation of a valid trust.

There are two sets of formal requirements which must be met before a valid trust can exist. On the one hand, there are those rules imposed by statute – principally the **Law of Property Act 1925** – which establish formality requirements for the creation of trusts of certain kinds of property. These are requirements of writing and the like which are not inherent in the concept of the trust *per se*, although failure to comply with them will render the trust unenforceable. Rather, they are 'external' requirements imposed in order to ensure the proper working of the trust concept, especially the prevention of fraud by the trustee. Second, there are those rules of common law and equity which require the declaration of trust and/or the transfer of ownership of the trust property to the trustee to be achieved in specific ways according to the particular type of trust property. Examples include the need for a deed or registered disposition for the transfer of land to the trustee and entry in the company's register for the transfer of shares. These rules are not peculiar to the law of trusts, but given that the property which is the subject matter of the trust must pass into the hands of the trustee before the trust can exist (if it is not already there), the mode of transfer appropriate to each particular kind of property must be used if the trust is to be regarded as properly constituted. Failure to constitute the trust because of a failure to transfer the trust property to the trustee by the appropriate method has serious consequences.

Thus, the issues covered in this chapter require an understanding of the following matters:

(a) the different formality requirements for the creation of trusts of land and those for the creation of trusts of other property;

(b) the distinction between the creation of a trust and the 'disposition' of a 'subsisting' equitable interest under an existing trust and the reasons why an accurate distinction must be made;

(c) the necessity of properly constituting a trust and the manner in which this may be achieved relative to specific types of trust property; and

(d) the consequences of failure to constitute the trust properly.

QUESTION 1

'Although equity will not aid a volunteer, it will not strive officiously to defeat a gift' (*per* Lord Browne-Wilkinson in Choithram International SA v Pagarani (2001)).

▶ **Evaluate this statement by reference to decided cases.**

How to Read this Question

This is a broad essay question on the constitution of a trust and the consequences of creation. The focus of the question is whether the court is prepared to relax the Milroy v Lord rule in favour of volunteers in order to give effect to the clear intention of the transferor.

How to Answer this Question

A good answer to this question will deal with the principle in Milroy v Lord by reference to structured discussion of the relevant cases. The main issue is when would a gift or trust be fully created and do the courts have a discretion to develop the law in this area? The permutation of legal principles determining this question are required to be discussed as well as the effects of constitution and the ineffectual creation of an express trust or gift.

Up for Debate

Students are urged to read the judgments in the controversial decision **Pennington v Waine**. In this case, Arden LJ's view of unconscionability was based on the discretion of the court and varies with the circumstances of each case. This approach introduces notions of justice and fairness in outcomes to transactions that involve the process of the transfer of the legal title to property. In **Pennington v Waine**, what would have been the position if registration of the shares were declined by the company? If the constructive trust theory is to be maintained, despite the refusal to register the new owner, this would result in equity treating an ineffective transfer as a valid declaration of trust. But in **Pennington v Waine** the donor had not declared a trust, nor made a gift, nor had she done everything in her power to make a gift, yet the court decided that the transfer was effective in equity.

The following articles are instructive in order to get a better understanding of the subject: J Morris 'Questions: when is an invalid gift a valid gift? When is an incompletely constituted trust a completely constituted trust? Answer: after decisions in *Choithram* and *Pennington*' (2003) 6 PCB 393; M Halliwell 'Perfecting imperfect gifts and trusts: have we reached the end of the Chancellor's foot?' (2003) Conveyancer 192.

Answer Plan

- ❖ The Milroy v Lord test.
- ❖ Transferor completing everything required of him.
- ❖ No self-declaration following imperfect transfer.
- ❖ The principle in Re Ralli.
- ❖ Multiple trustees, including the settlor.
- ❖ Trust of a chose in action.
- ❖ Consequences of a trust being perfect.
- ❖ Exceptions to the rule that equity will not assist a volunteer.

Answer Structure

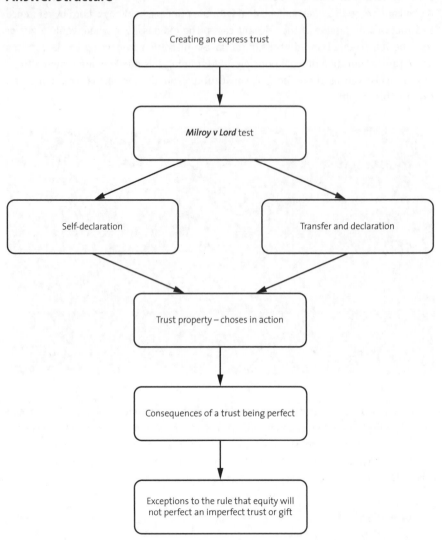

This diagram illustrates the methods and consequences of creating trusts, including gifts.

ANSWER

This statement by Lord Browne-Wilkinson highlights two fundamental principles of equity: the notion that equity will not assist a volunteer and that there is no policy in equity to defeat a perfect gift. These are self-evident propositions. However, a number of landmark cases have striven to perfect gifts which, on orthodox theory, ought to be considered as imperfect.[1]

1   Identify and address the issues posed by the question directly.

The principle laid down by Turner LJ in Milroy v Lord (1862) identifies the two modes of constituting an express trust. The onus is on the settlor to execute one (or in exceptional circumstances both) of these modes for carrying out his intention. The two modes of creating an express trust are:

(a)   a self-declaration of trust; and
(b)   a transfer of property to the trustees, subject to a direction to hold upon trust for the beneficiaries.

A settlor may declare that he presently holds specific property on trust, indicating the interest, for a beneficiary. In this respect he simply retains the property as trustee for the relevant beneficiaries. Clear evidence is needed to convert the status of the original owner of the property to that of a trustee, see Paul v Constance (1977). The test that is applicable here is the 'three certainties' test, i.e. certainty of intention, subject matter and objects.

The alternative mode of creating an express trust involves a transfer of the relevant property to another person (or persons) as trustee(s), subject to a valid declaration of trust. In this context the settlor must comply with two requirements, namely a transfer (gift or sale) of the relevant property or interest to the trustees complemented with a declaration of the terms of the trust. If the settlor intends to create a trust by this method and declares the terms of the trust, but fails to transfer the property to the intended trustees, it is clear that no express trust is created.[2] The court will not automatically imply a self-declaration of trust: see Richards v Delbridge (1874) and Jones v Lock (1865).

The formal requirements, if any, concerning the transfer of the legal title or equitable title to property vary with the nature of the property involved, in accordance with the Milroy v Lord (1862) principle; but if the transferor has done everything required of him to transfer the legal title to property and something has yet to be done by a third party, the transfer will be effective in equity: see Re Rose (1952); contrast Re Fry (1946) in respect of the transfer of shares in a private company. The effect of this rule (known as the rule in Re Rose) is that although the transfer of the legal title is not complete, the transferor will nevertheless hold the legal title to the property as constructive trustee for the transferee. Indeed, in Pennington v Waine (2002), the Court of Appeal decided that the delivery of the share transfer form to the company could be dispensed with if it would be *unconscionable* for the transferor to recall what she intended to donate, the transfer would be effective in equity. This notion of unconscionability was based on analogy with the principle laid down by the Privy Council in Choithram International SA v Pagarani (2001). However, the Privy Council in that case had decided that the trust was perfectly created and thus it would have been unconscionable for the settlor to deny the existence of the trust, whereas in Pennington the donor had neither declared a trust nor made a perfect gift nor had she done everything required of her to make the

....
2   Highlight the significance of the modes of creating an express trust.

gift. Accordingly, Pennington may be treated as an unjustifiable extension of the Milroy v Lord principle.[3] More recently in Zeital v Kaye (2010), an element of orthodoxy was reinstated when the Court of Appeal applied the strict Re Rose principle and distinguished Pennington.

Up for Debate

Is the principle of 'unconscionability' laid down in Pagarani and Pennington an appropriate test to determine whether a gift is complete and a trust perfect? When would this test be satisfied?

In Re Ralli (1964), the High Court decided that a settlor may expressly manifest an intention to transfer the relevant property to third-party trustees (transfer and declaration mode) and, prior to completing the transfer, to declare himself a trustee for the beneficiaries (self-declaration mode). In this event, the trust will be perfect, provided that the third-party trustee acquires the property during the settlor's lifetime. The court had also decided that it was immaterial how the third-party trustee acquired the relevant property. The mere fact that the property had reached the hands of the intended trustees was sufficient to constitute the trust. The logic of this test extended the Milroy v Lord principle.

Moreover, in Choithram International SA v Pagarani (2001), the Privy Council decided that where the settlor appoints multiple trustees, including himself, and declares a present, unconditional and irrevocable intention to create a trust for specific persons, a failure to transfer the property to the nominated trustees is not fatal, for his (settlor's) retention of the property will be treated as a trustee. Trusteeship for these purposes is treated as a joint office so that the acquisition of the property by one trustee is equivalent to its acquisition by all the trustees. There was no distinction between a settlor declaring himself to be the sole trustee and one of a number of trustees.

In Fletcher v Fletcher (1844), the court construed the subject matter of a covenant (to transfer property on trust) as creating a chose in action, namely the benefit of the covenant. This intangible property right may be transferred to the trustees on trust for the relevant beneficiaries, thus perfecting the trust. What is needed to assign such a right or chose is a clear intention on the part of the assignor to dispose of the chose to the transferee, but it is questionable whether the settlor had the benefit of the covenant. In any event, the Fletcher principle was subsequently restricted in Re Cook (1965) to debts enforceable at law, as distinct from any other choses in action.[4]

---

3   Express the controversial nature of the *Pennington* rule.
4   The *Fletcher* rule is highly controversial and ought to be stated accompanied by its limitations.

Where a trust is perfectly created, the beneficiary is given a right *in rem* in the trust property and may protect his interest against anyone, except a bona fide transferee of the legal estate for value without notice. He may bring the claim in his own name and is entitled to join the trustee as a co-defendant. On the other hand, if the intended trust is imperfect, the transaction operates as an agreement to create a trust. This involves the law of contract, as opposed to the law of trust. An agreement to create a trust may only be enforced in equity by non-volunteers. The rule is that 'equity will not assist a volunteer' and 'equity will not perfect an imperfect gift'. To obtain an equitable remedy, the claimant is required to establish that he has furnished consideration, see Pullan v Koe (1913). Valuable consideration refers either to common law consideration in money or money's worth or marriage consideration in equity. The persons who are treated as providing marriage consideration are the parties to the marriage and the issue of the marriage, including remoter issue.

In conclusion, Lord Browne-Wilkinson's statement is vindicated by a number of exceptional cases including Ralli, Fletcher, Pagarani and Pennington.

Common Pitfalls

Students are urged to approach this question by highlighting the various occasions when the court in purporting to apply the **Milroy v Lord** principle, in effect, extended the test in a number of landmark decisions. Simply 'trotting out' the popular cases without a structure will not stand you in good stead with the examiners. Students should be clear as to the significance of the principles in the controversial decisions, Choithram v Pagarani, Pennington v Waine and Fletcher v Fletcher.

QUESTION 2

In 2010, Alfred, in contemplation of his marriage with Bette, covenanted with Tim to transfer £50,000 to him to be held on trust for Bette for life, remainder to any of the children of the marriage absolutely. The marriage duly took place. A few months later Alfred made a bargain with his father-in-law, Freddie, that in consideration of receiving 10,000 shares in Cashflow Ltd (a private company), Alfred will settle his yacht, *Orca*, on trust for Bette for life, remainder to her brother, Charlie, absolutely. Alfred duly executed another covenant with Tim to settle his yacht, *Orca* on trust for Bette for life with remainder to Charlie.

❖ Alfred failed to make any transfers to Tim in accordance with the covenants although he has been registered as the new owner of 10,000 shares in Cashflow Ltd.

❖ In 2012, Bette died leaving a son, Donald. Alfred still refused to transfer any of the properties to Tim in respect of the covenants.

❖ In 2013 Alfred met Ede and decided to spend his declining years with her.

❖   In February 2014 Alfred died. Amongst his personal effects was a will, executed in January 2014, which declared that all his property was to be distributed to Ede. Ede was also appointed executrix of Alfred's will.

▶ Advise Donald, Charlie, Freddie, Tim and Ede as to their rights, if any, in the above transactions.

[Ignore any applications under the Inheritance (Provision for Family and Dependants) Act 1975.]

How to Read this Question

This problem question raises issues on the enforcement of covenants to create trusts. Material issues in this question are whether Bette's son, Donald, her father, Freddie and brother, Charlie as well as Tim, the covenantee may enforce the agreement to create trusts.

How to Answer this Question

We are told that Alfred failed to transfer the relevant properties. Are the trusts of the covenants perfect? If not, are the claimants volunteers? The status of each of the claimants is required to be analysed to ascertain whether the nature of the remedies each may have against Albert's heir.

Common Pitfalls

It is at this point of an answer to an exclusion clause question that many students will be unable to resist reciting all they know about the **UCTA**, whether or not it is relevant to the problem. You will impress the examiner much more if you isolate the really relevant sections, and focus your attention on them – in this case **s2** and the issue of 'reasonableness'.

Aim Higher

In attempting questions on the constitution of trusts, students ought to adopt a more holistic approach and consider related issues. These may include the three certainties; the remedies, if any, available to a claimant who wishes to enforce an agreement to create a trust; the exceptions to the rule that equity will not assist a volunteer; and the statutory formalities, if any, that are applicable to the transaction.

Answer Structure

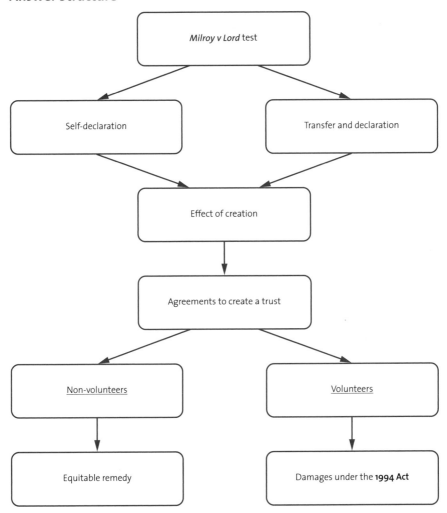

This diagram indicates the requirements for the creation of an express trust, notes its effect and lists the remedies that may be available to a claimant.

ANSWER

Alfred executed two covenants with Tim on separate occasions to transfer £50,000 and the yacht, *Orca*, to him to hold on various trusts, but failed to transfer the properties. Two questions arise in these circumstances: whether the covenants create trusts of the relevant properties in favour of the intended beneficiaries; alternatively, whether the covenants are enforceable as agreements to create trusts.

The test for creating a perfect trust was laid down by Turner LJ in Milroy v Lord (1862). This involves the settlor, Alfred, choosing one of two modes of creating the trust:

(a) a transfer of property to the trustees, subject to a direction to hold upon trust for the beneficiaries; or

(b) a self-declaration of trust.

Applying this test to the facts of the problem, we have been informed that Alfred failed to transfer the relevant properties (£50,000 and the yacht) to Tim, the intended trustee.[5] Thus, it would appear that the intended trust is imperfect. Further, the court will not automatically imply the second mode for creating an express trust as laid down in Milroy v Lord, namely, a self-declaration of trust, in order to constitute Alfred a trustee: see Richards v Delbridge (1874). The reason for the rule is that, despite the transferor's intention to benefit another by means of a transfer (whether on trust or not), the transferor ought not to be treated as a trustee if this does not accord with his intention, for otherwise all imperfect trusts will become perfect.

Up for Debate

Was the settlor's intention in **Fletcher v Fletcher** clear enough to signify an intention to create a trust of his promise to transfer the money?

Alternatively, the intended beneficiaries may argue that the subject matter of the covenant involves the 'benefit of the covenant', as distinct from the cash and the yacht, which constitute choses in action. Such properties are intangible personal property rights that are transferred by operation of law in accordance with the intention of the transferor. If this argument were to succeed, it would follow that Tim would have acquired the respective properties from Alfred and would be required to hold the same on trust for the beneficiaries: see Fletcher v Fletcher (1844). However, the Fletcher rule is restricted to one type of chose in action, namely debts enforceable at law: see Re Cook (1965). A debt enforceable at law involves a legal obligation to pay a quantified amount of money. It does not concern a covenanted obligation to transfer shares, paintings or indeed yachts. It follows that in accordance with the Fletcher principle only the covenant to transfer £50,000 is capable of constituting a perfect trust. No trust exists of the covenant to transfer the yacht. It may be noted that the Fletcher rule is a highly controversial principle and it is arguable that it is restricted to occasions where the covenantor has agreed that his executor will transfer the property to the covenantee trustee. This argument has the tendency to restrict the principle to its own facts.[6]

If the trust in respect of the covenant to transfer £50,000 to Tim is perfect (in accordance with the Fletcher v Fletcher rule) it follows that the beneficiaries, who are given proprietary rights in the trust property, are entitled to enforce the trust: see Jeffreys v Jeffreys (1841). Thus, Bette, during her lifetime, and Donald acquire equitable interests in the

---

5 State the principle of law as clearly as possible and apply the same to the facts.

6 The *Fletcher* rule with its limitation ought to be considered when dealing with constitution questions.

covenanted sum and are entitled in their own right to bring claims to protect their interests. Similarly, Tim, as trustee, may bring claims on their behalf.[7]

On the other hand, if the trusts of the covenants are imperfect (i.e. the covenant to transfer £50,000 and the yacht) on the ground that the subject matter of the trust has not been transferred to Tim, the intended trustee, the trust is imperfect and the principle is that 'equity will not perfect an imperfect trust' and 'equity will not assist a volunteer'. The unfulfilled covenants will amount to agreements to create trusts and be enforceable, if at all, in contract law.

Subject to the **Contracts (Rights of Third Parties) Act 1999**, in order to enforce the covenants to create trusts, the claimants are required to establish that they have furnished valuable consideration. Consideration refers either to common law consideration in money or money's worth or marriage consideration. Common law consideration is the price paid by each party to an agreement. 'Marriage consideration' takes the form of an ante-nuptial settlement made in consideration of marriage, or a post-nuptial settlement made in pursuance of an ante-nuptial agreement.[8] The persons who are treated as providing marriage consideration are the parties to the marriage and the issue of the marriage, including remoter issue. Relating this principle to the facts of the problem, it would appear that Bette (and her estate on her behalf) and Donald (if he is an issue of the marriage between Alfred and Bette) are non-volunteers, having provided marriage consideration. Freddie appears to have provided common law consideration and is also treated as a non-volunteer. The other parties connected with the covenants, namely Tim and Charlie, are volunteers and are not entitled to equitable remedies.

The non-volunteers are entitled in their own right to seek equitable assistance and, if necessary, obtain equitable remedies. At the instance of these claimants (Bette's estate, Donald and Freddie) the imperfect trusts will be treated to all intents and purposes as though they were perfect. In other words, the claimants who had furnished valuable consideration will derive from the agreements to create trusts all the benefits accorded to a beneficiary under a perfect trust: see Pullan v Koe (1913). In particular, Freddie, as a non-volunteer, is entitled to bring a claim in equity for specific performance to enforce the agreement to transfer the yacht to Tim, subject to a trust: see Beswick v Beswick (1968). This is the position even though Charlie is a volunteer and may obtain a benefit from the claim of Freddie; but it must be appreciated that neither Tim nor Charlie, as volunteers, may be able to force Freddie to bring such a claim in equity for specific performance: see Re Pryce (1917) and Re Kay (1939).

By virtue of **s1** of the **Contracts (Rights of Third Parties) Act 1999**, a third party to a contract is entitled 'in his own right' to enforce a term of the contract if, *inter alia*, the 'term of the contract purports to confer a benefit on him'. This is clearly covered by the covenant to transfer the yacht to Tim on trust *inter alia* for Charlie. **Section 1(5)** declares that

---

7   State the effect of the trust being treated as perfect.
8   It is imperative to state clear definitions of relevant concepts.

'any remedy' will be available to the claimant, on the assumption that he is a party to the contract. The effect is that Charlie, a volunteer, is entitled only to damages against the estate of Alfred for breach of contract. The quantum of damages may be calculated by reference to the value of the yacht on the date of the breach of contract.

In summary it would appear that a trust of a chose of £50,000 may be constituted and the subject matter of the remaining properties embodied in the covenants may be enforceable by the intended beneficiaries as non-volunteers or under the 1999 Act.

Common Pitfalls

Students sometimes perform poorly in this type of problem question because of inadequacy in analysing the issues and presenting clear statements of law and applying this to the facts.

QUESTION 3

'In order for a settlor to create a valid *inter vivos* trust of property he owns absolutely, it is necessary both to constitute the trust perfectly and to meet certain statutory requirements.'

▶ Discuss.

How to Read this Question

This broad essay question requires you to consider the various methods of constituting an express trust as laid down in Milroy v Lord as well as the formal requirements for the *inter vivos* creation of a trust enacted in s 53 of the **Law of Property Act 1925**.

How to Answer this Question

This question requires you to deal with a variety of issues including the need for control over the trust property to be effectively conveyed to the trustee, or alternatively retaining the property as trustee as laid down in Milroy v Lord. In addition you are required to outline the statutory requirements for the validity of trusts of certain kinds of property (s 53 of the **Law of Property Act 1925**) and consider the consequences of imperfect creation (briefly).

Up for Debate

The traditional and contemporary principles for creating express trusts were critically explored by J Morris 'Questions: when is an invalid gift a valid gift? When is an incompletely constituted trust a completely constituted trust? Answer: after decisions in *Choithram* and *Pennington*' (2003) PCB 393. Students are advised to study these arguments.

Answer Structure

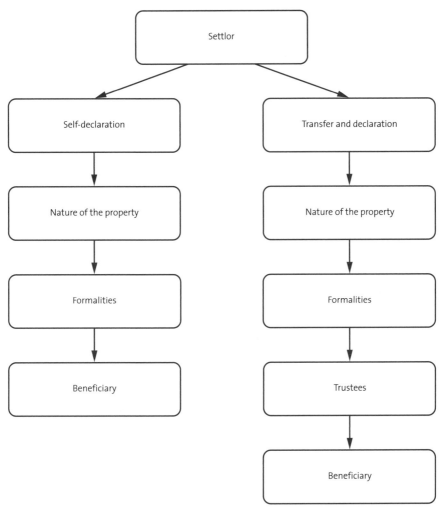

This diagram refers to the various steps that are required to be complied with in order to create a valid express trust.

ANSWER

In considering the creation of trusts, it is important to realise that there are only two ways of creating an express trust *inter vivos*. These are a self-declaration of trust and a transfer to the trustees complemented by a declaration of trust. Unless one of these modes of creation has been adopted, the trust is said to be incompletely constituted and the intended beneficiaries will have no claim in trusts law to the property (Milroy v Lord (1862)). An innovation created by the Privy Council involves the occasion where the settlor appoints multiple owners as trustees, including himself. If he manifests an irrevocable intention to create a trust, his retention of the property may be construed as one of the trustees, thereby constituting the trust, whether with or without a transfer to the other trustees. The maxim, 'equity regards as done that which ought to be done' will be applicable: see Choithram v Pagarani (2001).[9] In cases where the trust property needs to be conveyed to a trustee, it is necessary to examine the particular type of trust property in order to determine what must be done for an effective transfer of the title. The requirements will be different for each type of property. In addition, there are 'external' formality rules, imposed by statute, which regulate the way in which trusts per se can be created. These are to be found in the **Law of Property Act (LPA) 1925** and they are designed to ensure that the creation of trusts of certain kinds of property is not open to doubt and to minimise the potential for fraud by the trustee. Failure to fulfil these requirements renders the trust unenforceable or void (s 53 of the **LPA 1925**).

In the case of a self-declaration of trust, the person who is to be the trustee already has title and, therefore, there is no need to transfer the property. All that is needed is an effective declaration of trust – or rather, a declaration by the current owner of himself as trustee – sufficient evidence of a present and irrevocable declaration of trust is needed, as in Paul v Constance (1977) and Re Kayford (1975), and generally this evidence may take any form except in relation to land; see below. The general rule is summarised in the maxim 'equity looks at the intent rather than the form'.

The second way in which trusts may be created involves the effective transfer of property to the trustee, subject to the trust. Unless the trustee has title to the property, the trust is incompletely constituted and the beneficiaries have no enforceable claim to the property under the failed 'trust' (Jones v Lock (1865)). On a practical and theoretical level it is essential to know how title to different types of property may be transferred. In the context of trusts, the trustee receives the property on behalf of someone else and not for his own use. It is clear that the particular requirements for the effective transfer of title to a trustee depend upon the nature of the property being transferred. It must be noted that an ineffectual transfer of the relevant property to the nominated trustee will not automatically be treated by the courts as a valid self-declaration of trust, otherwise all imperfect trusts will become perfect. The intention to declare oneself a trustee is very different from the intention to transfer property to another as trustee and they are mutually exclusive: see Richards v Delbridge (1874).

Before considering the 'external' formality requirements for the creation of a trust, it is necessary to consider briefly one or two exceptions to the general principle just considered. First, a trust may be held to have been validly constituted, despite the fact that the trustee has not formally received the legal title, if failure to be invested with that title is because of some requirement outside the control of the settlor or trustee. The test is whether the transferor has done everything required of him, see Re Rose (1952). The trust

---

9   This case (*Pagarani*), or principle, has had an impact on the question whether the trust is perfect. Examinees will find that a reading of the judgment may assist in understanding where this principle fits within the scheme of things.

will be constituted with the equitable interest in the property. Controversially, in Pennington v Waine (2002), the Court of Appeal extended this principle to occasions when it is unconscionable for the transferor to deny his promise. Second, according to Re Ralli (1964), it may be immaterial that the trustee acquires title to the trust property in a manner different from that which the settlor originally intended. It was decided in this case that the capacity in which the trustee acquires the property is immaterial. Third, there are several other methods by which imperfect gifts may be perfected in equity. Examples include the principles of *donatio mortis causa*, the law of proprietary estoppel and the rule in Strong v Bird (1874).

We shall look now at the other major requirement for the valid creation of a trust: the external formality rules imposed by statute. Trusts of property other than land may be created orally or in writing and all that is needed is a self-declaration of trust or an effective transfer of title to another as trustee. In the case of land, however, the creation of a trust must be 'manifested and proved' in writing. Although the trust does not have to be *in* writing, there must be written evidence of it, even if that evidence is not contemporaneous with the date of the creation of the trust (s 53(1)(b) of the LPA 1925 and Rouchefoucauld v Boustead (1897)). Failure to comply with this evidential requirement renders the trust of land unenforceable, although there are exceptions for resulting or constructive trusts of land (s 53(2) of the LPA 1925). Likewise, the court may, in exceptional circumstances, allow oral evidence to prove the existence of a trust of land if this is necessary to prevent fraud by the trustee, as where the trustee dishonestly claims that there is no trust and that he may keep the property *because* of an absence of the necessary writing (Rochefoucauld v Boustead).

Up for Debate

How would you classify the trust created in Rochefoucauld v Boustead?

Of course, if the trust is to be created by will, then different considerations will apply (see s 9 of the Wills Act 1837, as amended) and if the subject matter of the trust is itself an equitable interest (so that the trustee holds an equitable title on trust for another), there may be further formality requirements springing from the requirements of writing found in s 53(1)(c) of the LPA 1925. Finally, it is relevant to note that, in some circumstances, it may be difficult to distinguish between, on the one hand, the creation of a trust of pure personalty (no writing) or of land (evidenced in writing) and, on the other, the transfer of an equitable interest in personalty or land under a trust which already exists. The difference is, however, crucial, for the transfer of any equitable interest under an existing trust – be it of personalty or realty – must actually be *in* writing under s 53(1)(c) of the LPA 1925. As the cases of Grey v IRC (1960) and Vandervell v IRC (1967) demonstrate, such a distinction is not always easy to draw.

In summary the underlying rules for the creation of an express trust satisfy the twin needs for clarity and certainty for all the parties concerned.

Common Pitfalls

This is a fairly broad question that deals with the key elements related to the creation of an express trust. It is imperative to adopt a clear structure in presenting the principles raised in the cases and avoid simply trotting out a catalogue of cases. It is unnecessary to deal with exceptions to the rule that 'equity will not assist a volunteer' in any detail.

QUESTION 4

Alfred is the sole beneficial owner under a trust that comprises 20,000 shares in Trident Co Ltd (a private company). The trustees are Thomas and Trevor. Discuss the proprietary effect of the following alternative actions:

(i)   Alfred orally declares that he henceforth holds his beneficial interest in the Trident shares on trust for himself for life with remainder to Bernard absolutely.

(ii) Alfred orally instructs his trustees to convey his legal title to the Trident shares to Bernard, at the same time informing Bernard that he is now the outright owner of the shares.

(iii) Alfred enters into an oral contract with Bernard for the purchase of Alfred's beneficial interest in the Trident shares.

How to Read this Question

This question requires you to consider whether the transactions initiated by Alfred are effective to dispose of his equitable interests.

How to Answer this Question

In answering this question you are required to deal with the following issues:

❖   What are the requirements of s 53(1)(c) of the **Law of Property Act 1925** and would the sub-section be applicable to personal property (i.e. shares)?

❖   What constitutes a disposition within s 53(1)(c) of the **LPA 1925**? See Romer LJ's pronouncement in Timpson's Executors v Yerbury.

❖   Whether a declaration of trust of part of an equitable interest is treated as a disposition?

❖   Would the unification of the legal and equitable interests in the hands of a third party constitute a disposition within s 53(1)(c) of the **1925 Act**?

❖   Would a constructive trust that may arise from an oral contract be exempt from the requirements of s 53(1)(c) of the **1925 Act**?

Up for Debate

Do you think that a declaration of trust of part of an equitable interest ought to be excluded from **s 53(1)(c)** of the **Law of Property Act 1925**? Consider the analysis by B Green 'Grey, Oughtred and Vandervell: a contextual re-appraisal' (1984) 47 MLR 385.

Applying the Law

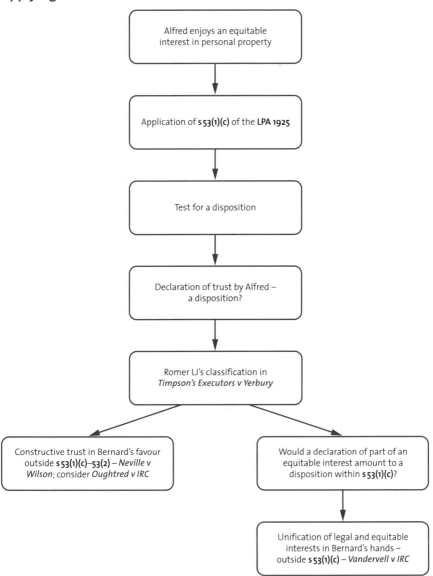

This diagram represents the legal effect of the various transactions entered into by Alfred.

ANSWER

The circumstances indicate that Alfred is an equitable owner of 20,000 shares in Trident Co Ltd and he is the sole beneficiary. His interest is enjoyed under a 'subsisting' trust for the purposes of s 53(1)(c) of the **Law of Property Act 1925 (LPA)**. A 'subsisting' trust refers to any form of trust that exists irrespective of whether it is express, resulting, constructive or indeed statutory. **Section 53(1)(c)** requires a 'disposition' of an equitable interest under a subsisting trust to be in writing signed by the disponer or his agent lawfully authorised in writing.[10] Failure to comply with the requirements of the sub-section will result in the attempted disposition being void and the interest will remain with Alfred.

Before considering the effect of each individual transaction entered into by Alfred there are two preliminary points that underpin the issues. First, s 53(1)(c) of the **LPA 1925** is applicable to equitable interests in land and personalty. Despite s 205(1)(x) of the **LPA 1925** defining equitable interests by reference to land, the courts have extended the application of the sub-section to personal property in a series of high profile decisions. The mischief or purposive interpretation of the sub-section, namely to prevent fraud, vindicates the extension of the provision. It is thus unnecessary and too late in the day for the sub-section to be given its literal meaning. Second, the expression 'disposition', has been classified by Romer LJ in Timpson's Executors v Yerbury as including:

- ❖ assignments of interests to donees;
- ❖ directions to the trustees to hold upon trust for another or others;
- ❖ contracts entered into for valuable consideration in order to sell the interest to the other contracting party;
- ❖ self-declarations of trust in favour of other beneficiaries.

(i) Alfred's Oral Declaration of Trust in Favour of Bernard

The question in issue here is whether Alfred's self-declaration of trust of his interest constitutes a disposition within s 53(1)(c) of the **LPA 1925**. Romer LJ's classification of a disposition in Yerbury includes a self-declaration of trust and this transaction involves a sub-trust. Prima facie the oral declaration by Alfred constitutes an attempt to dispose of his equitable interest and, since it does not comply with the requirement of writing, is therefore void.

On the other hand, academics of the calibre of Professors Pettit and Hayton have advanced arguments to the effect that the expression 'disposition' within s 53(1)(c) does not include the creation of trusts but merely the continuance of trusts. Accordingly, a creation of an interest under a sub-trust by way of a declaration of trust does not constitute a disposition if the declarant has active duties to perform. The reason is that the declarant will not be able to drop out of the picture but is required to perform his duties. Where there are only passive duties on the part of the trustees to perform, the declaration will amount to an intended disposition: see Grainge v Wilberforce and Re Lashmar. The nature of the transaction seems to vary depending on whether the declarant has active or

10 This is a summary of the statutory provision. It is advisable to narrate the provision verbatim.

passive duties to perform. The declaration of trust by Alfred is in respect of part of his equitable interest, namely the remainder interest in favour of Bernard, and therefore imposes active duties on Alfred. The effect is that, according to this view, s 53(1)(c) is not applicable to the creation of this sub-trust. The opposing view was put forward by Brian Green, who, after analysing the main cases, concluded that the sub-section does not draw a distinction between a disposition with or without active duties to perform. In both cases of sub-trusts a disposition is intended and will be effective only when the formal requirements are satisfied. There is some support for this view in Nelson v Greening & Sykes (2007). On this basis the oral declaration of trust will be ineffective to dispose of Alfred's equitable interest.

(ii) Transfer of the Legal and Equitable Interests to Bernard

The transfer of the legal title to shares in a private company is complete when the intended new owner of the shares (Bernard) is registered in the company's share register. Alfred as the sole equitable owner of the shares is entitled under the Saunders v Vautier principle to direct Thomas and Trevor, the legal owners of the shares, to transfer these shares to Bernard. Once the trustees have dispatched an executed share transfer form along with the share certificates to the company, a constructive trust will be created in favour of Bernard. The basis for this trust is that the transferors would have done everything in their power to transfer the shares and the decision whether to register Bernard is beyond their control: Re Rose and Pennington v Waine. This constructive trust would be outside the formal requirements of s 53(1)(c) by virtue of s 53(2) of the LPA 1925: see below.

On the assumption that the transfer of the legal title to the shares has been completed, the next issue is the effect of Alfred's oral statement to Bernard. The House of Lords in Vandervell v IRC decided that the transfer of the equitable interest, when coupled with the transfer of the legal title to the same individual, was outside the requirements of s 53(1)(c). The reason is that the trust will be terminated and there is unlikely to be a fraud, and specifically there will be no need for the trustee to chart the movement of the equitable interest. The effect is that this transaction by Alfred will be effective to dispose of the property to Bernard.

(iii) Alfred Contracts to Sell his Interest in the Shares to Bernard

Applying Romer LJ's *dictum* in Yerbury it would follow that a contract for valuable consideration to sell Alfred's equitable interest in the Trident shares to Bernard is potentially a disposition within s 53(1)(c) of the LPA 1925. Assuming the consideration is valuable the contract will be valid and binding on the parties. The question in issue is whether Alfred's equitable interest will be transferred to Bernard by virtue of this oral contract. The solution depends on whether a constructive trust arises in favour of Bernard and, if so, whether the trust would fall within s 53(2) of the LPA and exempt the donor from the requirements of s 53(1)(c). In Oughtred v IRC the House of Lords decided that when one party executes his part of the bargain, a constructive trust arises in his favour on the basis of the maxim, 'equity regards as done that which ought to be done': see also Chinn v Collins. The next question as to whether s 53(2) exempts the disponer from the requirements of s 53(1)(c), was surprisingly only adequately dealt with by one Law Lord, namely

Lord Radcliffe. He decided that since a constructive trust (as well as a resulting trust) is created by the courts, it would be regarded as outside the requirements of s 53(1)(c). His view has now been endorsed by the Court of Appeal in **Neville v Wilson**. The effect is that once Bernard has performed in part or as a whole his side of the bargain by paying the purchase monies to Alfred, he, Bernard, will acquire Alfred's equitable interest.

QUESTION 5

A young couple, Wendy and Harold, decided to get married. On the happy occasion, Wendy's father, Frank, who was a pioneer heart surgeon, covenanted with his friends, John and Smith (who were also the executors under his will), to transfer to them £200,000 and a house in Chelsea, to hold on trust for the benefit of Wendy and Harold for their respective lives, thereafter for their children and thereafter for their grandchildren. Failing issue, the trust properties were to be conveyed to Norman, his next of kin, absolutely.

The day after the wedding, Frank, who had made a fortune from his practice at Harley Street, received the shocking news that he had an inoperable brain tumour and that he was unlikely to live longer than 12 months. Frank then decided to sort out his affairs. He called the trustees of the above settlement and told them that he would shortly be transferring the house and cash to them. He also executed a further covenant with the trustees to transfer to them within seven days his portfolio of 20,000 shares in Lazerdot.com.

Later that night, Frank executed the necessary documents relating to the various properties, except for the cheque for £200,000, which he had filled in but forgotten to sign. He gave the documents to his solicitor to effect the transfers. When he went to the door to see the solicitor off, a bolt of lightning suddenly struck and killed both men instantly.

▶ Consider the issues raised by the events above and advise the executors whether any of the intended beneficiaries and donees are entitled to an interest in any of the properties.

How to Read this Question

This question raises issues as to whether Frank's intention to create trusts of the house in Chelsea, £200,000 and 20,000 shares in Lazerdot.com have been perfected and the consequences of the various events that have unfolded.

How to Answer this Question

You are required to analyse and apply the methods of creating trusts by reference to the principles in **Milroy v Lord**. Consider the consequences of Frank executing the relevant documents in order to transfer the properties, save for the cheque for £200,000. If the trusts of the relevant properties are imperfect who is entitled to enforce the covenants and what remedies will such parties be entitled to?

Up for Debate

How would you reconcile the rule in **Fletcher v Fletcher** with the principle in **Milroy v Lord**?

Aim Higher

In dealing with questions on the constitution of trusts, students are advised to bear in mind that additional issues may include the exceptions to the general rule that equity will not assist a volunteer.

Answer Structure

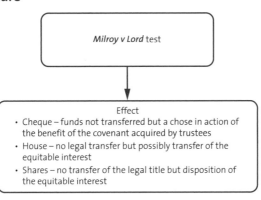

This chart identifies the legal effect of the transactions concerning Frank's properties.

ANSWER

One of the primary issues in this problem is whether a trust attaches to each of the properties specified. A trust is perfect if the settlor, Frank, declares himself a trustee for the relevant beneficiaries or transfers the property to the trustees, subject to a declaration of trust, see Milroy v Lord.

Cheque for £200,000

Frank had forgotten to sign the cheque that would have transferred the funds to the nominated trustees, John and Smith. Accordingly, there is no transfer of the funds to the trustees. In any event, a cheque is a revocable mandate which is revoked on death, see Re Beaumont. The effect is that Frank had manifested an intention to settle funds specified in the cheque, without a transfer of the funds.[11]

At the same time an imperfect transfer will not automatically be construed as a self-declaration of trust with the effect of imposing a trust obligation on Frank, for otherwise all imperfect transfers will be treated as perfect (Richards v Delbridge (1874)).

In accordance with the principle in Fletcher v Fletcher (1844), the covenant to transfer £200,000 may be treated as a transfer of a chose in action (i.e. the benefit of the covenant) provided that the cash existed (or its equivalent) at the time of the covenant,

---

11 Application of the principles of law to the facts.

and Frank intended the chose to be the subject matter of the trust. Whether Frank intended to create a trust of a chose in action would depend on the circumstances of each case. This involves a question of fact to be construed by the courts. There is very little evidence that Frank intended the subject matter of the trust to be the right created under the covenant, as distinct from the cash sum of £200,000.[12]

On the assumption that there is no transfer of property to the trustees (either as funds in a bank account or a chose in action), the intended trust of the covenanted sum will involve an imperfect trust and the maxims that are applicable are 'equity will not assist a volunteer' and 'equity will not perfect an imperfect transfer'. The consequences of such an omission by Frank will be considered later.

The House in Chelsea

The transfer of the legal title has not been effective because the transfer documents have not been sent to the Land Registry. The issue here is whether Frank had done everything required of him to transfer the legal title to his trustees John and Smith. This is a question of degree, but, if he had, a constructive trust (involving Frank, or his estate after his death, holding the property as constructive trustee) would arise transferring the equitable interest to the trustees, John and Smith, on trust for the named beneficiaries: see Re Rose (1952) and Mascall v Mascall (1984). In the recent case of Pennington v Waine (2002) the Court of Appeal introduced an alternative basis for resolving the dispute, namely, whether it would be unconscionable for the transferor to deny the transfer. This is a question for the court to decide on the facts of each case. The fact that in Pennington the subject matter was shares in a company, as opposed to land (as in the present case), is not material. Frank appears to have been motivated by the marriage of his daughter, Wendy, to execute the covenant and, following the tragic news of his poor heath, informed the trustees and his solicitor of his intention to transfer the relevant properties. Drawing the evidence together, it would appear that there is strong evidence to suggest not only that Frank felt that he had done everything required of him to transfer the house, but that it may be unconscionable for Frank's estate to deny the transfer.

The Fletcher v Fletcher rule (trusts of choses in action) is distinguishable on the ground that the subject matter is land, rather than a debt enforceable at law, see Re Cook (1965).

20,000 Shares in Lazerdot.com

The legal title to shares is only transferred if the new owner is registered in the share register of the company. The **Companies Act 2006** and the **Stock Transfer Act 1963** impose an obligation on Frank to execute a share transfer form and send the share certificates, along with the form (personally or through his agent), to the company at its registered office in order to secure registration. Frank had 'executed the necessary documents' and delivered these to his solicitor (his agent). Has he done everything required of him? This is a question of fact – see Re Rose, Pennington v Waine (above) contra Re Fry (1946). If he has, the transfer would be effective in equity and he (or his executors) would become a

---

12   In constitution questions it is important to consider the *Fletcher v Fletcher* rule.

constructive trustee of the shares. In Pennington v Waine the court decided that the delivery of the executed transfer documents to an intermediary to secure registration was sufficient compliance with all that was required from the transferor.

General

It is evident that the intended trust of some of the properties may be perfect. Much depends on the view taken by the court. However, if the trust of any of the properties is imperfect, the question that arises is whether the respective claimant is entitled to enforce the covenant to create a trust.

It was stated earlier that the two equitable maxims are applicable with regard to imperfect trusts. A volunteer would not be entitled to equitable assistance if the trust is imperfect. The issue therefore is whether the respective claimants are volunteers and, if so, what claims they may pursue.

A volunteer is one who has not provided valuable consideration, i.e. money or money's worth, or a person who does not come within the marriage consideration. The latter requires a marriage settlement, i.e. an ante-nuptial settlement made in consideration of marriage or a post-nuptial settlement made in pursuance of an ante-nuptial agreement: see Re Park (No 2) (1972). The persons within the marriage settlement are the parties to the marriage as well as the issue of the marriage, including grandchildren. Applying this principle to the facts, it would appear that Wendy and Harold, as parties to a marriage settlement, are deemed to provide marriage consideration. The effect is that Wendy and Harold are entitled to enforce the covenant in equity as non-volunteers. Thus, they are entitled to claim specific performance of the agreement as if they were beneficiaries under a perfect trust: see Pullan v Koe (1913).

The next of kin is a volunteer and unable to enforce the covenant in equity: Re Plumtree (1910). But under the **Contracts (Rights of Third Parties) Act 1999**, the next of kin (third party) is given the capacity to bring an action in his own right. Effectively, this is only in respect of damages, for the rule remains that equity will not assist a volunteer. The volunteer therefore does not have a claim in priority over the non-volunteers.

Despite John and Smith being appointed executors of Frank's will the rule in Strong v Bird (1874) is not applicable. Frank manifested a future intention to transfer the properties, see Re Freeland (1952).

Common Pitfalls

It is significant to recognise that in **Re Cook**, the settlor's intention was construed as an intention to create a trust as and when the subject matter came into existence and was transferred to the trustees. Thus, **Fletcher v Fletcher** was distinguished on the ground that, in the latter case, the subject matter involved was existing property, whereas in **Re Cook** the subject matter was future property.

Further Reading

Delany D and Ryan D 'Unconscionability: a unifying theme in equity' (2008) Conv 401.
Luxton P 'In search of perfection: the Re Rose rule rationale' (2012) Conv 70.

Note

The questions raised in this section involve the fundamental principles for the creation of an express trust – formalities and the constitution of a trust. This is a popular collection of topics with examiners.

2

Secret Trusts

INTRODUCTION

Secret trusts are a peculiar animal. They are special because they allow the creation of valid trusts even though the normal formality rules for the creation of trusts by will have not been met. In this sense, they are exceptions to the principles discussed in Chapter 1. However, as we shall see, although 'secret' trusts arise out of testamentary dispositions (that is, wills), there is often little that is secret about either their existence or their terms. Originally, the doctrine of secret trusts was developed to allow testators to make provision for beneficiaries whose identity, or even existence, was best kept quiet, such as illegitimate children or mistresses. Today, however, they are more likely to provide an indecisive testator with a means of avoiding the strict forms required by the **Wills Act 1837** (as amended).

Secret trusts are of two types: 'fully secret' trusts and 'half-secret' trusts. In essence, the difference between the two is that nothing of the existence of the trust is revealed in the will of a testator with a fully secret trust, whereas with a half-secret trust, the fact of a trust, but not the identity of the beneficiaries, is revealed in the will. This difference in purpose is reflected in the somewhat different conditions which must be met before the existence of each type of secret trust can be recognised and enforced by the 'secret' beneficiaries. In addition, because both forms of secret trusts do not meet the strict requirements of the **Wills Act 1837**, there is considerable academic interest in the theory behind the validity of secret trusts, especially how they gel with statutory and common law rules which would otherwise require their invalidity.

There are two general issues which may face a student dealing with secret trusts. First, there are the conditions for the existence of both types of trusts and the manner in which they operate. This requires a knowledge of substantive law and some appreciation of the requirements of the **Wills Act 1837** and general equitable principles concerning the validity of trusts. Second, there is the largely theoretical argument about the rationale or theory behind secret trusts. While not necessarily of great practical importance, this is fertile ground for examination questions.

QUESTION 6

To what extent is it possible to develop a coherent theory to explain the validity of so-called secret trusts?

How to Read this Question

This essay question raises a fundamental issue that involves a potential conflict between the primacy of Parliamentary provisions (s 9 of the Wills Act 1837 and s 53 of the Law of Property Act 1925) and the jurisdiction of equity to suppress unconscionable conduct. The upshot has been a number of different views expressed in a quest to identify the rationale for the validity of secret trusts.

How to Answer this Question

In answering this question the examinee should state and evaluate the various justifications that have been expressed for the creation of secret trusts. In doing so it is necessary to distinguish fully secret from half-secret trusts. The quest for laying down a theoretical basis for enforcing secret trusts may prove to be illusive and the examinee is required to evaluate the merits of each theory.

Up for Debate

The lawyer's natural instinct is to search for (and expect) a rational, coherent theory which will explain why the normal rules of statute and common law do not apply. As we shall see, it may be that such a search is fruitless, or that such theories as do exist are not coherent or all-embracing. With that in mind, what can be said about the rationale for secret trusts? There are a number of different views. Relevant articles to read on this subject include G Allan 'The secret is out there: searching for the legal justification for the doctrine of secret trusts through analysis of the case law' (2011) 40 CLWR 311; P Critchley 'Instruments of fraud, testamentary dispositions and the doctrine of secret trusts' (1999) 115 LQR 631.

Aim Higher

This is a typical 'bookwork' question on the law of secret trusts. It is imperative when answering such a question to avoid a lengthy repetition of the rules concerning the validity of secret trusts – they are straightforward – and to concentrate instead on addressing the precise issue raised by the question, namely, the justification for the courts' jurisdiction in enforcing secret trusts. A useful article that attempts to reconcile the differences between fully and half-secret trusts is D Wilde 'Secret and semi-secret trusts: justifying distinctions between the two' (1995) Conv 366.

Common Pitfalls

The theories of enforcement of secret trusts are extremely complex to evaluate within the conventional norms of the law of equity. Students are best advised to analyse the subject carefully as part of their revision plan before attempting this type of question in the examination and to avoid simply stating the requirements for the creation of secret trusts.

Answer Plan

❖ The context of secret trusts: their special status with respect to formalities for the creation of trusts.

❖ Fully secret and half-secret trusts briefly distinguished.

❖ Theories based on fraud: using a statute as an instrument of fraud or disregarding the intention of the testator (old fraud and new fraud).

❖ The declaration and constitution theory.

❖ *Dehors* the will theory.

❖ Views on the different communication requirements.

Answer Structure

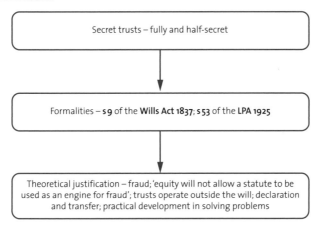

This diagram illustrates the theoretical bases for enforcing fully and half-secret trusts.

ANSWER

The starting point in answering this question is to state the obvious: that is, that both fully secret and half-secret trusts may be valid and enforceable despite lack of compliance with the formalities laid down by **s 9** of the **Wills Act 1837** and other statutes. Fully secret trusts are not declared in the will at all, with the trustee apparently taking the property absolutely, while in the case of half-secret trusts the existence of the trust is acknowledged in the will, so bringing partial compliance with **s 9** of the **Wills Act 1837**, but the identity of the beneficiaries is not.

Perhaps the most prevalent theory was that secret trusts would be enforced by a court of equity in favour of a secret beneficiary on the ground that 'equity will not permit a statute to be an instrument of fraud' (*McCormick v Grogan* (1869), noted with approval in *Box v Barclays Bank* (1998)). That is, if a fully secret trust was declared void because it did not comply with the **Wills Act 1837**, the legatee/trustee would be able to keep the trust property for himself despite the fact that he had accepted the trust obligation during the testator's lifetime.

Certainly, this rationale has the attraction of simplicity and, indeed, the equitable maxim used here is familiar and well established (see, for example, *Rochefoucauld v Boustead* (1897)). However, a moment's thought will reveal that this rationale cannot explain the validity of half-secret trusts. In half-secret trusts, the testator leaves property to the legatee 'on trust' for unnamed beneficiaries. There is thus no possibility that the half-secret trustee may commit fraud, as he or she is forever barred from the property and a resulting trust will arise (*Re Keen* (1937); *Re Rees* (1950)).

The impossibility of explaining both fully secret and half-secret trusts on the basis of *McCormick v Grogan*-type fraud has led to the development of theories that secret trusts are founded on a redefinition of what 'fraud' actually means. Traditionally, 'fraud' would mean the trustee taking a personal benefit when he or she was meant to hold the property for another and this is what is meant by the *Grogan* rationale. However, some commentators have argued that this is a far too narrow definition of 'fraud' and that a wider view might be taken, which can then be used to justify both fully secret and half-secret trusts. This was the view of Lord Westbury in *McCormick v Grogan* (1869). Here, however, lies the flaw in this theory, because it amounts to no more than the bald assertion that a testator's wishes and the beneficiaries' interests should be respected even if he has put them into effect in a manner that is not acceptable (that is, not in compliance with the **Wills Act 1837**, see Lord Buckmaster in *Blackwell v Blackwell* (1929). There is nothing here to explain why the formalities prescribed by statute for facilitating that intention can be ignored.

A final theory seeks to prise secret trusts away from its link with the **Wills Act 1837** altogether and to explain them as ordinary trusts created *inter vivos*. According to this view – sometimes called the declaration and constitution theory (or *dehors* principle) of secret trusts – both fully secret and half-secret trusts operate outside the testator's will and should not be regarded as dependent upon it (*Blackwell v Blackwell*). The evidence for this is, apparently, provided by *Re Young* (1951), where a witness to a will was permitted to be a beneficiary under a secret trust, and *Re Gardner (No 2)* (1923), where a beneficiary under a secret trust died before the testator but, nevertheless, his interest passed to his estate. Both of these results would have been impossible if the trust was governed by the **Wills Act 1837**.

Assuming, then, that the **Wills Act 1837** is not central to the whole matter, how are secret trusts formed under this theory? The rationale is that the communication by the testator to the trustee of the trust and/or its terms amounts to a normal *inter vivos* declaration of trust which is then completed on the testator's death when the property passes into the hands of the trustee. The will is simply the mechanism by which the trustee obtains the property and the trust becomes constituted. The logical effect of this argument is that secret trusts also depart from trust rules. A trust may not be created in respect of after-acquired property.

It is trite law that the trust does not come into existence until the testator dies, that being when the property passes and the trust becomes constituted. Yet, as ever, there are difficulties. If secret trusts are express trusts, this should mean that such trusts of land must be evidenced in writing as required by **s 53(1)(b)** of the **Law of Property Act 1925**. However, at least with fully secret trusts, *Ottaway v Norman* (1972) suggests that writing is not required and it would be strange for written evidence to be necessary for compliance with **s 53** of the **LPA 1925** when none such was required for compliance with the **Wills Act 1837**. Nevertheless, *Re Baillie* (1886) is unequivocal that writing is needed for half-secret trusts of land. There are other problems, too. If the secret trust does not come into existence until the testator's death, *Re Gardner (No 2)* (1923) must be wrongly decided, as the trust did not exist when the beneficiary died! More importantly, if the relevant date for constitution of the half-secret trust might be the testator's death, why is the date of the will so important for communication purposes? Why is it necessary to declare the trust before the will is made if the will is only a trigger for the constitution of the trust? It is difficult to answer these criticisms,[1] save only to say that the communication rule for half-secret trusts is wrong and that post-testamentary communication should be possible. Support for this radical proposition comes from other common law jurisdictions where the distinction between fully secret and half-secret trusts has been abolished (for example, Australia). Nevertheless, there are other explanations of why there is a difference in this respect between the two types of secret trust, although none is altogether convincing. Two of the more cogent theories are, first, that the rule allowing acceptance after the will in fully secret trusts was originally procedural, in that evidence of events occurring after the will (that is, acceptance of the trust obligation) could be admitted by a court to prove a fully secret trust in order to prevent fraud by the legatee/trustee, whereas with half-secret trusts, where the legatee is clearly stated to be a trustee, there is no possibility of fraud and therefore no need to examine events (for example, acceptance) occurring after the will. Second, it may be that the half-secret trust rule is a mistake because of confusion with the law of incorporation of documents. A will may be said to 'incorporate' another document if the will makes reference to that document and if that document was in existence at the time the will was made. It is easy to see how this rule could have been carried over to require acceptance of the half-secret trust at the time the will was made. Of course, it is clear that neither of these theories (nor any other) is wholly satisfactory, and they do not help in finding a rationale for secret trusts generally. What they do illustrate, however, is that any theory concerning any aspect of the law of secret trusts is not watertight.

There may be no coherent theory underlying secret trusts and perhaps the best we can say is that the law in this regard has developed organically, with judges solving practical problems in real cases according to the needs of the parties at the time. That they may have had no real theory in mind is not in itself a serious criticism.[2]

QUESTION 7

Thomas executed his will on 1 April, which contained a legacy of £5,000 to Arnold and a legacy of £10,000 to Betty. In his will, Thomas directed Betty to hold her legacy 'as a matter of trust for such persons as I have communicated to her'. On 1 May, Thomas told

1   It is permissible to state that the current law is inaccurate provided that the point is clearly argued.

2   Explanation of the confused state of the law.

Arnold that he wished Arnold to pay his legacy to Thomas's illegitimate son, Zeus. One month later, after a quarrel with Zeus's mother, Thomas told Arnold to keep the money for himself. On 30 March, Thomas telephoned Betty and asked her whether she would be prepared to be a trustee of the money he would leave her in his will. Betty said she would think about it, and received a letter on 2 April enclosing a key to a safe where Thomas said he had deposited instructions as to the destination of the money. Betty immediately telephoned Thomas to assure him she would carry out his wishes. After Thomas's death, a letter was found in the safe directing Betty to pay the money to Lucy. Thomas died on 1 August without altering his will in any way.

▶ Advise Arnold and Betty as to their rights concerning the legacies.

How to Read this Question

Problem questions require careful reading and analysis. The main issues here involve the extent to which Thomas may alter the identity of the intended beneficiary during his lifetime and ascertaining the date of acceptance of a half-secret trust obligation.

How to Answer this Question

The examinee is required to define fully secret and half-secret trusts and apply the relevant issues to the facts. The specific issues raised need to be identified and discussed in depth. The issues involve the date of creation of a fully secret trust and the possible date of acceptance of half-secret trust obligations. These issues may require objective and balanced arguments to be presented.

Up for Debate

Secret trusts are subject to a number of controversial issues. One of these is to ascertain the date of creation of fully secret trusts. Closely related to that issue is the notion of the status of fully secret trusts. Are they express or constructive trusts? These matters have not been conclusively determined by the courts but have significant, practical ramifications with regard to statutory formalities.

Aim Higher

The peculiarity of secret trusts is that they are regarded as valid and enforceable despite the fact that they do not comply with the strict requirements of formality found in s 9 of the **Wills Act 1837**. Secret trusts may be valid where either or both the fact of the trust and its details are declared orally or by post-testamentary writing. Although the matter is not free from doubt, it is arguable that secret trusts operate under the court's equitable jurisdiction which has always been flexible enough to assist those believed worthy of its protection. Articles that explore the rationale of secret trusts include P Critchley 'Instruments of fraud, testamentary dispositions and the doctrine of secret trusts' (1999) 115 QR 631; D Kincaid 'The tangled web: the relationship between a secret trust and the will' (2000) 64 Conv 421.

Common Pitfalls

The danger with problems of this type is that students are content to remain with the most obvious answer, namely that the half-secret trust fails. A moment's thought will reveal the danger in this, since it must always be remembered that equity encompasses a flexible set of principles, not rules written in concrete.

Answer Plan

❖ Fully secret trusts: communication and acceptance, validity of revocation of trust and substitution of trustee/legatee as sole legatee.

❖ Half-secret trusts: date of communication and acceptance, method of communication and acceptance, possible contradiction of the will.

Answer Structure

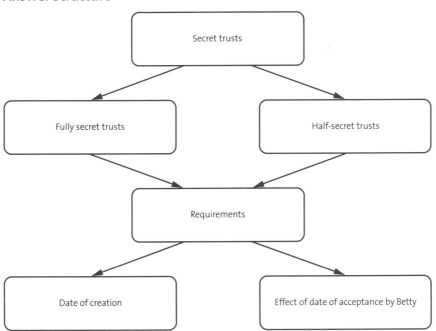

This diagram illustrates a number of fully and half-secret trusts issues raised in the transactions involving Arnold and Betty.

ANSWER

This question concerns the law of secret trusts. In essence, secret trusts are those trusts which operate in relation to a testamentary disposition but where either the very fact and details of the trust are not declared in the testator's will (fully secret trusts) or where, although the fact of the trust is declared in the will, the identity of the beneficiaries is not (half-secret trusts) (*McCormick v Grogan* (1869); *Re Keen* (1937)). In this question, there appear to be issues concerning the validity of fully secret trusts and half-secret trusts. Each attempted disposition will be discussed in turn.[3]

First, we shall consider the legacy to Arnold, with oral instructions to hold the property for another under a potential secret trust.

In his will, Thomas makes a bequest of £5,000 to Arnold without any limitation on the way in which Arnold may use his gift. On the face of the will, this is an absolute gift to Arnold. Consequently, any claim that Zeus may have to the money may arise only under a fully secret trust.[4] A fully secret trust will arise where, despite an apparently absolute gift, the testator has communicated his intention to the legatee that the property should be held for another, which expressed desire has been accepted by the legatee (*Thynn v Thynn* (1684)). In our case, there is no doubt of Thomas's intention to create a trust (contrast *Margulies v Margulies* (2000)) and, providing that the legatee/trustee accepts the obligation at any time before the testator's death, there is every chance that the secret trust will be enforced in favour of the intended beneficiary. Arnold's acceptance of the trust obligation is clear enough and, prima facie, a potential fully secret trust seems to have arisen. Arnold's acceptance may take the form of silence or acquiescence, see *Re Keen* (1937). However, before his death, Thomas attempts to revoke his secret trust intention and revert to the position as it is expressed on the face of the will; namely, an absolute gift to Arnold. This poses a far-reaching question about the time at which a fully secret trust comes into existence. If, for example, the secret trust comes into existence the moment the legatee/trustee accepts the trust obligation, then clearly Arnold will hold the property on trust for Zeus, as once a trust is created, the beneficiaries' rights become perfect (see *Milroy v Lord* (1862)). If, on the other hand, the secret trust comes into existence at the testator's death, then clearly the intended trust can be revoked at any time prior to that event and alternative arrangements can be made.[5]

The former view, which would enable Zeus to claim the £5,000, is superficially attractive because it prevents the testator from using fully secret trusts to alter his testamentary dispositions without making another will. It is one thing to allow secret trusts to avoid the **Wills Act 1837** in their formation, but should they also be used to circumvent the requirements of writing by giving the testator a power of unattested disposition right up to his death? Such a view of secret trusts is implicit in the decisions in *Re Gardner (No 2)* (1923) and *Sonley v Clock Makers Company* (1780), although *Sonley* was a half-secret trust and *Re Gardner (No 2)* has attracted considerable academic criticism.

The alternative view sees the secret trust as arising on the testator's death and therefore revocable until then. The judgments in *Blackwell v Blackwell* (1929) and *Re Maddocks* (1902) support this view. The logic of this approach is that the communication to the trustee during

---

3   It is important to define relevant legal concepts.
4   Application of the legal principle to the facts.
5   On controversial issues examiners require you to raise the issue and evaluate your opinion.

his lifetime, and acceptance thereof, is simply an *inter vivos* declaration of trust and that the trust becomes constituted when the property passes into the hands of the trustee on the testator's death. Thus, the trust may be revoked by the settlor prior to his death. If this is the better view (despite the fact that it allows oral post-testamentary dispositions of property), then clearly Thomas can revoke the trust in favour of Zeus. Further, it seems from the facts that Arnold is to revert to being the beneficiary of an absolute gift as stated on the face of the will and, if the revocation is effective, this will be the final position. Indeed, even if one were to argue that Arnold is to be the new beneficiary under the secret trust (that is, holding on trust for himself), *Irvine v Sullivan* (1869) is clear authority for the proposition that a fully secret trustee can be a beneficiary under his own trust. Arnold may claim his legacy.

▶ **Next, there is the gift on trust to Betty, holding for Lucy.**

There is a clear intention in respect of the bequest in the will to Betty that she is to be a trustee. Hence, whatever conclusion we come to about the persons ultimately entitled to the £10,000, we know that Betty will not be able to claim the gift. At the very least, she will hold the money on resulting trust for Thomas's estate (*Re Keen* (1937) and *Re Rees* (1950)). However, in order that Lucy may claim the property, she must establish a half-secret trust, wherein the details of the trust were communicated to Betty and accepted by her prior to, or simultaneously with, the execution of the will (*Re Bateman* (1970)). Here is Lucy's first problem as the facts make it clear that, although Thomas asked Betty to be a trustee before the date of the will, acceptance thereof was not made until after the will was executed on 1 April.[6] There are four possibilities. First, the communication rule is applied strictly and the half-secret trust is invalid, with Betty therefore holding on resulting trust for Thomas's estate. Although a perfectly defensible result on the authorities, this seems harsh in the circumstances. Second, it might be argued that Betty had impliedly accepted the trust at the date of the initial telephone call. This seems untenable on the facts and *Moss v Cooper* (1861) is not applicable. Third, we could take the robust view that the communication rule for half-secret trusts is wrong and that the proper approach is that of other common law jurisdictions where the rules for fully secret trusts and half-secret trusts are assimilated. This is attractive, especially because there is no totally convincing explanation for the difference between the two types of trust. However, unfortunately, both *Re Keen* (1937) and *Re Bateman* (1970) are clear enough. Fourth, it can be argued that it is not certain that the communication rule is violated in this case. As *Re Keen* establishes, communication and acceptance must be made before or *simultaneously with* the execution of the will and it is arguable that a process of communication and acceptance that began prior to the execution of the will and which was completed soon after is 'simultaneous' for this purpose.

Assuming, then, that the communication and acceptance of the trust were validly made, Lucy faces other problems. It might be thought that the terms of the trust contradict the terms of the will and this is prohibited by *Re Keen* (for example, as I 'have' communicated). However, this point is met if the above argument about the simultaneous nature of the communication and acceptance of the details is adopted. Likewise, although Betty is not

---

6 Identification of the issue as clearly as possible is necessary.

given the precise details of the trust, because they are contained within a locked safe, it is clear from *Re Boyes* (1884) that communication of the means of identifying the beneficiaries is acceptable if it is made at the relevant time (the simultaneous argument again) and if it is out of the power of the testator to change those details. Thus, assuming that Thomas has not kept a key to the safe and cannot change the identity of the beneficiary after his will has been executed, Lucy will be able to claim the £10,000.

QUESTION 8

Sam has recently died. By his will, he bequeathed his large collection of rare stamps to 'Peter and David absolutely'. In addition, in a separate clause in the will he left his house to William 'on trust for purposes I have communicated to him'.

Before he died, he told Peter that both he and David were to hold the stamps on trust for Becky, his illegitimate daughter. A letter repeating the same instruction to David was found amongst Sam's personal effects after his death. David has informed you that he only became aware of Sam's wishes regarding the stamp collection following his death. Before his death, Sam orally told William that the house was also to be held on trust for Becky.

◗ Advise Becky as to whether she is entitled to any of the properties.

How to Read this Question

This problem question raises issues concerning both fully and half-secret trusts. On a careful reading of the question you will notice that we have not been told when the will was made. This is significant to determine whether David is a trustee and to decide on the validity of the potential half-secret trust that may be imposed on William.

How to Answer this Question

This problem requires you to state and apply the requirements for the creation of fully and half-secret trusts and to consider the extent to which David and William may be bound to hold on trust. In addition students are required to consider the standard of proof that must be discharged before a claimant may succeed in proving the existence of a secret trust as well as the formal requirements under s 53 of the **Law of Property Act 1925**.

Up for Debate

This problem question raises a number of controversial issues with crucial facts deliberately left vague in order to tease out arguments that may be raised for and against the validity of the trusts. One such issue is the solution and its justification when one of several intended trustees has agreed to become a secret trustee. Bryn Perrins explores the rationale of the court's solution in 'Can you keep half a secret?' (1972) 88 LQR 225. Another difficult issue involves non-compliance with formal requirements created by statute, see G Allan 'The secret is out there: searching for the legal justification for the doctrine of secret trusts through analysis of the case law' (2011) CLWR 40.

Answer Plan

- ❖ Requirements in order to create a fully secret trust.
- ❖ Communication to one of several intended trustees.
- ❖ Standard of proof.
- ❖ Requirements for a half-secret trust.
- ❖ Section 53(1)(b) of the **Law of Property Act 1925**.

Answer Structure

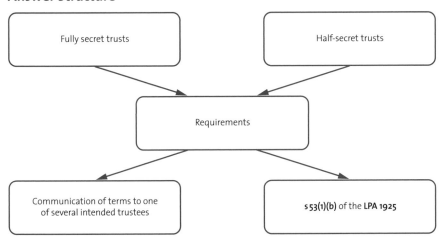

This diagram highlights secret trusts requirements and a number of related issues connected with Sam's will.

ANSWER

Sam's will has effected two transfers – the first concerning a large collection of rare stamps to Peter and David, the second in respect of a house to William. We will deal with the consequences of each of these dispositions in turn.

The stamp collection

The transfer in the will is to Peter and David apparently beneficially on the face of the will. There is no indication that these two individuals take other than for their benefit. However, before Sam died he told Peter that both he and David were required to hold the collection on trust for Becky, Sam's illegitimate daughter.[7] This arrangement raises the possibility of a fully secret trust being created in favour of Becky. We will now examine how far this is the case.

A fully secret trust is one where the legatee takes the property beneficially on the face of the will but subject to an understanding between the testator and themselves concerning the property during the lifetime of the testator. The *existence* of the trust, as well as

---

7   It is advisable to extract salient facts from the problem in order to focus on the issue.

its *terms*, are fully concealed by reference to the will. This appears to be evident in the problem. In this context, the court draws a distinction between a mere legacy on the one hand, and a legacy subject to a secret trust.[8] The essence of the distinction is that in a legacy subject to a secret trust, the testator communicates the terms of the trust during his lifetime to the legatees. In this respect, it is immaterial that the communication of the terms is made before or after the execution of the will, provided that it is made before the testator's death. Applying this principle to the facts of the problem Sam, during his life-time, has communicated the terms of the trust to Peter, namely that both legatees are required to hold on trust for Becky. Thus far, it is clear that Peter has knowledge of the terms of the trust and is subject to an equitable obligation to carry out the testator's wishes. Has Sam, during the relevant time, communicated the terms of the trust to David? We are told that a letter was found among Sam's personal effects repeating the instruction to David. But the issue is whether this letter was received by David during Sam's lifetime.[9] It would appear that this is not the case. The conclusion here is that David was unaware of Sam's wishes. The implications of this finding will be explored below.

The next requirement for the creation of a fully secret trust is that the intended trustees must accept the terms of the communication made to them. Acceptance for these pur-poses may be expressly declared by the trustees in the sense that they positively acknow-ledge the existence of an obligation to act as trustees. There is no evidence that this is the case on the facts of the problem. But acceptance may also be inferred by the silence or acquiescence of the trustee, during the testator's lifetime, see *Moss v Cooper* (1861). Of course this can only be the case where the trustee is aware of the terms of the communi-cation. The rationale is that it would be a fraud on the testator (not to mention the intended beneficiary under the trust) for the trustee to deny the agreement made with the testator. Accordingly, Peter, by implication, has agreed to become a trustee for Becky.

Would David be obliged to hold on trust or would he take part of the property beneficially? To put the question another way, the issue is when a testator leaves property by will to two persons apparently beneficially, but informs one of the apparent legatees of the terms of the trust, would the person who is unaware of the trust be bound to hold upon trust or not? The solution adopted by the courts, which is far from adequate, depends on the status of the co-owners and the time when the communication was made to those who are aware of the trust. If the informed legatee or devisee was told of the terms of the trust before or at the time of the execution of the will and the multiple owners take as joint tenants, the uninformed legatee is bound by the terms of the trust communicated to the informed legatee. The reason commonly ascribed for this solution is that no one is allowed to claim property under a fraud committed by another. This was stated by Farwell J in *Re Stead* (1900). The assumption that is made is that the informed trustee attempted to defraud the testator, irrespective of the reason for failure to inform the ignorant trustee. On the other hand, if the communication of the terms was made subsequent to the

----

8   Application of the legal definition to the facts.
9   The legal issue may be identified in the form of a question. It is important to address that issue by refer-ence to the law.

execution of the will only the person aware of the terms of the trust is bound, for in this case there is no fraud. On the facts of the problem, Peter and David take as joint tenants for they are co-owners without any words of severance, but we are not told when Sam communicated the terms of the trust to Peter. If the communication was made before or at the time of the execution of the will, this would be sufficient to subject David to a trust in favour of Becky. If the communication was made later, David will take part (half) of the property beneficially, and Peter will hold the other portion on trust, see *Re Stead*.

The final point involves the standard of proof to establish the trust. If there is no fraud the standard of proof is a balance of probabilities, but if there is an allegation of fraud the standard exceeds a balance of probabilities but is not as high as beyond a reasonable doubt, see *Re Snowden* (1979). There is no clear definition of fraud, but it has been suggested that where the intended trustee denies the existence of a trust, this involves an allegation of fraud. Since David disputes the existence of an obligation on his part (failure to communicate), it is arguable that this imposes a higher standard of proof on Becky.

The house

The terms of the will indicate the existence of a trust but the details of the trust are concealed. This is consistent with an intended half-secret trust. In order to create such a trust, the testator is required to communicate the terms before or at the time of the execution of the will. If the terms of the trust are communicated after the execution of the will, even during the testator's lifetime, the evidence is not admissible, see *Blackwell v Blackwell* (1929). The reason commonly attributed to this rule involves compliance with the formal requirements under **s 9** of the **Wills Act 1837** in respect of post-will communications. Commentators have suggested that it is a confusion of probate rules with trusts rules. In any event the courts have not demonstrated a willingness to modify the principle. Applying this principle to the facts of the problem, we are told that Sam told William of the terms of the trust before his death. But we are not told specifically at what time the communication was made.[10] If the communication was made before or at the time of the execution of the will, Becky would be entitled to prove the terms of the trust, otherwise the intended trust will fail and the property will be held on resulting trust for Sam's estate.

There are additional problems in that William has pre-deceased the testator; would this have an effect on the potentially valid half-secret trust? Although there are no decided cases, it is arguable that since the trustee takes as trustee on the face of the will, the trust ought not to fail, provided that the terms of the trust could be established. This is in accordance with the maxim, 'equity will not allow a trust to fail for want of a trustee'. The alternative is that the intended half-secret trust fails by virtue of the probate doctrine of lapse. This rule, it may be pointed out, is applicable where a person takes beneficially under a will. In half-secret trusts this is not the case. An additional issue is whether the terms of the trust could be established in the absence of both William and Sam. If this is not the case, a resulting trust will arise in favour of Sam's estate.

....

10 Where a significant fact is unclear you should assume both ways and apply the appropriate legal principles.

Another issue concerns the lack of writing in respect of the terms of the trust. The argument here is that s 53(1)(b) of the **Law of Property Act 1925** enacts that a 'declaration of trust in respect of land or any interest therein must be manifested and proved by some writing signed by the person able to declare the trust or by his will'. Clearly, the will does not declare the trust and the subject matter is land, but the issue is whether Sam ought to have manifested the terms of the trust in writing. We are told that he orally told William of the terms. Is s 53(1)(b) of the **LPA 1925** applicable to the transaction or does s 53(2) of the **LPA 1925** exempt the testator from the requirements of s 53(1)(b) of the **LPA 1925**? **Section 53(2)** of the **LPA 1925** enacts that 'This section shall not affect the creation or operation of implied resulting or constructive trusts.' This involves the classification of half-secret trusts. If they are treated as intended express trusts, s 53(1)(b) of the **LPA 1925** may be required to be complied with. In *Re Baillie* (1886) the court decided that half-secret trusts are required to comply with the predecessor to s 53(1)(b) of the **LPA 1925**. Non-compliance with the sub-section makes the trust unenforceable for lack of evidence in writing. Thus Becky may not be able to enforce the trust of land. If, on the other hand, the trust is treated as constructive, s 53(2) of the **LPA 1925** will exempt Sam from the requirements of s 53(1)(b) of the same Act. An argument in support of this view is that the trust is created to prevent fraud. This was the original basis for such trust and may still be applicable today.

3 The Inherent Attributes of a Trust: The Three Certainties and the Beneficiary Principle

INTRODUCTION

In the previous two chapters we have looked at the formalities needed to create a trust, the necessity for the trustee to be invested with title to the trust property in order that the trust be properly constituted and the curious exception to some of these rules found in the law of secret trusts. We have not yet begun to explore the factors which are elemental in the trust concept. In this chapter, two of the inherent characteristics of the trust will be examined: the requirement of the 'three certainties' and the 'beneficiary principle'.

The 'three certainties' is simply a shorthand description for a set of conditions which, when fulfilled, epitomise the trust. These certainties constitute the minimum set of requirements or terms necessary in order to declare the trust. In simple terms, every express trust must be established with:

(a) certainty of intention, so as to indicate that the holder of the property is under a trust obligation and must use the property according to the terms of the trust;

(b) certainty of subject matter, so as to ensure that the property which is the subject matter of the trust obligation is clearly defined or definable; and

(c) certainty of objects, so as to ensure that the beneficiaries to whom the trustee owes his onerous duties are clearly ascertainable and in whose favour the court can enforce the trust should the trustee fail in those duties.

As we shall see, the method of determining whether the three certainties exist may vary from trust to trust, especially with certainty of objects. In addition, where charitable trusts are concerned, the certainty of objects rules to be discussed below are not applicable and reference should be made to Chapter 4 for the definition of 'charity'. Finally, there is no statutory guidance as to the nature of the 'three certainties' and there is no substitute for a thorough grounding in case law.

The 'beneficiary principle' is very closely related to the need for certainty of objects for it expresses the idea that every non-charitable trust must have a human beneficiary. In other words, it is generally impossible in English law to establish a trust for a purpose, unless that purpose can be regarded as charitable (see Chapter 4). Thus, nearly every attempt to place a duty on a trustee to achieve non-charitable aims instead of holding the property for ascertainable individuals is doomed to failure. Once again, the beneficiary principle is easy to state, but difficult to apply in concrete cases because of the sometimes confusing precedents which are available.

QUESTION 9

Does the 'is or is not' test propounded by the House of Lords in *McPhail v Doulton* (1971) provide clarity in relation to the need for certainty of objects in the creation of a discretionary trust or power?

How to Read this Question

This essay question requires you to analyse the 'any given postulant' test for certainty of objects and evaluate the various approaches that have been advocated. In the light of the discussion the ultimate question is whether the test has provided clarity in the law.

How to Answer this Question

In answering this question you will be required to explain not only the test but to state the justification for the assimilation of the test for powers and discretionary trusts in 1971. In addition you will be required to state and evaluate the various judicial approaches that have been laid down.

Up for Debate

This is a highly contentious area of law because of the uncertainty created by the courts in respect of a fundamental issue regarding the validity of discretionary trusts and powers of appointment. Some of the issues have been explored by C Emery 'The most hallowed principle: certainty of beneficiaries in trusts and powers of appointment' (1982) 98 LQR 551.

Aim Higher

This is an extremely complex and fluid area of the law and students are advised to carefully read the judgments in the leading cases. The distinction between certainty of gifts (*Re Allen* certainty of conditions) and certainty of trusts ought to be understood and the various approaches of the Lords Justices of Appeal in *Re Baden (No.2)* and *Re Tuck* (1978) carefully considered. Careful reading of the following articles may significantly enhance your understanding of the subject: Y Gribch, 'Baden: awakening the conceptually moribund trust' (1974) 37 MLR 643; L McKay, 'Re Baden and the third class of uncertainty' (1974) 38 Conv 269.

Common Pitfalls

Students attempting this type of question do not always appreciate the rationale and ramifications behind each of the interpretations of the 'is or is not' test. Since there is no consistency in the approach of the courts, students are encouraged to be assertive, provided that they base their arguments on rational grounds.

Answer Plan

❖ Explain the 'is or is not' test.

❖ The move to the 'is or is not' test.

❖ Three views of the test: *Re Baden* and redefining concepts.

❖ Other tests of certainty.

Answer Structure

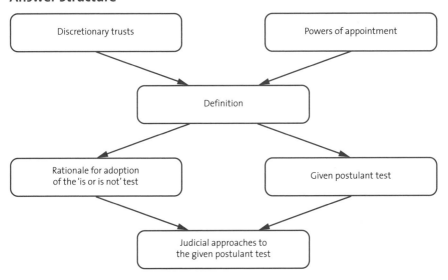

This diagram refers to the rational and judicial approaches underlying the 'any given postulant' test for certainty of objects.

ANSWER

The narrow 'list' test for certainty of objects in respect of discretionary trusts was abandoned by the House of Lords in *McPhail v Doulton* (1971) in favour of the broader 'is or is not' test that has always been applicable to powers of appointment. The justification for this change involved the inappropriateness of subjecting such a broad concept as a discretionary trust to the extremely limited 'list' test as illustrated in *IRC v Broadway Cottages Trust* (1955). In addition, the discretionary trust, in form though not in substance, is closer to a power of appointment as opposed to a fixed trust. A discretionary trust is an express trust that imposes an obligation on the trustees to distribute property in favour of any or all of the members of a class of objects. A power of appointment is similar in form but does not impose an obligation to distribute but merely permits the trustee or donee of the power to do so. The 'is or is not' test for certainty of objects is whether the trustees may say with certainty that any given postulant is or is not a member of a class of objects and it is unnecessary for the trustees to draw up a comprehensive list of the objects. Unfortunately, this test is easy to state but difficult to apply. Following the change in the law in *McPhail v Doulton* the case was remitted to the High Court (*Re Baden (No 2)* (1973)) to determine the validity of the trust. The decision of the High Court was affirmed by the Court of Appeal in favour of the validity of the trust. The three Lords Justices of Appeal in the Court of Appeal took the opportunity to provide a thorough explanation of the 'is or is not' test. What emerged was three individual interpretations of what the test required in practice.

When considering the test, it is important to distinguish between 'conceptual' uncertainty and 'evidential' uncertainty. A class description is conceptually uncertain when the words used by the settlor or testator do not have a precise legal meaning in themselves, irrespective of the factual circumstances surrounding the particular case e.g. 'friends'. Conversely, a class description is evidentially uncertain when it is impossible to determine whether, in fact, a person falls within the class description. The issue is one of evidence, not of the meaning of the words used to define the class. Thus, a trust 'for my employees' may be evidentially uncertain if there is no method of determining who is in fact an employee. As we shall see, it is disputed whether the 'is or is not' test requires conceptual certainty of the class of objects, evidential certainty of the class of objects or both.

Starting first with the judgment of Stamp LJ in *Re Baden (No 2)* (1973), it is clear that he approached the 'is or is not' test literally. In his view, conceptual and evidential certainty of the class are required, for otherwise it would not be possible to say whether anyone *was not* a member of the class. It will be appreciated that this is a rigorous standard as it may mean that a trust or power is declared void even though the settlor has drafted his dispositions very carefully, the fault lying in lack of evidence outside of his or her control. Consequently, there has been much criticism of this view of the *McPhail* test, not least because it requires a degree of certainty barely less than the 'complete list' test so decisively rejected by the House of Lords in that case.[1]

A recognition of these difficulties was at the heart of Sachs LJ's rejection of this literal approach in the second judgment in *Re Baden (No 2)*. In his judgment, the crucial question was whether the class was conceptually certain. If there was conceptual certainty the trust or power would not be invalidated by evidential uncertainty. A person who could not prove evidentially that he or she was within the conceptually certain class would be regarded as outside it. This very practical and workable view has much to commend it because it avoids confusing questions about the inherent validity of the trust or power (conceptual certainty) with difficulties surrounding its execution (evidential certainty). It is, perhaps, the most justifiable of the views to emerge from *Re Baden (No 2)*.

---

1 It is acceptable to present rational criticism of a judgment.

The third judge in the case, Megaw LJ, adopted the least stringent approach – the test was satisfied if it could be said of 'a substantial number' of persons that they were within the class conceptually, even if it were not possible to make a clear decision about every potential beneficiary or object. His reasoning was simply that the trustees/donees of the power could effectively administer the trust or power in such circumstances and, therefore, it should not be invalidated. As indicated, this test will be satisfied by most class gifts because there will be few class descriptions that do not have a central meaning and where it is not possible to say of a 'substantial number' (whatever that means) whether they are in the class or not. Indeed, Megaw LJ's analysis does not sit well with the House of Lords' formulation in *McPhail* that it must be possible to say of *any given person* whether they are or are not within the class. Indeed, it is arguable that Megaw LJ's approach is but a variant from the 'one postulant approach' that was overruled by the House of Lords in *Re Gulbenkian* (1970).

Another difficulty is that there is no agreement as to whether questions of conceptual certainty can be delegated by the settlor to a third person, as where the settlor directs that his brother may conclusively determine who is a 'friend'. On the one hand, this removes the question of objective validity of the trust or power from the hands of the court (*Re Wynn* (1952)) but, on the other, it has merit in that it clearly reflects the settlor's wishes (*Dundee General Hospital Board v Walker* (1952)). If we then remind ourselves that absolute gifts to individuals subject to a condition precedent (for example, '£100 to any person who is my friend') are subject to a completely different test of certainty (namely, whether it could be said of just one person that he or she satisfies the condition (*Re Barlow* (1979))) and that class gifts and gifts subject to a condition precedent can be easily confused, it is apparent that the certainty rules for discretionary trusts and powers are not defined with as much clarity as we might like. Again, even if the objects of the trust or power are sufficiently certain, there are the further hurdles of 'administrative unworkability' in discretionary trusts (*R v District Auditor ex p West Yorkshire MC* (1986)) and 'capriciousness' with powers (*Re Manisty* (1974)) to surmount. All in all, a person predicting in advance whether a discretionary trust or power has sufficiently certain objects may make a well-informed estimate, but cannot be entirely confident that he or she will be right.[2]

QUESTION 10
To what extent have the courts withdrawn from the fundamental principle that private purpose trusts are invalid?

How to Read this Question
This essay question is pitched by promoting an assertion that the courts have founded new techniques for validating apparent private purpose trusts. This issue may be explored by reference to case law.

2   It is acceptable in questions like these to conclude that the law is far from clear.

How to Answer this Question

A very good answer would require a clear justification of the rule against the validity of private purpose trusts (beneficiary principle) and an identification of the traditional exceptions to the general rule as concessions to human weakness. In addition students need to discuss the limitations to the lack of beneficiary rule as illustrated by numerous court decisions in respect of gifts to unincorporated associations.

Up for Debate

The *Denley* principle has been re-interpreted by the courts in dubious manner in *Re Grant's Will Trust* and *Re Lipinski*. The modern equivalent of the beneficiary principle is respect of gifts to unincorporated associations. Prominent articles to read on the subject include: J Warburton, 'The holding of property by unincorporated associations' (1985) Conv 318; P Matthews, 'A problem in the construction of gifts to unincorporated associations' (1995) Conv 302.

Answer Plan

❖ The beneficiary principle and its purpose.
❖ Recognised exceptions and the problem of perpetuity.
❖ *Re Denley* principle.
❖ Unincorporated associations: exception to, or application of, the beneficiary principle.
❖ *Quistclose* trusts.

Answer Structure

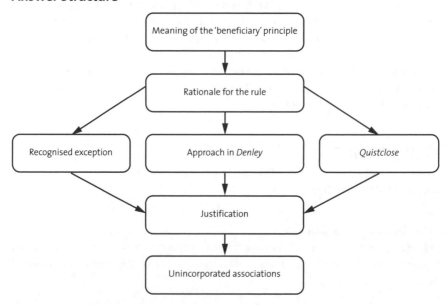

This diagram depicts the justification and exceptions to the 'beneficiary' principle.

ANSWER

When a person accepts the obligation of a trustee, he or she submits both to the jurisdiction of the court of equity and to the onerous duties of trusteeship. It is inherent in the concept of a trust that a court must be able to control and enforce the trusteeship and, if necessary, compel the trustees to carry out their duties.[3] There are several methods by which a court can exercise an effective enforcement jurisdiction, not least by requiring that all trusts have certain objects. Similarly, it is equally important that there must actually be *someone* in whose favour the court can decree performance of the trust and who can apply to the court to enforce its terms. Consequently, with the exception of charitable trusts (which can be enforced by the Attorney General on behalf of the Crown as *parens patriae*), a trust must be made for the benefit of human beneficiaries. There must be a *cestui que trust* in whose favour the court can decree performance (*Morice v Bishop of Durham* (1804); *Re Wood* (1949)). This is the 'beneficiary principle', and it means that, with the exception of charities, nearly all trusts for a purpose are void (*Re Endacott* (1960); *Re Astor* (1952)). Not surprisingly, therefore, there are a number of exceptional situations where trusts have been held valid despite being apparently or actually for a non-charitable purpose.

The first point to remember is that the meaning of every trust must be determined in the light of the words used by the settlor or testator. It is perfectly possible for a trust which, on its face, appears to be for a purpose to be construed as a trust for an individual or individuals (*Re Sanderson* (1857)).[4] A good example is provided by *Re Osoba* (1979), where a trust 'for the training of my daughter' was construed to be a trust absolutely for the daughter, the testator's expression of purpose (that is, 'for training') having no legal effect.

In contrast to the above category, it is also clear that special kinds of purpose trusts which actually benefit individuals directly or indirectly may be upheld by the court, providing certain conditions are met. This is known as the *Re Denley* principle. They are trusts for purposes which the court holds valid simply because there are individuals with *locus standi* who can apply to have the purpose carried out.[5] The essence of the matter, as explained in *Re Denley* (1969), is that the beneficiary principle is designed to eliminate purpose trusts of an abstract or impersonal nature, so that any purpose which may be accomplished with certainty and which does thereby confer a benefit directly or indirectly on human beneficiaries should not be declared void. Thus, in *Re Denley*, a trust for the maintenance of a sports ground (a purpose) for use by the employees of a company (the individuals indirectly benefited) was valid on the ground that the employees had *locus standi* to ensure that the trustees put the purpose into effect.

Moreover, private trusts are subject to the full rigour of the rule against perpetuities and may be a ground for invalidating the gift, see *Re Grant* (1980). In order to avoid perpetuity,

---

3 Justification for the beneficiary principle.

4 This is a question of construction and illustrates the flexibility of the court's jurisdiction.

5 Separate justification for adopting this approach.

the purpose trust must be expressly or impliedly limited to operate within the perpetuity period by the terms of the trust. In *Re Denley* itself, the trust was limited specifically to the perpetuity period and so was upheld by the court. But in *Re Grant* there was no power of disposal of the capital and the gift failed.

The *Re Denley* principle is a refinement of the rule against purpose trusts and, in principle, it can operate to validate any purpose trust that meets both the requirements of perpetuity and the need for ascertainable individuals indirectly benefited. In addition there are some purpose trusts for very specific purposes which are regarded as valid as being anomalous exceptions to the beneficiary principle. These are so-called 'trusts of imperfect obligation'; 'imperfect' because there is no beneficiary as such to enforce the trust. Although the categories may not now be extended (*Re Endacott* (1960)), they have been held valid because the trustees were prepared to undertake the purpose, because the purpose was certain, because there was no perpetuity and because the court had sympathy with the specific motive of the testator on the occasion the validity of the trust was challenged.[6]

The specific purpose trusts which may be valid under these principles are, first, trusts for the erection or maintenance of tombs or monuments, either to the testator or some other person (*Mussett v Bingle* (1876)). Second, trusts for the upkeep of animals after the testator's death, provided, again, that they are limited to the perpetuity period (*Mitford v Reynolds* (1848)). But see *Re Dean* (1889) which involved a peculiar application of the perpetuity rule. Third, trusts for the saying of masses for the soul of the testator may be upheld (*Re Gibbons* (1917)). Fourth, and very exceptionally, a trust for the promotion of fox hunting was upheld in *Re Thompson* (1934) on a spurious analogy with the animals' cases.

Finally, brief mention should be made of two other matters which relate to the beneficiary principle. First, there are many examples of settlors and testators attempting to give property to *unincorporated* associations – such as the local brass band or gardening club – which appear to fall foul of the beneficiary principle. The problem is simply that unincorporated associations have no legal personality and cannot, therefore, be beneficiaries under a trust. The difficulties this poses have been avoided by construing gifts to unincorporated associations not as gifts on trust for their purposes but as gifts to the individual members of the association who will then use the property to carry out the functions of the association (*Re Recher's Trust* (1972), *Artistic Upholstery Ltd v Art Forma (Ltd)* (1999) and *Re Horley Town Football Club* (2006)). This is so even if the settlor's or testator's gift is expressed to be for a purpose, see *Re Lipinski*. Once again, what seems to be a purpose trust is not so taken, because of a favourable construction by the court. Likewise, so-called *Quistclose* trusts (from *Barclays Bank v Quistclose Investments* (1970)), whereby a person (A) gives money to another (B) for the single purpose of enabling (B) to pay his debts to a creditor (C), appear to be purpose trusts – the payment of a debt. However, they have been variously analysed as either a form of the *Re Denley* trust (*Re Northern Developments (Holdings)* (1978)) or as a trust for the

---

6   Independent justification for these exceptions.

creditors with a resulting trust for the provider of the money (A) should the recipient (B) not use the money to pay his debts (*Carreras Rothmans v Freeman Mathews Treasure* (1985) and *Burton v FX Music* (1999)). Whatever their true basis, such trusts are not easily proven – as in *Box v Barclays Bank* (1998)).

In conclusion, it remains true that English law refuses to admit the validity of non-charitable purpose trusts as a matter of principle. However, the *Re Denley* principle, the anomalous exceptions, the imaginative constructions placed on gifts to unincorporated associations and, above all, the wide meaning given to charity, means that only the purest examples of purpose trusts which have no element of community benefit are likely to be invalid today.

QUESTION 11

Consider the validity of the following dispositions in the will of Elizabeth, who died in 2014:

'(a) £10,000 for the erection and maintenance of a suitable monument to myself in the village of my birth and for an annual memorial service in the parish church;
(b) £15,000 to the vicar of St Mary's Parish Church to be used as she pleases in the knowledge that nothing will be done which diminishes respect for the church; and
(c) £50,000 to my trustees to be spent on the provision of tennis courts for use by the residents of my home village.'

How to Read this Question

The three problem questions are essentially gifts to promote purposes and are therefore subject to the beneficiary principle. The student needs to focus on the anomalous exceptions to the *Astor* principle, the rule against perpetuities and the *Denley* principle.

How to Answer this Question

In (a) there are two purposes that are required to be considered the validity of the gifts to erect and maintain monuments and the memorial service for private purposes. In (b) there is a hint of charitable purposes that needs to be addressed, even though it may be impossible to draw firm conclusions because of the lack of evidence. In (c) discussion needs to be centred on the *Denley* principle.

Up for Debate

The main contentious issue in this type of question involves the scope of the *Denley* rule. What is the rule and what are the limits to principle? Articles published by leading academics on the subject include: P Lovell, 'Non-charitable purpose trusts: further reflection' (1970) Conv 77; L McKay, 'Trusts for purposes: another view' (1973) Conv 420.

Aim Higher

The beneficiary principle is fundamental to the law of trusts and manifests itself in different guises. Problems of perpetuity should not be avoided or ignored as even an otherwise valid purpose trust might thereby fail. The law regarding the perpetuities rule was brought up to date by the **Perpetuities and Accumulations Act 2009**. **Section 18** of the Act retains the common law concerning the duration of gifts for private purpose trusts. C Emery, 'Do we need a rule against perpetuities?' (1994) 57 MLR 602 provides a detailed account of the rule with proposals for reform.

Common Pitfalls

In dealing with questions on purpose trusts, the prospect of the gift being charitable must be borne in mind and mention must be made of the possibility of a resulting trust on a failure of the intended express trust.

Answer Plan

❖ Anomalous exceptions to the beneficiary principle: severability of gifts and perpetuity.
❖ Trusts, absolute gifts and purposes.
❖ *Re Denley* gifts: the appropriate perpetuity rule.

Answer Structure

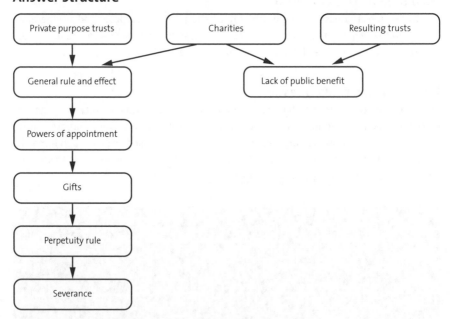

This diagram depicts a holistic view of purpose trusts.

ANSWER

(a) £10,000 for Monuments, etc.

This is an attempt to establish a purpose trust or, more accurately, a purpose trust with three different aims: the erection of a monument, the maintenance of that monument and the holding of an annual memorial service. The starting place must be *Re Endacott* itself, for not only does this firmly establish the beneficiary principle in English law, it was a case involving an unsuccessful attempt to establish a trust for the provision 'of some useful memorial to myself'. However, *Endacott* also accepted that there were a limited number of specific purpose trusts whose validity had been accepted by the court, albeit for reasons of sentiment or expediency. One of these, as demonstrated by *Mussett v Bingle* (1876) and *Re Hooper* (1932), is trusts for the erection or maintenance of monuments or graves, at least if the executors of the will are prepared to carry out the trust. Prima facie, this would seem to be authority for the validity of Elizabeth's trust for the erection and maintenance of a monument to herself, providing questions of perpetuity can be resolved. Indeed, our case is distinguishable from the failed trust of *Re Endacott*, as that involved a 'memorial', although it seems that even 'monuments' must have a funereal character to fall within the limited exception.

Unfortunately, however, apart from perpetuity problems, there is a further difficulty as the trust is also for an annual memorial service for Elizabeth. While it is possible that a trust for the purpose of saying a mass in private for a testator may be a valid purpose trust (*Re Gibbons* (1917)), it seems that Elizabeth's purpose falls outside that limited exception to the beneficiary principle. There is authority from a former colonial court that a private, non-Christian ceremony to perpetuate the memory of a person may be the subject of a valid purpose trust (*Re Khoo Cheng Teow* (1932)), but it is unlikely that such a trust would be accepted today, especially in the light of the clear direction from *Re Endacott* that the categories of valid purpose trusts are not to be extended. Consequently, questions of perpetuity aside, we seem to have one potentially valid purpose trust and one that is certainly void. It then becomes a matter of construction whether the invalidity of one part of the gift invalidates the whole, for it may be possible to sever the presumptively valid purpose trust, especially if some discrete portion of the £10,000 can be set aside for its completion.[7] The remainder would result to the testator's estate, as would the whole amount if there is no severance or if there were a general perpetuity problem (see below).

(b) £15,000 to the Vicar of St Mary's, etc.

The validity of this gift depends almost entirely on the construction that is placed upon it. There are four possible alternatives.[8] First, this might be an attempt by Elizabeth to give the vicar of St Mary's a power of appointment over the £15,000, where the object of the power is a purpose. There is no rule in English law that makes it impossible to create a power for a purpose. However, there must be an intention to establish a power (an

---

7   The issue of severance is inherent in the problem.
8   This is a very good technique to identify the possible solutions.

intention to establish a void purpose trust is not sufficient (*IRC v Broadway Cottages* (1955)), the objects of the power must be certain and there must be no perpetuity. In any event, it is likely that the purpose of the power would be regarded as too uncertain within the test for certainty of objects of powers (the 'is or is not' test) established in *Re Gulbenkian* (1970). The second possibility is that this disposition is regarded as neither a trust nor a power, but as an absolute gift to the vicar of St Mary's per se. The point is of some importance as, if this is an absolute gift, the vicar may keep the property for herself and do with it as she pleases. There are several examples of gifts being regarded as absolute despite the fact that the testator has attached some expression of motive or desire to the bequest, including *Re Osoba* (1979) and *Re Andrews* (1905). It may be important that the vicar of St Mary's is not named, but identified by her office. This does suggest that the money is not intended for that person individually, but in virtue of her official capacity.

A third possibility may be that this is a gift for charitable purposes, being for the advancement of religion (*Re Fowler* (1914)), see **s 3(1)(c)** of the **Charities Act 2011**. In some cases, a gift to a clergyman on trust to do as he pleases has been taken to indicate a trust for the advancement of religion (*Re Flinn* (1948)). However, once again, in our case, there is no clear indication that any trust was intended and, even if it were, the general vagueness of the testator's instructions suggests that the gift may be used for other purposes that are not wholly for the advancement of religion: advancement is not the same as non-obstruction. Fourth, this may be a straightforward, non-charitable, purpose trust which is void under *Re Endacott*. So, depending on the construction of the gift, this disposition discloses either no trust or power at all, being an absolute gift; a power for a purpose, which is probably uncertain and therefore void; a charitable purpose; or a void purpose trust.

(c) £50,000 on Tennis Courts

This appears to be a simple purpose trust: after all, the trustees will be under a mandatory obligation to erect tennis courts. However, instead of being void for want of a human beneficiary, this purpose trust appears to be valid under the *Re Denley* (1969) principle. According to this case, the rule against purpose trusts is intended to invalidate only those trusts which are abstract and impersonal. If a purpose trust directly or indirectly benefits a class of ascertained or ascertainable individuals, it will be valid as the individuals may be given *locus standi* to apply to the court in the event that the trustees do not carry out the trust. The individuals directly or indirectly benefited have no equitable interest in the trust property itself, although they do provide the means of enforcement. Indeed, with the exception of the perpetuity issue, our case is very similar to that in *Re Denley* itself where the purpose was the provision of a sports ground for employees. Applying that case, this disposition is presumptively valid.

Finally, we come to problems of perpetuity.[9] According to the rule against perpetual trusts, those non-charitable purpose trusts which, as an exception to the beneficiary principle, equity regards as valid, must not last longer than the perpetuity period, being a period not exceeding a life or lives in being and/or 21 years, see **s 18** of the **Perpetuities and**

---

9 Good technique to adopt a holistic approach to the question.

Accumulations Act 2009. Furthermore, the question of perpetuity must be resolved at the date the disposition comes into effect and, to be valid, there must be no possibility of the purpose lasting longer than the perpetuity period. This usually means that it is necessary for the testatrix to make some express or implied limitation to perpetuity in the trust instrument itself (*Leahy v Attorney General for New South Wales* (1959)). In our cases, although a trust for the erection of a monument will be presumed to be completed within the perpetuity period, a trust for its maintenance must be specifically limited to the period. The same is true for the trust for the annual memorial service, even if it is otherwise valid. Likewise, the *Re Denley* type trust must be limited to perpetuity. There are no such limitations and all these trusts would seem to fail for perpetuity if nothing else. Similarly, any power given to the vicar of St Mary's would fail were it not exercised within the perpetuity period.

QUESTION 12

In 1990, pursuant to a meeting 20 individuals formed the Benevolent Parachutists Club by each transferring £5,000 to their appointed trustee-treasurer to hold as a fatal accident fund. The minutes of the meeting disclosed that the fund was to be invested and monies paid out on a certain payment scale to the surviving spouse of a member who died as a result of a parachuting accident. Further contributions to the fund had been received by gifts from anonymous donors and by entertainment organised by the members. The payment scale had been updated from time to time but involved one-off capital sums to the recipients. In 2014 the funds of the Club were valued at £20,000.

▶ Advise the treasurer-trustee as to the beneficial ownership of the funds on the assumption that he is the only surviving member of the Club.

How to Read this Question

This problem question in respect of unincorporated associations involves the status of contributions of funds to the Club and the method of distributing surplus funds on the date of liquidation. It is significant that the Club has only one surviving member.

How to Answer this Question

It is advisable to first define an unincorporated association and deal with the legal status of the Club. The legal effect of donating funds to the Club needs to be examined in accordance with the case law. The main issue in the problem concerns the ownership of assets of the Club when only one subsisting member exists. The exclusion of charitable status ought to be expressly stated.

Up for Debate

The status of ownership of assets held by unincorporated associations and the destination of such property on liquidation has been the subject of some controversy. This issue has been explored by S Panesar, 'Surplus funds and unincorporated associations' (2000) 14 T&T 698.

Aim Higher

Students are urged to approach problem questions on purpose trusts holistically. First, consider whether the gifts are capable of subsisting as charitable trusts, second, whether the gifts create valid private purpose trusts and, if not, the consequences of failure, in particular, whether resulting trusts will arise or some alternative solution adopted by the courts. See C Rickett, 'Unincorporated associations and their dissolution' (1980) CLJ 88; P Smart, 'Holding property for non-charitable purposes: mandates, conditions and estoppels' (1987) Conv 415.

Common Pitfalls

Insufficient appreciation of the various approaches adopted by the court to avoid the beneficiary principle in the context of unincorporated associations.

Answer Plan

- ❖ Consideration of whether the Club is charitable.
- ❖ Status of unincorporated associations.
- ❖ Status of gifts to unincorporated associations.
- ❖ Status of gifts on trust for unincorporated associations.
- ❖ Distribution of surplus funds on dissolution.

Answer Structure

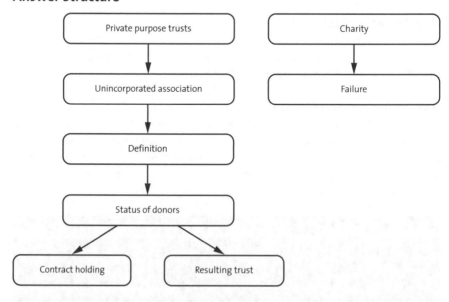

This diagram illustrates the nature of unincorporated associations and the status of holding its assets.

ANSWER

Clearly the Club is not charitable for the public benefit test laid down in **s 4** of the **Charities Act 2011** is not satisfied. There is a contractual nexus between the donors and donees that would deprive the Club of charitable status, see *Oppenheim v Tobacco Securities* (1951). This is evident in a private members' club.

The Club is an unincorporated association which is not a legal person but comprises a group of individuals joined together with common aims usually laid down in its constitution creating mutual duties and rights, see *Conservative and Unionist Central Office v Burrell* (1982).[10] The label, Benevolent Parachutist Club, is a means of identifying the members of the Club and claims may be made or defended by the members collectively or through the officers of the association as representatives of the members. The issue in these types of cases involves the identity of the owners of assets of the association. In this respect Cross J in *Neville Estates Ltd v Madden* (1962), in an *obiter* pronouncement, outlined various constructions concerning gifts or trusts in favour of unincorporated associations. He laid down three propositions:

- ❖ gifts to the members of the association as joint tenants, see *Cocks v Manners* (1871);
- ❖ gifts to the existing members as an accretion to the funds of the Club; and
- ❖ gifts on trust for the purposes of the association, see *Re Lipinski* (1977).

The prima facie rule with regard to gifts to the association concerns the second of these propositions, see *Re Recher's Will Trusts* (1972).[11] In this case Brightman J in an *obiter* pronouncement declared that a gift to the association may be construed as a gift to the members of the association on the date of the gift, not beneficially, but as an accretion to the funds of the society which is regulated by the contract (evidenced by the rules of the association) made by the members *inter se*. Thus, a subsisting member on the date of the gift is not entitled *qua* member to claim an interest in the property but takes the property by reference to the rules of the society. A member who leaves the association by death or resignation will have no claim to the property, in the absence of any rules to the contrary. Accordingly, the transfer in 1990 of £5,000 by each of the members of the Club will be construed as a gift to the members collectively for their benefit, but subject to the contract made with each other as manifested in its constitution. The effect is that no one member is unilaterally entitled to claim any part of the fund except in accordance with the rules of the Club.

The donations to the Club by anonymous persons and entertainment are construed in a similar vein. On the dissolution of the Club these donors are not entitled to a return of the funds donated by these means. A material factor concerns the intentions of the transferors.[12] First, the donors in the same category are treated as having the same intention. Accordingly, all the anonymous donors are deemed to have a like intention. Second, since the intention has not been expressed, the court is required to consider whether there is any evidence of an implied intention that the transferor retained an interest in

---

10 Definition of an unincorporated association.

11 Where there are several judicial solutions to an issue it would be prudent to express a preference.

12 Status of donation to the club.

the property. In *Re Gillingham Bus Disaster Fund* (1958), the High Court decided that funds donated anonymously were contributed for a specific purpose which failed and the funds were to be held on resulting trust for the contributors; but the court could easily have come to the opposite conclusion, namely the donors, being anonymous, manifested an intention not to have the property returned to them. They would then have parted with their funds 'out and out', leaving no room for a resulting trust. In other words, the transfer of the funds anonymously creates an irrebuttable presumption that the donors had parted out and out with the funds. This is the better view and the solution adopted by the High Court in *Re West Sussex Constabulary Trusts* (1971).

With respect to the fund-raising activities for the Club by means of entertainment, it would appear that on authority the donors are not entitled to a return of the funds on a dissolution of the Club. Those who attended these events with the motive of increasing the endowment of the Club created a relationship of contract, not trust. The contributors received the consideration for which they bargained, namely entertainment. Indeed, there were no direct contributions to the Club funds; only the profits of the entertainment were received by the Club. This was the view of Goff J in *Re West Sussex Constabulary* (1971). The effect is that the surplus funds of the Club originating from a variety of sources form an endowment which becomes available for distribution on a dissolution of the association.

Turning to the issue regarding the surplus funds on the date of the dissolution of the Club, it is worth pointing out that, subject to any liquidation clauses in the constitution, the modern rules governing the distribution of funds is based on the law of contract rather than the law of trusts. The court will infer a contract between all the members to the effect that ex-members of the Club on the date of dissolution cease to have any interest in the funds, see *Re Bucks Constabulary Fund (No. 2)* (1979). The earlier solution based on a resulting trust has fallen out of favour. The effect is that only subsisting members on the date of dissolution are entitled to participate in the distribution.

The issue posed in the problem involves the destination of property rights in the event that all the members have passed away save for one. The question is whether the sole surviving member of an unincorporated association is entitled to the surplus funds of the Club or whether the Crown is entitled to it on a *bona vacantia*. It is clear that the association will cease to exist because the contract between the members will come to an end. There can be no association since one cannot associate with oneself, see *Re Bucks Constabulary* (1979). On the death of the last surviving member, prior to the liquidation of the Club, the Crown will be entitled to the surplus as opposed to the estate of the last deceased member, see *Cunnack v Edwards* (1896); but the issue in the problem is distinguishable because the treasurer-trustee (member) is still alive and wishes to establish an interest in the surplus funds of the Club. On this issue Walton J in *Re Bucks Constabulary* (1979) in an *obiter* pronouncement declared that if the society is reduced to a single member, neither he, nor his personal representatives, will be entitled to the surplus funds and thus the assets become ownerless and may be taken by the Crown.

However, in the recent case, *Hanchett-Stamford v AG* (2008), the High Court refused to follow the *obiter* pronouncement of Walton J and decided that the sole surviving member was entitled to the surplus funds of the association. The court pointed out that the thread that runs through the main cases is that the property rights of an unincorporated association are vested in its members subject to their contractual rights and duties. On the date of the dissolution of the association the subsisting members are entitled to the assets. It would be illogical if a different rule were to be adopted where the membership of the association falls below two. In addition, the deprivation of the property interest in the surviving member would be a breach of **Article 1** of **Protocol 1** of the **European Convention on Human Rights** which guarantees the peaceful enjoyment of possessions. No pubic interest is served by the appropriation by the state of such member's share in the Club's assets.

In conclusion, the treasurer-trustee as the sole surviving member of the Benevolent Parachutist Club will be able to claim the surplus assets of the Club.

QUESTION 13

Assess the validity of the following dispositions in the will of Thomas, who died in December 2013:

(a) £10,000 to my Aunt Agatha, knowing that she will use the money in order to secure the future of my daughters;

(b) the residue of my estate to my executors for such of my colleagues at work as they shall in their discretion think fit.

Thomas worked for the National Health Service at various hospitals throughout his life, but spent the last ten years of his working life in Claremont General Hospital, which was destroyed by fire just after his retirement in 2010.

Aim Higher

It is important to appreciate that the three versions of the *Baden* test may cause different results for the validity of the trust or power. All must be considered and *Baden* should *not* be regarded as having a clear *ratio decidendi*.

Common Pitfalls

It is not necessary to decide whether the *Baden* test will be satisfied on the facts of the problem. What is needed are rational arguments demonstrating knowledge of the law, as opposed to conclusions on difficult issues of law.

How to Read this Question

This problem question requires you to analyse and apply two of the three certainties test for the creation of an express trust namely, certainty of intention and objects. Q 13(a) concerns the validity of transfers subject to precatory words and 13(b) deals with a transfer subject to a discretion as to the class of objects.

How to Answer this Question

(a)   You need to state and apply the test of construction regarding precatory words and consider the various outcomes when such expressions are used in a will.

(b)   The residue of Thomas's estate is subject to a discretion vested in his executors. Would this create a special power of appointment or alternatively a discretionary trust? Would the transfer be valid as satisfying the 'any given postulant' test? What are the consequences of failure to satisfy the test?

Up for Debate

The 'any given postulant' test for certainty of objects has attracted a great deal of attention in the courts and the academic sphere. Students are advised to read the following articles that have explored these issues: Y Gribich, 'Baden: awakening the conceptually moribund trust' (1974) 37 MLR 643; C Emery, 'The most hallowed principle: certainty of beneficiaries in trusts and powers of appointment' (1982) 98 LQR 551.

Answer Plan

Brief introduction to the concept of the three certainties:

❖   certainty of intention: precatory words, construction of the gift;
❖   certainty of objects: trust or power; test for certainty; construing the gift; evidential difficulties; administrative unworkability.

Answer Structure

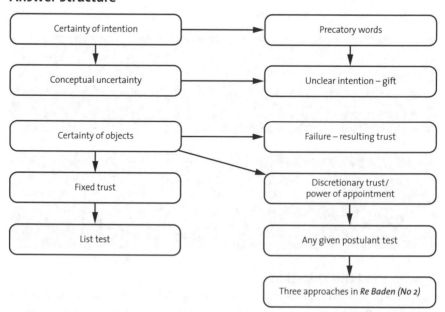

This diagram identifies the 'three certainties' test as an essential feature for the creation of an express trust.

ANSWER

It is a cardinal principle of the law of equity that a trust may only be valid – that is, enforceable by the beneficiaries against the trustee – if it has been created with certainty of intention, certainty of subject matter and certainty of objects (*Knight v Knight* (1840)). This particular problem concerns various aspects of the 'three certainties', and each limb of Thomas's testamentary disposition will be considered in turn.

(a) £10,000 to Aunt Agatha

The issue raised by this disposition is whether the legacy of £10,000 to Aunt Agatha is by way of trust or an absolute gift – in other words, whether there is sufficient certainty of intention to create a trust.[13] If a trust is created, then it becomes necessary to consider whether there are any valid objects of the trust and whether they are defined with sufficient certainty.

The imposition of a trust over the money requires Thomas to have imposed a mandatory obligation upon Aunt Agatha to carry out his wishes. This is purely a matter of construction of the words used and the surrounding circumstances (*Lambe v Eames* (1871)). It is clear that precatory words (words of expression, hope or desire) will not of themselves impose a trust on the recipient of property in the absence of corroborative evidence (*Re Conolly* (1910)).[14] In our case, the words used by Thomas are stronger than precatory words: Thomas does not 'hope' or 'wish' that Agatha will carry out his wishes, he 'knows' that she will. However, it is still not certain that this is enough to constitute a trust obligation. For example, in *Re Adams and the Kensington Vestry* (1884), a gift 'in full confidence that …' was held to be absolute and not mandatory in the way of a trust. On balance, it is likely that the bequest to Aunt Agatha will be construed as an absolute gift, essentially because of the absence of any other indication that this is intended to be a trust.[15] Moreover, even if this disposition was construed to be a trust, there might well be certainty of objects problems. While it is obvious that a trust in favour of 'my daughters' is perfectly certain as to objects, the disposition in this case is 'in order to secure the future of my daughters'. A literal reading of this suggests that this is a trust for *purposes* connected with Thomas's daughters, and trusts for purposes are void (*Re Endacott* (1959)). Of course, it might be possible to construe the disposition (if it were a trust in the first place) in favour of the daughters per se (compare *Re Osoba* (1979)) or as a trust saved by the *Re Denley* principle. However, these difficulties in defining the objects of the trust precisely only add to the doubts surrounding the lack of certainty of intention (e.g. *Re Kayford* (1975)). Consequently, in all probability, this is an absolute gift to Aunt Agatha, who may use the property for the benefit of Thomas's daughters if she chooses, but cannot be compelled to do so (*Lassence v Tierney* (1849)).

13 This is good examination technique; identifying the issues raised in this part of the question first before launching into a discussion about the issues.

14 Clear statement of the approach of the courts to precatory words.

15 Application of the principle to the facts of the problem. Tentative conclusion on a flexible issue is advisable.

(b) The Residue of Thomas's Estate

The gift of residue for 'such of my colleagues at work' raises, once again, the problem of certainty of objects, those objects being defined by reference to a class description. As regards this disposition, it is clear that the executors are given a discretion as to whom from among the class they shall select to receive a portion of the residue, and in what proportions. So, this part of Thomas's will discloses either a discretionary trust for the class or a special power of appointment given to the trustees to appoint among the class. Of course, the difference is crucial so far as the executors are concerned because, if this is a discretionary trust, they are under a mandatory obligation to make a selection from among the class and distribute the property whereas, if this is a power, they may decide not to distribute and cannot be compelled to do so. Whether this disposition discloses a trust or a power is a matter of construction and, as *McPhail v Doulton* (1970) shows, the distinction is not always easy to draw. In our case, it is important that there is no gift over in default of appointment, perhaps suggesting that the executors *must* choose from among the class, although the absence of a gift over does not always foretell a trust, since the testator may be content to allow the property to revert to the next of kin if the power is not exercised (*Re Weekes* (1897)). On balance, however, given that the gift to this class is already of the residuary estate and consequently the beneficiaries in default would be difficult to identify, we can legitimately surmise that Thomas intended this to be a discretionary trust.

Since *McPhail v Doulton*, the test for certainty of objects of a discretionary trust and a power have been assimilated and, even if this is a power, the test we must apply is whether it is possible to say with certainty that any given person is, or is not, a member of the class (*McPhail*). Unfortunately, although this test is easy to state, it is difficult to apply because the leading case on its application (*Re Baden (No 2)* (1973)) gives us three alternative approaches.[16] According to Stamp LJ, the traditional, rigid approach is required to be adopted and this requires the class to be defined with precision. This is a strict test and in view of the fire at his last place of work, will there be sufficient employment records to indicate with whom he worked, even if it were possible to say who then qualified as a 'colleague'? Second, even if we take Sachs LJ's approach, it may be difficult to decide whether this discretionary trust is valid. In his view, the test is satisfied if members of the public may prove that they are within the class. The corollary is that evidential difficulties will not invalidate a trust because any person who cannot prove that he or she is a member of the class will be deemed to be outside it. Would the concept of a 'colleague' be clear enough for the courts to determine validity? Finally, we come to Megaw LJ who proposed the least strict version of the 'is or is not' test, believing it to be satisfied if it could be said of a substantial number of persons that they were inside the class, even if it could not be said of every potential person whether he or she was or not. It may be that Thomas's dispositions would satisfy this version of the test. Unfortunately this lax approach has been heavily criticised by commentators.

The conclusion is then that Thomas's third disposition may fail for uncertainty of objects. It may be that a court would be prepared to redefine the concept of 'colleague' so as to make it more certain and then apply the 'is or is not' test to the class description so

16 It is advisable to state and apply each of three approaches to the test.

redefined (as in *Re Baden*), but that cannot be guaranteed. Indeed, even then, the executors face one more hurdle, for it may be that the class of the discretionary trust is 'administratively unworkable' and so void for 'secondary uncertainty'. This concept was expounded by Lord Wilberforce in *McPhail* and it is clear from *R v District Auditor ex p West Yorkshire MC* (1986) that if the settlor or testator stipulates a class so large that the trustees cannot effectively fulfil their duties, nor exercise their discretion properly under a discretionary trust, that trust will fail. In our case, Thomas's large number of former places of work may bring the class description within this principle. This will be a matter of judgment. If the gift under the residuary clause is void then the next of kin would be entitled to such surplus funds.

4

The Law of Charities

INTRODUCTION

Charitable trusts are valid public purpose trusts. This means simply that it is perfectly possible to establish a trust for the achievement of a purpose, provided that the purpose in law is regarded as charitable. As far as charities are concerned, it is not important if there is no human beneficiary capable of enforcing the trust, because the Attorney General can take action in respect of all charitable trusts on behalf of the Crown. Moreover, valid charitable trusts are not subject to certain aspects of the perpetuity rule and may be of unlimited duration. Furthermore, when compared to valid private trusts (that is, trusts for human objects), charitable trusts have other advantages; they enjoy considerable fiscal privileges including exemption from many taxes. Hence, many of the decided cases involve HM Revenue & Customs seeking to deny charitable status. Likewise, there are special rules applicable to the failure of charitable trusts (the principles of *cy-près*) which may oust the normal rules of resulting trusts, and there is a separate body of rules dealing with the administration of charities and the conduct of business by charitable trustees.

Obviously it is of singular importance to be able to distinguish between charitable purposes and non-charitable purposes. The former will be valid and enforceable, as well as having other advantages over private trusts, and the latter will be void unless they fall within one of the exceptions to the beneficiary principle considered in the previous chapter. The **Charities Act 2006** enacted for the first time a statutory definition of charities after centuries of reliance mainly on case law to lead the way on the type of activities that would be given charitable status. The **2006 Act** introduced a statutory definition by reference to a two-step approach – the listing of a variety of charitable purposes and the public benefit test. The **2006 Act** has been repealed and replaced by the **Charities Act 2011**. This is a consolidating statute that repeals the diverse statutory provisions that are applicable to charities and insert the same in one statute. The **Charities Act 2011** came into force on 14 March 2012. The **2011 Act** contains a list of 13 charitable purposes – 12 specific charitable objects, and a residual category of charitable purposes designed to maintain the courts' discretion to determine the type of novel activity that ought to be treated as charitable. This is intended to be a comprehensive list of charitable activities. Most of the purposes, in any event, were charitable before the Act was passed. The meaning of 'charity' is to be found principally in case law and the opinions of the Charity Commissioners (now the Charity Commission).

QUESTION 14

Bernard died last year leaving a will providing the following legacies:

(a) £1,000,000 to be used to train Great Britain's most promising young amateur athletes for the forthcoming Olympic Games;

(b) £2,000,000 to be used to raise awareness of schoolchildren in London of the dangers of possessing a knife in a public place.

▶ Consider the validity of these bequests.

Aim Higher

In *IRC v McMullen* (1981), the majority of the Law Lords adopted a restrictive construction to recreational facilities by deciding that the persons who may benefit from the trust must be deprived of the facilities in the first place.

How to Read this Question

This problem question requires you to analyse and consider whether the various bequests in Bernard's will create valid gifts on trusts for the respective purposes. In both parts of the question you are required to discuss whether the gifts create valid charitable trusts and in the alternative whether private purpose trusts have arisen. In the event of an express trust failing resulting trusts of the funds will arise in favour of Bernard's heirs.

How to Answer this Question

In (a) the question is whether the stated purpose falls within the definition of the promotion of amateur sport within **s 3(1)(g)** of the **Charities Act 2011**. In addition the provision of recreational facilities under **s 5** of the **2011 Act** needs to be considered. In all questions concerning charitable gifts you are required to analyse and apply the public benefit test. In (b) the main issue concerns the advancement of education.

Up for Debate

The public benefit test which pervades all charitable trusts is a fairly case centred subject. Recent cases such as *ISC v Charity Commission* and *AG v Charity Commission* have affirmed that there was no evidence that the courts adopted a presumption in favour of the validity of gifts for some charitable purposes. An issue that arises in question (b) is whether the limitation of the beneficiaries to London will satisfy the test.

Answer Plan

- ❖ Trusts for the advancement of amateur sport within **s 3(1)(g)** of the **Charities Act 2011**.
- ❖ The provision of recreational facilities within **s 5** of the **Charities Act 2011**.
- ❖ Advancement of education within **s 3(1)(b)** of the **Charities Act 2011**.
- ❖ Resulting trust.

Answer Structure

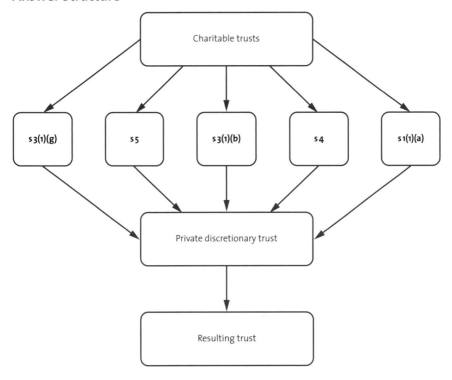

This diagram illustrates the tests to determine the charitable status of gifts in Bernard's will.

ANSWER

A charitable trust is a public purpose trust that may result in individuals or members of the public deriving direct benefits. It is enforceable by the Attorney General on behalf of the Crown. If any of the purposes, as stated in Bernard's will, fail to satisfy the tests for charitable status, consideration is required to be given as to the validity of the purposes as private trusts. If the purposes fail on this score, the relevant property will be held on resulting trust for the residuary beneficiaries under the will.[1]

(a) £1,000,000 to be Used to Train Great Britain's Most Promising Young Amateur Athletes for the Forthcoming Olympic Games

Prior to the **Charities Act 2011** the promotion of sport was not regarded as a charitable activity: see *IRC v City of Glasgow Police Athletic Association* (1953), where the House of Lords held that the provision of facilities for the recreation of police officers was not exclusively for charitable purposes. However, s 3(1)(g) of the **Charities Act 2011** has now recognised that the advancement of amateur sport is to be treated as a charitable

---

1 Analysis of the issues that will be considered.

activity and the training of athletes for the Olympic Games clearly promotes such activity. 'Sport' for these purposes has been broadly defined 'as sports or games which promote health by involving physical or mental skill or exertion': see s3(2)(d) of the **Charities Act 2011**. Thus, the charitable status of such activity is dependent on the way the facility is organised. The facts of the problem indicate that the sporting activities are restricted to amateur sport and this would appear to satisfy the requirements laid down in s3(2)(d) of the Act.

The public benefit requirement is now obligatory to prove in respect of all charities without the aid of presumptions: see ss4(1) and (2) of the **2011 Act**.[2] **Section** 4(3) consolidates the case law meaning of public benefit that existed before the passing of the Act. This involves a two-step test of demonstrating a benefit to society. The change in the law introduced by s3(1)(g) has this effect by reference to the purpose. In addition, those eligible to receive benefits must comprise a large enough group to be considered as the public and without a personal or private relationship being used to limit those who may benefit. Again this test appears to be satisfied in that there is no connection between the donor, Bernard and the intended beneficiaries.

Further, s5 of the **Charities Act 2011** confirms the charitable status of recreational activities provided that a number of basic conditions are satisfied. The facilities are required to improve the 'conditions of life' of those who will use them and these persons have need for the facilities because of their youth, disability, and social and economic circumstances. In *Guild v IRC* (1992), the Law Lords adopted a 'benign construction' of the test of 'deprivation' and decided that recreational facilities are provided with the object of improving the conditions of life of the beneficiaries, irrespective of whether or not the participating members are disadvantaged. It would appear that the gift to train promising young athletes for the Games will satisfy this test.

In any event the gift is capable of being charitable under s3(1)(m) of the **2011 Act**, the miscellaneous category.

(b) £2,000,000 to be Used to Raise Awareness of Schoolchildren in London of the Dangers of Possessing a Knife in a Public Place

The issues created by this gift in Bernard's will concern the advancement of education within s3(1)(b) of the **Charities Act 2011** as well as s3(1)(j) (relief of those in need by reason of their youth) and s3(1) (m) (the miscellaneous category).

The first issue is to determine what is meant by education and second to consider whether this gift promotes education. Prior to the **Charities Act 2011** the advancement of education was treated as a charitable purpose within the preamble to the **Statute of Elizabeth 1601**. **Section** 3(1)(b) of the **2011 Act** consolidates this purpose. **Section** 3(3) enacts that terms used in the Act are to be given the same meaning under existing charity law.

---

2   Charities questions require discussion of the purposes and public benefit.

Thus, the interpretation of the term 'education' under the general law will be consistently applied. Education has been interpreted fairly broadly by the courts. It is not restricted to teaching activities in schools and universities but covers any form of worthwhile instruction, including research or cultural advancement. In *Re Shaw's Will Trust* (1952), the court decided that the promotion in Ireland of self-control, elocution and the arts of personal contact was charitable. Likewise in *South Place Ethical Society* (1980), the promotion of ethical principles was treated as a charitable purpose under this head.

It would appear that the gift in Bernard's will may be treated as a form of education of schoolchildren. Nothing has been said in the will concerning the methods of raising such awareness. One such method may involve activities within the school setting. In this event, the narrower meaning of education that was considered in *Re Shaw* (1957), involving an element of teaching, will be satisfied.

The public benefit test will be satisfied if the subject of education is for the public benefit. In other words, the court takes into consideration the usefulness to society or educational value of the subject matter that will be advanced. In *Re Pinion* (1965), the gift of a collection of paintings to the National Trust lacked any artistic merit and failed on this ground. In view of the spate of senseless attacks on young people involving knives, there cannot be any doubt that measures to deter the carrying of weapons in public places have a great deal of public value. An additional consideration is whether the restriction to schoolchildren in London only will fail to satisfy the public benefit test. The satisfaction of the test is a question of law for the judge to decide on the evidence submitted to the court.[3] In essence, this test will be satisfied if the potential beneficiaries of the trust are not numerically negligible and there is no bond or link between the donor and the intended beneficiaries. The number of schoolchildren in London is not negligible and there is no nexus with Bernard.

One minor point ought to be made and that is whether this gift includes a political element masquerading as education.[4] A trust for political purposes will fail as a charity on the ground that the court is incapable of deciding whether a political programme is for the public benefit: see *McGovern v AG* (1982). There is very little evidence that the gift in Bernard's will promotes a political purpose. The gift is not designed to change the law but simply to raise awareness of the dangers in carrying a weapon.

Common Pitfalls

Students do not always appreciate that the pre-2011 case law on charities is still relevant today. **Sections 3(1)(m)(i) to (iii)** and **3(3)** of the **2011 Act** endorse the common law approach to charitable objects and **s4(3)** consolidates the case law meaning of public benefit.

---

3 Identify questions of law and distinguish these from questions of fact.
4 Address and expressly exclude related issues.

QUESTION 15

Mark, who has recently died, made a will in 2008 in which he made the following gifts:

(i)   £250,000 to the University of London upon trust to establish and maintain in perpetuity a School of Law Reform;

(ii)   £3,000 to the trustees of the South Blankshire Methodist Conference for the promotion of physical recreation for Methodists in South Blankshire.

▶ Consider whether these gifts are charitable.

How to Read this Question

This problem question on charities requires you to deal with the facts to determine
whether the gifts are charitable only. You are not required to deal with private purpose
trusts although you may state that on failure of any of the stated purposes resulting
trusts will arise in favour of the residuary beneficiaries under the will or the next of kin.
The first part of the question raises the issue of the charitable status of the gift for the
advancement of education and the second part involves trusts for the advancement of
amateur sports or recreational activities.

How to Answer this Question

In the first part of the question the material issues are whether the University of London
is intended to be a trustee and whether the stated purpose is within the definition of
charity. The second part of the question requires you to consider whether the promotion
of recreational activities is a recognised charitable activity and the public benefit test.

Up for Debate

The public benefit test was considered by the Upper Tribunal in *ISC v Charity Commission* and *AG v Charity Commission* where the court decided that the pre-2006
court decisions did not adopt a presumption of public benefit with regard to trusts
for the advancement of education. Accordingly the Charity Commission was required
to amend its guidelines on public benefit.

Answer Plan

❖   Trusts for the advancement of education.
❖   Exemption of charities from the perpetuity rule – excessive duration principle.
❖   Trusts for the promotion of sport.
❖   **Section 5** of the **Charities Act 2011** – promotion of recreational facilities.
❖   Public benefit test.

Answer Structure

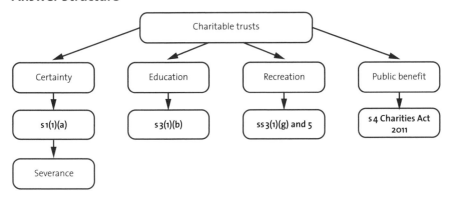

This diagram illustrates the construction and effect of the various purposes stated by Mark in his will.

ANSWER

(i) £250,000 to the University of London upon Trust

In this problem, the issue is whether the donation of £250,000 to the University for the stated purpose is charitable. Does the gift advance education as declared in **s 3(1)(b)** of the **Charities Act 2011**? The donation is to the University of London. This clearly is a charitable body that exists to advance education. If, as is possible, the University is the trustee to promote the stated purpose, the question arises as to whether the stated purpose is charitable. A School of Law Reform within the University exists as a department to undertake the task of examining the extent to which the current law is satisfactory and in appropriate cases to suggest proposals for reform. **Section 3(3)** of the **Charities Act 2011** endorses the common law approach to charitable objects. In the law of charities, education has been interpreted generously and is not restricted to the classroom mode of disseminating knowledge, but requires some element of instruction or supervision. Thus, research is capable of being construed as the provision of education: see *Re Hopkins Will Trust* (1964). In *McGovern v Attorney General* (1981), a definition of advancement of education by way of research was laid down by Slade J. He posited that the requirements are that: (a) the subject matter of the proposed research is a useful object of study; (b) it must be contemplated that the knowledge acquired as a result of the research will be disseminated to others; (c) the trust is for the benefit of the public, or a sufficiently important section of the public. It would appear that the establishment of a school to study the extent to which the law is in a satisfactory state would clearly satisfy the test laid down by Slade J. An additional issue is whether this purpose is political – for if that is the case the gift will fail as a charity.[5] Political activities include attempts to change the law and gifts to further the objects of political parties. A trust for political purposes is incapable of subsisting as a charity, for the court may not stultify itself by deciding that it is in the public good for the law to be changed: see *National Anti-Vivisection Society v IRC* (1948), concerning the activities of the stated society and

---

5   Related issues ought to be expressly and clearly excluded.

McGovern, where Amnesty International was declared to be a political organisation. The School exists only to study the extent to which the law is satisfactory; it is not designed to lobby Parliament for changes to be introduced. On this basis it is a charitable activity.

A further point involves the reference to the School being maintained perpetually. Would this infringe the perpetuity rule? Although charitable trusts, like private trusts, are subject to the rule against remote vesting, charitable trusts, as distinct from private trusts, are not subject to the rule against excessive duration. Indeed, many charities (schools and universities) continue indefinitely and rely heavily on perpetual donations. Accordingly, if the purposes are charitable the gift will not fail for infringing the perpetuity rule.

(ii) £3,000 to the Trustees of the South Blankshire Methodist Conference

The purpose as stated in this problem raises a number of issues. Is the purpose as declared in the will, namely physical recreation, a charitable activity? In any event, would the public benefit test be satisfied? The donation contemplated appears to promote recreation under the guise of advancing religion, i.e. Methodists in South Blankshire. In other words, the religious element seems to be purely incidental and the real purpose is to promote physical recreation *simpliciter* for such beneficiaries. A similar purpose was considered by the court in *IRC v Baddeley* (1955). Here the House of Lords decided that the gift was void, as recreational activities or sport are not within the preamble to the Statute of Elizabeth or the 'spirit and intendment of the preamble': see *Re Nottage* (1895) and *IRC v City of Glasgow Police Athletic Association* (1953). **Section 3(1)(g)** of the **Charities Act 2011** includes the advancement of amateur sport within the list of charitable purposes. 'Sport' for these purposes has been broadly defined as sports or games which promote health by involving physical or mental skill or exertion: see **s 3(2)(d)** of the **Charities Act 2011**. The effect is that the charitable status of such activity is dependent on the way the facility is organised. However, there is little evidence in Mark's will to indicate that the funds are to be used for the promotion of amateur sport.

Section 5 of the **Charities Act 2011** consolidates the law regarding the provision of recreational facilities. **Section 5** of the Act stipulates that the provision of recreational facilities shall be charitable if two criteria are fulfilled, namely: (1) the public benefit test is satisfied; and (2) the facilities are provided in the interests of social welfare. The 'social welfare' test will be complied with if two 'basic conditions' are satisfied as enacted in **s 5(3)**. The first requirement is continuous as stipulated in **s 5(3)(a)**. The second requirement may be satisfied in alternative ways, either by proving that the facilities are available to a limited class of objects who have a need for such facilities by virtue of one or more of the factors enumerated within **s 5(3)(b)(i)** (such as a youth club or an organised outing for orphaned children) or **s 5(3)(b)(ii)** 'the facilities are available to the entire public' (such as a public swimming pool or a public park) or 'female or male members of the public at large' (women's institutes, etc.). In *Guild v IRC* (1992), the court decided that the test today is whether the facilities are provided with the purpose of improving the conditions of life of the beneficiaries, irrespective of whether the participating members of society are disadvantaged or not. In short, the material issue concerns the nature of the facilities rather than the status of the participants.

On this basis a strong case could be made out that the activities contemplated fall within the requirements of **s 5** of the **Charities Act 2011.**

The definitive issue in this problem is whether the public benefit test will be satisfied. The public benefit test is used to distinguish a public trust from a private trust. A public trust is required to exist for the benefit of the public (the community) or an appreciable section of society. A unique application of this test is reserved for trusts for the relief of poverty. The test of public benefit is laid down in **s 4** of the **Charities Act 2011. Section 4(3)** of the Act endorses the common law approach to the public benefit test that existed prior to the introduction of the **2011 Act**. The satisfaction of the test is a question of law for the judge to decide on the evidence submitted to the court. In *IRC v Baddeley* (1955) the court decided that the test will not be satisfied where the intended beneficiaries comprise a class within a class. The facts of the problem refer to Methodists (a class) in South Blankshire (another class) with the effect that the test may not be satisfied. In addition, the beneficiaries must not be numerically negligible and must comprise a sufficient section of the community to be treated as charitable. These are flexible questions for the court to decide.

QUESTION 16

Consider the validity of the following gifts in the will of Daphne, who died in 2014:

(a) £100,000 to my trustees for the establishment and maintenance of a walled garden within the precincts of St Luke's Church, for the quiet reflection of the parishioners;
(b) £10,000 to my trustees to be distributed to such organisations involved in the protection of the environment and related causes as they shall in their absolute discretion select; and
(c) £50,000 to my trustees for the promotion of tennis in the public schools of Derbyshire.

How to Read this Question

This question requires you to consider whether the legacies create valid charitable trusts within the **Charities Act 2011** and, if not, the destination of the funds by way of private purpose trusts or as a last resort by way of resulting trusts.

How to Answer this Question

❖ In part (a) you will need to consider how far the stated purpose promotes religion, other purposes beneficial to the community or private purposes.
❖ Part (b) involves issues of construction of exclusivity of charitable purposes and discretionary trusts.
❖ Part (c) concerns the extent to which charitable status may be established under the following headings, the advancement of education, the promotion of amateur sport and recreational facilities.

Up for Debate

An issue for discussion concerns the judiciary's approach to the public benefit test which led to the revised guidelines issued by the Charity Commission.

Aim Higher

Problem questions on charities may involve a variety of issues. It is necessary to present the points in a clear and logical order.

Answer Plan

- ❖ Brief introductory points about the definition of charity.
- ❖ Possible failure of the stipulated purposes as private purpose trusts.
- ❖ Trusts for the *promotion* of religion: activities within a religious context per se might not be enough.
- ❖ Trusts for other purposes beneficial to the community and questions of exclusivity of charitable purpose.
- ❖ Environmental protection – a charitable purpose within s3(1)(i) of the 2011 Act, but is 'related purposes' too vague?
- ❖ Trusts for education: issue of public benefit.
- ❖ Charitable purposes – the advancement of amateur sport, s3(1)(g) and s5 (provision of recreational facilities) of the **Charities Act 2011**.

Applying the Law

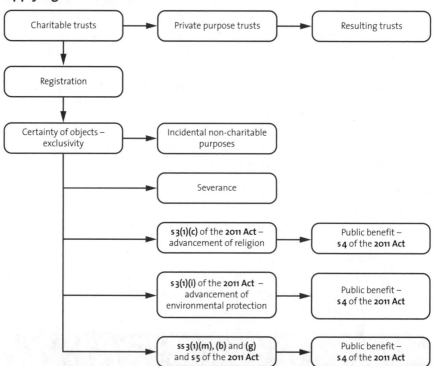

This diagram illustrates the holistic nature of dealing with purpose trusts first as charitable trusts, second as private purpose trusts and finally as resulting trusts.

ANSWER

All charities are required to be registered with the Charity Commission (**s 30** of the **Charities Act 2011**), subject to a number of limited exceptions. **Section 37** of the **Charities Act 2011** enacts that an institution that has been registered shall be 'conclusively presumed' to be a charity. Thus the first stage in determining the status of these institutions is the application to the Commission for registration. Second, charitable purposes under the **2011 Act** are construed in accordance with the wealth of case law decided over several centuries: see **ss 3(3)** and **3(1)m)** of the **2011 Act**.[6] As a general point if any of the gifts fail as a charity a resulting trust of the fund will arise for Daphne's heirs. It would not be possible to spell out valid private purpose trusts for any of these gifts.

(a) £100,000 to my Trustees for the Establishment and Maintenance of a Walled Garden within the Precincts of St Luke's Church, for the Quiet Reflection of the Parishioners

This particular trust does have the potential to fall within the *Denley* exception to the rule against purpose trusts, although this is unlikely in practice because of the donor's intention to establish a trust in perpetuity. However, it may be that this trust is within the scope of trusts for the advancement of religion within **s 3(1)(c)** of the **2011 Act** and is thereby charitable. There is no doubt here that the proposed trust is connected with a religious establishment and questions concerning the disputed status of some faiths and beliefs are not relevant. The definition of 'religion' within **s 3(2)(a)** is extremely broad and inclusive: see, for example, *Funnell v Stewart* (1996) 'faith healing'. Yet, it is unclear whether trusts for religious purposes per se can be charitable if they are not otherwise for the advancement of religion (*Oxford Group v IRC* (1949)).[7] Furthermore, in our case, the actual purpose seems to be the establishment of a walled garden 'for quiet reflection' and it might be argued that this is not even a religious purpose, as believers are not the only persons able and willing to engage in contemplation (*Re Macaulay's Estate* (1943)). On the other hand, gifts for the maintenance and enhancement of buildings within a church are routinely held to be charitable (*Re Raine* (1956)), as are some matters connected with the church even though they appear far removed from the promotion of the religion itself (*Re Royce* (1940): benefit of church choir).

The matter here is one of construction of the trust instrument in the light of existing case law.[8] The fact that the walled garden must be erected within the fabric of a church is powerful evidence in favour of a charity for the advancement of religion, as is the fact that the anticipated benefit will fall on parishioners (*Re Norton's Will Trusts* (1948)). The only other tenable view is that the reference to 'quiet reflection' may introduce a non-charitable element into the equation and may make the gift void as not being exclusively devoted to charity.[9] Finally, should it be held that this purpose falls within the

---

6   Concise statement of relevant points regarding charitable status.

7   Highlighting the relevant issue in the problem.

8   These are flexible questions of law.

9   This concerns the test of certainty of charitable objects.

definition of charity *per se*, it is clear that there is a sufficient element of public benefit. The walled garden would be open to all parishioners and we can legitimately assume that these are neither numerically negligible nor 'a class within a class' (*Williams Trustees v IRC* (1947)). This case is not on a par with *Gilmour v Coats* (1949). In that case, the contemplative nature of the purpose was held to confer no public benefit because the value of prayer could not be proven and because the nuns were cloistered, limited in number and did not participate in community life. Our case, however, may be similar to *Neville Estates v Madden* (1962), where there was a sufficient element of public benefit because the persons enriched by the advancement of religion continued to be members of the community.

(b) £10,000 to my Trustees to be Distributed to such Organisations Involved in the Protection of the Environment and Related Causes as they shall in their Absolute Discretion Select

A charitable trust may allow the trustees some discretion in the selection of charitable objects provided, of course, that the trustees are required to exercise that discretion in favour of objects that are exclusively charitable (*Houston v Burns* (1918)). In this particular case, there are two issues: first, whether the 'protection of the environment' is itself charitable; and second, whether the trustees' ability to use the money for 'related causes' has any bearing on the matter.[10]

As far as the protection of the environment is concerned, this is likely to be a purpose that falls within **s (3)(1)(i)** of the **2011 Act** 'the advancement of environmental protection' and/or **s 3(1)(m)** of the **2011 Act**, the category of 'other purposes beneficial to the community'. This is despite the fact that there is some doubt as to how we are to determine whether any given purpose is charitable within **s 3(1)(m)**. **Section 3(1)(m)(i)** to **(iii)** offers some guidance by reference to the approach adopted by case law. According to Russell LJ in *Incorporated Council for Law Reporting for England and Wales v Attorney General* (1971), a court is entitled to assume that if a purpose is in itself beneficial to the community, it is also charitable in law. On the other hand, the more traditional approach requires that there must be some precedent or analogy with charitable purposes or previous case law before a new purpose which is beneficial in itself can also be regarded as charitable (*Williams Trustees v IRC* (1947); *Peggs v Lamb* (1994)).

Fortunately in our case, a trust for the protection of the environment is undoubtedly regarded as charitable. Certainly, the preservation of historic buildings and gardens is charitable (*Re Verrall* (1916)), as are trusts for natural amenities (*Re Corelli* (1943)). In addition, the Charity Commission explained that a trust to promote conservation must *inter alia* satisfy the criterion of merit or conserve something which deserves protection. This will be dependent on expert evidence in marginal cases. Undoubtedly, the protection of the environment will satisfy the public benefit test. There is no stipulation limiting use of the property to any specific class or type of person and nothing that suggests that the benefits of the charity per se are private and intangible. What,

---

10 Concise statement of the issues in this question.

then, of the trustees' ability to use the money for 'related causes'? This, again, is a matter of construction. If 'related causes' can be interpreted to mean exclusively environmental purposes, then there should be no problem with the validity of this charitable gift and it is suggested that this is the most sensible view of Daphne's disposition. If, on the other hand, 'related causes' may encompass worthwhile but non-charitable purposes, then the gift may fail as not being exclusively devoted to charity (*Blair v Duncan* (1902)), at least unless the non-charitable purpose is merely subsidiary to the performance of the charitable object (*Re Coxen* (1948)) or can be severed from it (*Lambert v Thwaites* (1866)). Subject, then, to resolving the 'related causes' issue, this is a charitable gift.

(c) £50,000 to my Trustees for the Promotion of Tennis in the Public Schools of Derbyshire

This is the most straightforward of Daphne's dispositions. **Section 3(1)(b)** of the **2011 Act** confirms that the 'advancement of education' is a charitable purpose. The provision of sport within schools is clearly for the advancement of education in that it involves the development of the mind and body. It was recognised by the House of Lords in *IRC v McMullen* (1981) that a trust to provide sporting facilities for schools was itself charitable as furthering the education of pupils. This would seem to cover our case. In addition, the endowment and maintenance of independent (that is, 'public') schools is a charitable purpose, even if some charge is made to parents for tuition fees, providing that the school is not run for profit for the benefit of private individuals: see *Independent Schools Council v Charity Commission* (2011). Moreover, if it should be objected that the scope of Daphne's charitable purpose is limited to a particular area and might fail the test of public benefit (whereas in *McMullen* it was any school within the UK), the trust in *Re Mariette* (1915) was charitable and this concerned the provision of sporting facilities at just one school (and that was an independent one). A fortiori, a trust for the promotion of sport in several schools must be charitable.

In addition, the advancement of amateur sport by virtue of **s3(1)g** of the **2011 Act** is now treated as a charitable purpose. 'Sport' is defined in **s3(2)(d)** as sport or games which promote physical or mental skill or exertion. Clearly tennis satisfies this definition and there is no indication that it is other than the advancement of tennis amongst amateurs and therefore a charitable activity. Finally, the tests of 'public benefit' and 'interests of social welfare' under **s5** of the **2011 Act** appear to be satisfied on these facts and will serve as a separate ground to support its charitable status.

Common Pitfalls

Examinees do not always address the issues raised by reference to the instructions. This question requires analysis of the ultimate validity of the gifts and therefore examinees ought to consider *inter alia* private purpose trusts and resulting trusts in the event of the gifts failing as charitable purposes.

QUESTION 17

Consider the validity of the following dispositions in the will of Freddie, who died this year:

(a) £10,000 on trust for the preservation of the habitat of the colony of badgers that is threatened by the work on the Manchester ring road;

(b) £10,000 to the inhabitants of Littleham for the provision of a new swimming pool to be used solely by the residents thereof for such a period as the law allows;

(c) £10,000 to my trustees, the income to be used for 30 years by the Lifeboat Association for the provision of rescue crafts, thence on trust for the purposes of the Society for the Promotion of Tiddlywinks.

Aim Higher

This is a difficult problem as it combines the law of charities, non-charitable purpose trusts and perpetuities. It demonstrates the wisdom of a thorough treatment of all purpose trusts and an understanding of the close relationship between the charitable and non-charitable variety.

How to Read this Question

Freddie, the testator, has included a number of dispositions in his will, all of which involve consideration of purpose trusts or related concepts. At the outset, it is important to bear in mind two general principles, reliance on which will help determine the validity of Freddie's proposed gifts. First, it is not possible to create a trust for a non-charitable purpose, save in the most exceptional cases (*Re Endacott* (1960) and *Re Denley* (1969)). Such trusts are void and the property will result to the estate of the testator. Second, and in contrast, should a purpose fall within the legal definition of charity, there may be a perfectly valid purpose trust which may last in perpetuity and will enjoy considerable legal and fiscal advantages. In fact, the dispositions in this problem concern both charitable and non-charitable purpose trusts.

How to Answer this Question

The instructions are to discuss the validity of the gifts in Freddie's will. This indicates that you are required to consider, first, charitable trusts, second, private purpose trusts and, ultimately, resulting trusts. In question (a) the main issues are whether the trusts to advance animal welfare may be construed as charitable and the public benefit test. In question (b) the issue concerns the status of a trust to promote recreational activities. In question (c) the issue involves the validity of a gift to a charity with a gift over to provide for a non-charitable purpose. This requires consideration of the perpetuity rule.

Up for Debate

The material issue here is the application of the perpetuity rule in respect of a gift to a charity with a gift over for a non-charitable purpose.

Answer Plan

❖ A brief note that this question covers both charitable and non-charitable purpose trusts.

❖ Protection of the countryside, possible political objectives, trusts beneficial to the community.

❖ Recreational charities, restricted classes, *Re Denley* purpose trust.

❖ Gift to charity, followed by a gift to a purpose trust, perpetuity problems.

Answer Structure

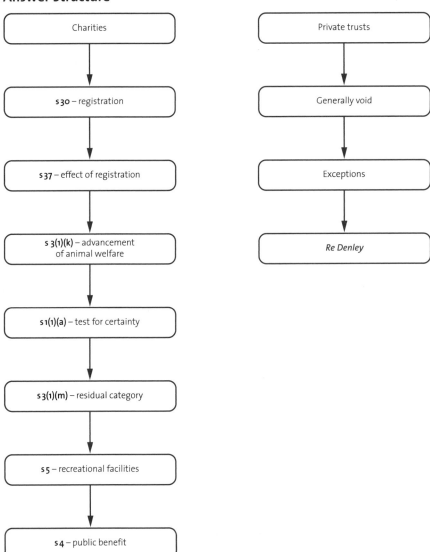

This diagram depicts the multiplicity of charitable purposes and effect of failure of the intended express trust.

ANSWER

(a) £10,000 on Trust for the Preservation of the Habitat of the Colony of Badgers that is Threatened by the Work on the Manchester Ring Road

Charitable purposes are specified in s3(1) of the **Charities Act 2011** and in addition are required to satisfy the public benefit test. There are 13 purposes stipulated in the subsection, including a general residual purpose in s3(1)(m). **Section 3(1)(k)** of the **2011 Act** identifies the advancement of animal welfare as a charitable purpose. **Section 3(3)** preserves the common law meaning of charitable purposes and the public benefit test. Prior to the enactment of the **2011 Act**, trusts for the protection of animals were held to be charitable as within the spirit and intendment of the preamble to the **Statute of Charitable Uses 1601**. In *Re Wedgwood* (1915) the court upheld an animal welfare trust, not for the benefit of the animals in their own right but on the ground that such trusts may promote feelings of humanity and morality amongst mankind. On this basis a trust has been upheld for a home for lost dogs, in *Re Douglas* (1887). The point is, however, that at common law such trusts are charitable because they benefit mankind – being displays of generosity and human kindness, or as protecting animals useful to man – and not because they benefit the animals per se (*Re Grove-Grady* (1929)). Consequently, Freddie's trust must demonstrate some benefit to the public from the protection of these animals, and while the display of human kindness in this purpose is evident, it might not be enough. However, s3(1)(k) of the **2011 Act** specifically enacts that the advancement of animal welfare is a charitable purpose in its own right. Despite these clear words it is reasonable to suppose that the court will imply a limitation, to the effect that in the event of a conflict of interests between humans and animals, the human interest will prevail, as was the case in *National Anti-Vivisection Society v IRC* (1948), where the court decided that the advancement of medical science and research far outweighed the welfare of animals used in such research. In addition, the public benefit test enacted in s4 of the **Charities Act 2011** requires the executors of Freddie's will to demonstrate positively the benefit that would be enjoyed by the community in preserving the habitat of the colony of badgers as opposed to the work on the Manchester ring road. This could prove to be extremely difficult to justify. Moreover, there is a risk that this purpose will be denied charitable status because of its actual or potential political overtones.[11] It is a clear principle that charities may not engage in political activities and may not attempt to cloak political objectives with more benign purposes (*Bowman v Secular Society* (1917); *McGovern v Attorney General* (1982); *Southwood v Attorney General* (2000)). In our case, this might be seen as an attempt to protect the countryside from transport policies approved by Parliament and this can too easily be regarded as political, especially if it involves a campaigning or propaganda element. So, even if this purpose does manifest a sufficient public benefit, the desire to protect animals may be so bound up with political objectives that its charitable status should be denied.

---

11 Identification of a non-charitable element.

(b) £10,000 to the Inhabitants of Littleham for the Provision of a New Swimming Pool to be Used Solely by the Residents Thereof for such a Period as the Law Allows

This is clearly an attempt to establish a trust for a recreational purpose. In general a trust for recreation or sport per se is not charitable (*Re Nottage* (1895)) (save for the advancement of amateur sport), although the matter would be different if the recreation was tied to an educational purpose (*IRC v McMullen* (1981)) or some other charitable object. Conversely, trusts for the provision of land for recreation can be charitable, even if limited to persons from a particular locality (*Re Hadden* (1932)), although this was not extended to an indoor swimming pool in *Valuation Commissioner for Northern Ireland v Lurgan BC* (1968). In the light of this rather clear authority, it seems unlikely that Freddie's trust will be charitable under the general law. Fortunately, that is not the end of the matter. First, it could be that this trust can be charitable under s 5 of the **Charities Act 2011** if the recreational facilities are provided in the interests of social welfare, this being where the facilities are provided with the object of improving the conditions of life of the people of Littleham, being persons in need of such facilities by reason of age, infirmity or social and economic considerations (s 5(2) and (3) of the **2011 Act**). Moreover, since *Guild v IRC* (1992), it is clear that the persons benefiting from the recreational purpose do not need to be 'deprived' in order to have their conditions of life improved. It is enough if the general conditions of life for members of the public are improved. In our case, provided that the people of Littleham constitute a section of the public (as they are almost bound to do, *Re Hadden* (1932)), this purpose may fall within the Act and be charitable, as was a trust for a similar leisure facility in *Guild*.

Second, even if this purpose is deemed non-charitable, it might still be valid as being within the *Re Denley* (1969) exception to the rule against purpose trusts. Indeed, this does seem to be a trust which indirectly benefits ascertainable individuals and it is limited to the perpetuity period by the reference to 'such a period as the law allows'. In fact, the case is very similar to *Denley* itself and Freddie's estate can be content that, at the very least, he has established a valid non-charitable purpose trust.[12]

(c) £10,000 to my Trustees, the Income to be Used for 30 Years by the Lifeboat Association for the Provision of Rescue Crafts, thence on Trust for the Purposes of the Society for the Promotion of Tiddlywinks

There is clear authority that trusts for rescue services are charitable, being for purposes beneficial to the community (*Re Wokingham Fire Brigade Trusts* (1951)). The Royal National Lifeboat Institution is a charitable organisation and, by analogy, so should be a gift to this Lifeboat Association for the provision of rescue craft. This principle has been affirmed in s 3(1)(l) of the Act – the promotion of the efficiency of the rescue services. However, the issue that requires consideration is the legal position with regard to the gift over. After 30 years, the £10,000 capital sum is to be given to the Society for the Promotion of Tiddlywinks, which is most unlikely to be regarded as charitable, being recreational and unlikely to fall within s 5 (*Re Nottage* (1895) and s 3(1)(g) of the **2011 Act**). This is, then, a gift

---

12 It is good technique to consider the validity of the gift as a private purpose trust after considering the law of charities.

to charity, followed by a gift over for a non-charitable purpose. In these circumstances, any potential perpetuities problem will be avoided by the clear, certain and generous perpetuity period of 125 years, introduced by the **Perpetuities and Accumulations Act 2009**. The effect is that the gift over to the non-charitable society will take effect 30 years after the Lifeboat Association had the use of the income.

Three additional issues may require consideration had the facts been clearer.[13] These are, first, that the position if the Tiddlywinks Society did not exist at the relevant time of vesting. In this event the possibility of a resulting trust of the funds would be a consideration. Second, the validity of a gift to an unincorporated association and the various solutions adopted by the courts would have warranted discussion had the facts been clearer. Finally, the issue arises as to whether the income alone from the trust fund or, alternatively, the entire fund is to be taken by the society. If, on construction, the income is devoted to the society, the gift may fail for infringing the perpetuity period. This issue will be avoided if the entire fund is to be transferred to the society.

Common Pitfalls

It is tempting for students to ignore the rule against perpetuities. But the introduction of the **Perpetuities and Accumulations Act 2009** has the effect of simplifying the law and no doubt increases its attraction as a subject for study.

QUESTION 18

Arnold made his will in 2010, in which he left three gifts of £50,000 each to:

(a) the National Association for the Homeless, an incorporated charity;
(b) the Whale Protection League, a voluntary association; and
(c) the Cook Home for the Disabled.

When Arnold died this year, it transpired that the National Association for the Homeless had become defunct two years previously and its premises purchased by the UK League Against Homelessness. Likewise, the Whale Protection League had disbanded after disagreements between its members, to be replaced by two organisations, the Whale and Dolphin Sanctuary and the Society for the Humane Harvesting of Whales. It also transpires that there never was a 'Cook Home for the Disabled'.

▶ **Advise as to the proper distribution of Arnold's estate.**

How to Read this Question

This question is centred on the *cy-près* doctrine that is applicable to charities. The issues are (a) whether the original purposes of the various bodies are charitable and (b) since they no longer exist on the date of Arnold's death whether the relevant funds may be applied *cy-près*.

---

13 Additional considerations where the facts are unclear.

How to Answer this Question

The *cy-près* points involved in this question focus on the issues of charitable gifts which fail to vest owing to initial or subsequent impossibility; the position regarding successive organisations and the various means of construing gifts to institutions, purposes or named funds.

Up for Debate

In appropriate cases trustees may need to prove a general charitable intent in order to apply the funds *cy-près*. This is a flexible concept as illustrated by the many cases on the subject. An incisive article on the subject is J Garton, 'Justifying the cy-pres doctrine' (2007) 3 Tru LI 134.

Answer Plan

- ❖ *Cy-près*: general purpose.
- ❖ Initial or subsequent impossibility.
- ❖ Gifts to institutions, purposes or named funds.
- ❖ Successor organisations.

Answer Structure

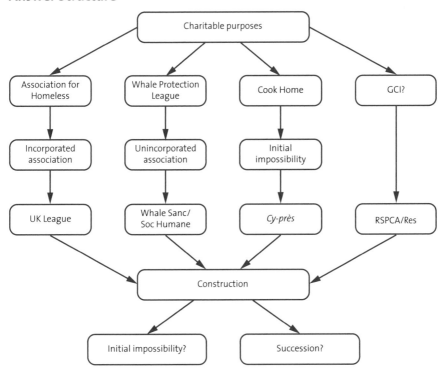

This diagram depicts the various procedures that need to be adopted in order to determine which body will acquire the property under Arnold's will.

ANSWER --

Arnold has attempted to distribute his property among several named organisations, none of which exists at the date of his death, at least in their original form. At the outset, it is necessary to determine whether all or any of these gifts are for charitable purposes. If any is not, then the property allocated to that organisation will return to Arnold's estate under a simple resulting trust consequent upon a void purpose trust (*Re Endacott* (1960)).[14] Fortunately, all of the original purposes selected by Arnold appear to be charitable. We are told that the National Association for the Homeless is 'an incorporated charity'; the Cook Home for the Disabled falls squarely within s3(1)(d) or (j) of the **Charities Act 2011**, being for the relief of the sick; the Whale Protection League will be charitable under s3(1)(k) of the **2011 Act** (*Re Wedgwood* (1915)), provided that it did not engage in political activities.

The importance of deciding that these three purposes are charitable is that it may help determine the distribution of Arnold's estate now that none of the original organisations remain in existence.[15] Simply put, the failure of a charitable trust does not always result in the property being returned to the donor or his estate but may, if certain conditions are fulfilled, be applied by the court or Charity Commission *cy-près* – that is, for purposes as near as possible to those originally stipulated (*Re Wilson* (1913)).[16] Broadly speaking, if a charity has failed for 'initial impossibility or impracticality', it may be applied *cy-près* if there is evidence that the donor had a general intention to benefit charity (*Re Wilson*). However, if the charity has failed for subsequent impossibility or impracticality, the property may be applied *cy-près* without the need for such an intention, since it has already been dedicated to charity in perpetuity (*Re Peel* (1921)). In our cases, it will be necessary to determine, first, whether the charitable trust has failed; second, whether such failure is initial or subsequent; and, third, if there is initial failure, whether there is a general charitable intention. Each of the four purposes identified by Arnold will be considered in turn.[17]

(a) £50,000 to the National Association for the Homeless, an Incorporated Charity

It is clear that Arnold has attempted to give his donation to a charity which, although once in existence, does not exist at the date the gift is to take effect, being on the testator's death. If anything, this may be a case of initial impossibility. However, we are told that the premises of the National Association for the Homeless have been purchased by the UK League Against Homelessness and it is arguable that this institution is in fact the successor in title to the National Association. If that is the case, the correct solution may well be that there has been no failure of Arnold's gift at all but, rather, a continuity between his named charity and its lawful successor, which may then receive the donation.[18]

....

14 Prevalence of the resulting trust where the *cy-près* doctrine is inapplicable.
15 Significance of charitable trusts and the *cy-près* doctrine.
16 Importance of the donor's intention and the *cy-près* doctrine.
17 Summary of issues to be considered.
18 Importance of determining whether there has been a failure or alternatively a succession of the charitable purposes.

Whether this is a case of initial failure or a case of a successor charity depends on the construction of Arnold's gift in the circumstances of the case. There are three possibilities. First, it may be construed that Arnold's gift is a gift specifically to the institution named in his will (*Re Rymer* (1895)). If this is the case, then there is initial impossibility and a general charitable intention needs to be found if the property is to be applied *cy-près*. Unfortunately, *Re Rymer* also decides that it is difficult to find a general charitable intention when a specific donee that once existed has been identified with such clarity although, as *Re Finger* (1972) demonstrates, this is not entirely impossible. Second, the original donation can be construed as a gift to the particular purposes undertaken by the original institution, so that if another institution has taken over those purposes, the property will pass to it automatically as the successor in title (*Re Roberts* (1963)). Third, the original donation can be construed as a gift to the charitable fund administered by the original institution, so that if there is another body now administering that fund, the property will pass to it automatically as the successor in title (*Re Faraker* (1912)).[19] In our case, it is unclear which construction to adopt. According to *Re Vernon* (1972) and *Re Finger* (1972), if the charity is incorporated – as here – then the gift should be construed as a gift to the specific institution per se (the first possibility above), while if it is unincorporated the gift should be construed as a gift for the purposes of the original institution. On the other hand, this guidance takes no account of the *Re Faraker* construction. If we follow *Re Vernon*, the donation to the National Association for the Homeless will fail for initial impossibility (being a gift to a specific institution) and will be applicable *cy-près* only if a general charitable intention can be found – something which *Re Rymer*, but not *Re Finger*, says is difficult. Failing such an intention, the property will result back to Arnold's estate. Again, on the basis of *Vernon*, a construction of the gift for purposes does not seem possible. This would mean that the UK League Against Homelessness could not claim the property as of right unless the *Faraker* construction is adopted and the League is now administering the National Association's funds. This we do not know. All in all, a resulting trust seems likely, or *cy-près* if a general charitable intention can be found.

(b) £50,000 to the Whale Protection League, now Dissolved and Replaced by the Whale and Dolphin Sanctuary and the Society for the Humane Harvesting of Whales

Once again, assuming this gift to be charitable, we must ask first what is the proper construction to be placed on Arnold's original disposition. This is particularly important in this case as there are two organisations who may claim to be the lawful successors in title to the Whale Protection League. We are told that the Whale Protection League was a 'voluntary association' and, therefore, it may be possible (should we wish – see below) to avoid construing this as a gift to a specific institution which has failed (that is, not *Re Rymer*) and so not a case of initial impossibility allowing for *cy-près* only if a general charitable intention can be found. However, it is not easy to choose between the *Re Roberts* construction (a gift for the particular charitable purpose) and the *Re Faraker* construction (a gift to a particular charitable fund). Again, following *Re Vernon* (1972), the unincorporated

---

19 Identification of the possible methods of construction.

nature of the original charity might lead us to choose the 'purpose construction', but then we have the dilemma of deciding exactly what the original purpose was. Was it the protection of whales, etc., in all circumstances, so that the Whale and Dolphin Sanctuary may claim the gift as carrying on those original purposes? Or was it a gift for the protection of whales from unnecessary hunting, in which case the Society for the Humane Harvesting of Whales may be the lawful successor to the original purpose? Indeed, precisely the same problem arises if we decide to adopt the *Faraker* construction (gift to a fund) instead of the purpose approach. It is not at all clear which of the rival organisations now administers the funds of the defunct society. Consequently, in the absence of further evidence, we might actually prefer a pragmatic solution and decide that this was, after all, a gift specifically to the Whale Protection League, which failed initially at Arnold's death, but where we can infer a general charitable intention so allowing the property to be applied *cy-près*. If the property is applied *cy-près* (as opposed to going to a successor in title), each rival organisation can receive a share, or none at all, as the court decides.

(c) £50,000 to the Cook Home for the Disabled

The Cook Home for the Disabled has never existed and therefore there is no doubt that this is a case of initial impossibility. Furthermore, there can be no successors in title to an organisation that never was. The property will result to Arnold's estate unless a general charitable intention can be found, in which case it will be applicable *cy-près*. In this regard, *Re Harwood* (1936) decides that, where a gift has been given to an institution which has never existed, a general charitable intention should be presumed unless there is convincing evidence to the contrary. Although somewhat arbitrary, this guidance has been followed in *Re Satterthwaite's Wills Trust* (1966) and in our case affords good authority for a *cy-près* application of the property.

5

Resulting Trusts

INTRODUCTION

Resulting trusts are an essential doctrine in the law of trusts. Apart from relatively rare occasions when the subject matter of a trust will pass to the Crown as ownerless property (*bona vacantia*), resulting trusts provide the last practical means of disposing of trust property should the original scheme of a trust fail. In fact, a resulting trust can arise in such a variety of circumstances that there is only marginal merit in considering it on an undergraduate course as a topic in its own right. For example, resulting trusts need to be considered in relation to secret trusts, the three certainties, the beneficiary principle, charities, formalities and constructive trusts. This is not an exhaustive list, and the use of the resulting trust in these and other cases is best considered alongside the substantive law which it services. Moreover, there is now much academic discussion about the proper theoretical basis of resulting trusts: for example, do they arise by reason of the intention of the parties, by operation of law, out of the implied or express acceptance by the resulting trustee of an obligation affecting conscience or for different reasons in different circumstances. This has practical consequences, as illustrated by the House of Lords' refusal to impose a resulting trust on the defendant in *Westdeutsche Landesbank Girozentrale v Islington LBC* (1996). As indicated above, much of this debate is outside the scope of an undergraduate course, but there are issues here which need consideration. In this chapter, brief attention will be paid to the attributes of the resulting trust per se (assuming that 'resulting trusts' share some common attributes), to issues touching on the rationale for the imposition of resulting trusts and to a typical problem-type examination question.

In very general terms, a resulting trust arises when the original arrangement envisaged by the testator or settlor has failed, has not been properly established or has been fully achieved without exhausting the trust's assets. To this extent, it arises out of a disappointed, failed or satisfied purpose of the testator/settlor. In reality the resulting trust arises in order to cure defective drafting of a trust instrument. Although this is a simplistic picture – see, for example, resulting trusts in the context of co-owned property – it explains why, under a resulting trust, the property returns or 'results' to the person originally entitled to it. To put it another way, resulting trusts may be seen as the consequence of the application of the old maxim that 'equity abhors a beneficial vacuum'. How, and in what cases, this is related to the intention of the person originally entitled to the property or to the state of mind (conscience) of the original trustee are difficult and complex issues.

Note

Section 199 of the Equality Act 2010 has abolished the presumption of advancement (i.e. the presumption of gifts) with regard to transactions that take effect after the subsection comes into force.

QUESTION 19

To what extent can it be said that resulting trusts operate to support the equitable maxim that 'equity abhors a beneficial vacuum'?

Aim Higher

Given that the categorisation of some resulting trusts as 'automatic' may now be incorrect – as all resulting trusts might spring from intention and a resulting obligation of conscience on the trustee – it could be the case that it may too simplistic to assert that resulting trusts may be seen as primarily filling a beneficial vacuum.

How to Read this Question

This essay question is structured for you to explore the extent to which the maxim stated in the question provides an adequate justification for the creation of resulting trusts

How to Answer this Question

Students are required to consider the different types of resulting trusts and the distinctions between them. There are many other situations in trusts law where, for one reason or another, the main purposes of the donor cannot be achieved. The question therefore arises as to who owns the trust property or, more accurately, who is entitled to the beneficial interest under the trust. The solution to this problem (sometimes known as cases involving failure of an express trust) is provided by the principles of resulting trusts. In short, if there are no beneficiaries entitled to the property, the trustee will hold the property on trust for the donor (or his estate): it will 'result back' to the person who provided it in the first place.

Up for Debate

The true rationale for the creation of resulting trusts has been the subject of academic research within the last four decades. Two incisive articles on the subject are P Millett, 'The *Quistclose* trust: who can enforce it?' (1985) 101 LQR 269; and W Swadling, 'Explaining resulting trusts' (2008) 124 LQR 72.

Answer Plan

❖   General nature of resulting trusts and the maxim that equity abhors a beneficial vacuum.

❖   Types of resulting trust.

❖   Differences between resulting trusts arising out of the failure of an express trust and other resulting trusts.

❖ Possible distinction between 'automatic' and 'presumed' resulting trusts.
❖ Rejection of such a distinction in *Westdeutsche Landesbank Girozentrale v Islington LBC* (1996).

Answer Structure

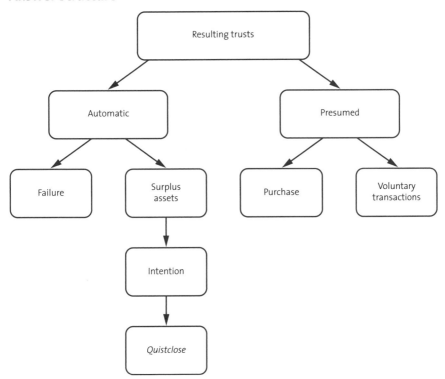

This diagram illustrates the thought processes in deciding which transactions attract the resulting trust.

ANSWER

Resulting trusts represent the solution of last resort when determining the ownership of trust property, failing which the property will fall to the Crown as *bona vacantia* (owner-less property), as happened with part of the gift in *Re West Sussex Constabulary Widows Fund* (1971). The circumstances in which a resulting trust may arise are numerous and varied and most cases are unique on their own facts, although this does not necessarily mean that the *concept* of resulting trusts cannot be explained by a general theory.[1]

First, one of the most common forms of resulting trust is that which arises when there has been an initial failure of the trust which the donor had intended to establish, either in respect of the whole or part of the trust property. For example, in *Vandervell v IRC* (1967)

1 Numerous 'trigger' events that create resulting trusts.

itself, the donor had attempted to dispose of his interest but had failed to divest himself fully of one portion of his property. Hence, that portion resulted to him. Likewise, if there is complete failure of the trust for uncertainty of objects, or lack of a human beneficiary (a purpose trust: *Re Endacott* (1960)), or where a charitable gift fails initially and cannot be applied *cy-près* (*Re Rymer* (1895)), the property will result back to the settlor. In all of these cases, the resulting trust arises in consequence of the failure of an express trust and, on one view, is said to operate 'automatically' upon that failure by operation of law (per Megarry J in *Re Vandervell (No 2)* (1974)). Whether such trusts are correctly described as 'automatic', suggesting, as it does, that they operate independently of the intention of the person originally making the gift, is open to doubt following *Westdeutsche Landesbank Girozentrale v Islington LBC* (1996). In that case, Lord Browne-Wilkinson said that resulting trusts operate because of an intention on the part of the donor to recover the property should the primary purpose fail. Hence, even in cases where there is failure of an express trust in the sense just discussed, a resulting trust will not arise if there is clear evidence of the donor's intention 'to part out and out' with his property. Such an intention, which would negate the existence of a resulting trust, means that the money is ownerless and will pass to the Crown as *bona vacantia* (*Re West Sussex Constabulary*). The equitable maxim raised in the question is supported only to the extent that the parties' intention does not dictate otherwise.

A second example of the use of resulting trusts arises where the primary trust established by the settlor has been completed, yet a surplus of undisposed trust property remains. Again, the traditional view is that the surplus is returned to the donor or his estate under a resulting trust because 'equity abhors a beneficial vacuum'. So, in *Re Abbott* (1900), the initial trust was completed and the surplus was held on resulting trust for the subscribers to the sisters' fund. Again, in *Re Gillingham Bus Disaster Fund* (1958), it was held that surplus funds should result back to the donors. Again, however, intention was an essential element in the use of resulting trusts: evidence of the donor's desire to part forever with his money meant that any surplus will not result (*Westdeutsche*). It is not sufficient that there was an absolute gift to an individual bound up with a non-binding motive to use the money for some specific purpose which then fails. So, in *Re Osoba* (1979), the gift was construed as an absolute gift to the testator's daughter with merely a non-binding direction to use the money for educational purposes. The original gift was absolute, not a gift on trust for educational purposes, and the doctrine of resulting trusts was irrelevant.

This leads us on to another area where resulting trusts may be important. It often happens that money is given in various ways to an unincorporated association for its members or general purposes, as where a local wildlife group raises money from donors and jumble sales. If this association then comes to an end, the surplus assets must be disposed of: equity abhors a beneficial vacuum. At one time, it was thought that these surplus assets should revert to the donors under a resulting trust (for example, *Re West Sussex Constabulary*). If a resulting trust is adopted, equity is filling the beneficial vacuum created by the failure of the initial gift (subject, as before, to questions concerning the relevance of intention). However, in a majority of recent cases, it is evident that the more favoured solution is to distribute the assets of a defunct unincorporated association among the surviving members of the association (that is, not necessarily among those people who provided the money in the first place). This is because a donation to the association need not be construed as a gift on a trust (which subsequently fails) but as an absolute gift to the members of the association subject to their contractual obligations *inter se*, as created by the rules of the association (*Re Recher's Trust* (1972); *Re Bucks Constabulary Fund Friendly Society (No 2)* (1979)). This construction, which ousts the resulting trust because it denies the existence of a primary trust, is more convenient as it does not require an extensive search for the original donors who may be very numerous and elusive.

Fourth, we come to a type of resulting trust that has come to the fore in recent years, especially in commercial transactions. Thus, if A (the donor) gives money to B (the trustee) solely in order that B may pay his debts to C, if those debts are not paid, the money will result to A under a resulting trust (*Barclays Bank v Quistclose Investments Ltd* (1970)). This may appear quite straightforward, but there are a number of difficulties with this arrangement. For example, if B pays the money to C, A has no claim, so the operation of the resulting trust in favour of A is dependent upon B not carrying out the specific purpose of paying his debts. Does this mean that the trust imposed on B is a purpose trust that is valid under *Re Denley* (1969) (see *Re Northern Developments (Holdings) Ltd* (1978))? Or that the equitable interest in the money is in suspense (*Carreras Rothmans Ltd v Freeman Mathews Treasure* (1985))? Or that A is the beneficiary under an express trust with a power to direct that the money be paid to C, hence excluding resulting trusts altogether? Furthermore, once the trust imposed on B is carried out (that is, he pays his debts), A will have a simple action in debt to recover the money from B: hence A has lost his proprietary right in the property under the resulting trust, to see it replaced by a personal right against B in debt, and all this by B's own actions.[2] In other words, this example of a resulting trust is used in a deliberate way to enable a donor to provide funds for another person (usually a company with which the donor is connected) and to restrict the use of those funds for a specific purpose, failing which the resulting trust comes into operation. The resulting trust is filling the beneficial vacuum, but only for the advantage of the donor, and the solution cannot be adopted where no primary trust existed (*Box v Barclays Bank* (1998)). Furthermore, it is an intended consequence of the parties' actions, in the nature of a deliberate 'failsafe'. It is very different from the 'automatic' resulting trusts considered above which might be thought to arise by operation of law because of an unintentional failure of the original arrangements. This type of resulting trust does seem consistent with the 'intention approach' put forward in *Westdeutsche*.

Finally, brief mention must be made of a different kind of resulting trust.[3] This is the so-called 'presumed' resulting trust. A presumed resulting trust does not arise automatically in order to fill a beneficial vacuum (assuming, post-*Westdeutsche*, that this is an acceptable analysis), but exists because of a presumed intention of the parties to create a trust over property. This presumption can be rebutted by evidence that the payment of money

....

2   Listing of various solutions advisable.
3   Status of the presumed resulting trust.

was as a gift or loan (*Cowcher v Cowcher* (1972)). Of course, in one sense, the resulting trust is filling the beneficial vacuum created by the payer's lack of express intention as to why he is paying the money at all but, in effect, this form of resulting trust is not used to determine ownership of apparently ownerless property, but to give effect to the unexpressed intentions of the parties.

Common Pitfalls

The answers to typical examination questions on resulting trusts are now complicated by the dictum that a resulting trust can exist only where supported by the original donor's intention (*Westdeutsche v Islington LBC*). It remains to be seen whether this goes unchallenged. If it becomes the accepted orthodoxy, the distinction between automatic and presumed resulting trusts will have been exploded.

QUESTION 20

The Over Village Association, a non-charitable, unincorporated body, existed to safeguard the amenities in the village of Over. It derived its funds from members' subscriptions, gifts by will and otherwise, the proceeds of local events such as jumble sales and raffles, money in collection boxes and one large anonymous donation. The village has now been granted Protected Status under European Union Regional Funds and its future is secure. The Village Association is about to be disbanded, but there is disagreement as to what to do with the considerable surplus funds that remain. The treasurer comes to you for advice.

How to Read this Question

The question requires you to consider the destination of funds on a liquidation of an unincorporated association. This is a matter of ascertaining the intentions of the donors as construed by the courts.

How to Answer this Question

In answering this question students will need to identify the peculiar nature of unincorporated associations and consider the status of transfer of funds to such associations. In doing so each source of finance will have to be considered separately to determine the intentions of the parties.

Up for Debate

The ownership of funds on a liquidation of unincorporated associations has been explored by a number of academics including G Green, 'The dissolution of unincorporated non-profit associations' (1980) 45 MLR 626 and S Panesar, 'Surplus funds and unincorporated associations' (2000) 14 T&T 698. You may find them rewarding.

Answer Plan

- ❖ The link between distribution of funds and validity of gifts.
- ❖ The need to consider each 'source' of finance separately.
- ❖ Resulting trusts, absolute gifts or *bona vacantia*.
- ❖ Rules to be adopted by the association, especially the establishment of a winding-up mechanism.

Answer Structure

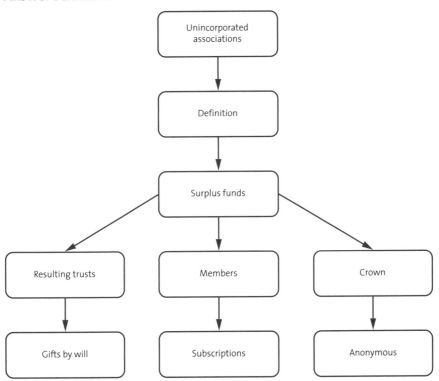

This diagram lists the principles for distributing funds on the liquidation of an unincorporated association.

ANSWER

(a) The Surplus Derived from Members' Subscriptions

It might be thought that money derived from members' subscriptions is most appropriately returned to those members under a resulting trust, on the basis that the primary purpose of their subscriptions has failed. Indeed, in some cases, this solution has been adopted and each subscriber (whether still a member at the date of dissolution or not) has received a share proportionate to his or her original contributions (*Re Printers and Transferrers Amalgamated Trades Protection Society* (1899), and see *Air Jamaica v Charlton* (1999) in the context of surplus funds of pensions). However, this solution presupposes that the members' subscriptions were given 'on trust' in the first place, which trust has now failed or has not exhausted the trust property. If true, this must have been a trust for the purposes of the association even though such trusts for purposes are void under the beneficiary principle (*Re Endacott* (1960)). Alternatively, it is now more likely that income derived from members' subscriptions will be treated as having been given to the association not by way of trust, but as an absolute gift to the members individually, albeit on the basis that the money is to be used in accordance with the rules of the association, this forming a binding contract between them (*Re Recher's Trust* (1972); *Re Bucks Constabulary Fund Friendly Society (No 2)* (1979); *Artistic Upholstery* (1999)).[4] This would mean that any surplus derived from subscriptions belongs to the members absolutely (that is, those at the date of dissolution) and may be distributed among them according to their contract (the rules). If the rules prevent the members taking any surplus assets personally when the association dissolves, then either the rules must be changed prior to dissolution (if permitted by the rules themselves) or the property will pass to the Crown as *bona vacantia*. In our case, therefore, the presumption will be that the members at the date of dissolution of the association may share in the surplus assets derived from subscriptions, provided this is permitted by their contract *inter se* under the rules.

(b) The Surplus Derived from Gifts by Will and Otherwise

This presents a similar problem to members' subscriptions, although now there is a real choice to be made between the resulting trust option and distribution of the surplus assets among the members. With gifts from identifiable persons, there is a distinct possibility that the money will be treated as having been given expressly for the purposes of the association and for nothing else. In other words, a primary trust for the association's purposes was intended which, having failed, the surplus assets attributable to that source result back to the donors unless there is evidence of a clear intention forever to have parted with the money (*Westdeutsche v Islington LBC* (1996)). Of course, there are problems with this interpretation, not least that trusts for purposes are void (*Re Endacott* (1960)) unless they fall within the *Re Denley* (1969) exception. So, unless this is a *Re Denley* trust, in theory the donors should be able to recover the whole of their original gifts – not merely the surplus after the void purpose had been undertaken and failed. However, although the pure logic of this is compelling, the case law suggests that only the *surplus* assets will result to the original donors and this would probably be the case if the resulting trust option was followed with our association (*Re West Sussex Constabulary Widows Fund* (1971)). Similarly, if gifts to the Over Village Association could indeed be construed on a *Re Denley* basis, the donors would be *entitled* only to the surplus funds under the resulting trust (*Re Abbott* (1900)), the primary purpose trust having been valid, but then failed. Finally, we should not discount the possibility that the *Re Bucks Constabulary* construction could be adopted and that specific donations could be construed as gifts to the individual members of the association under contract, in which case the same considerations are relevant as those considered above when discussing members' subscriptions.[5]

....

4   Modern view of the destination of surplus assets.
5   Contractual basis of donations by will.

(c) The Surplus Derived from a Large Anonymous Donation

The surplus attributable to this gift presumptively is to be dealt with in the same way as that arising from specific individual donations (as above). Of course, should the resulting trust option be followed, the anonymity of this donor creates a difficulty, although the court may well direct that the surplus assets be held in court until claimed by the donor on production of satisfactory evidence, as in *Re Gillingham Bus Disaster Fund* (1958). However, the fact that the donor wished for anonymity might lead to the conclusion either: that he or she had intended to disclaim any future interest in the gift and that it should be taken to be an absolute gift to the members of the association to be used according to their contractual rights *inter se* (*Re Bucks Constabulary Fund (No 2)*); or, that a trust for purposes existed but with a resulting trust excluded by intention, with the surplus going to the Crown (*Re West Sussex Constabulary; Westdeutsche v Islington LBC; Davis v Richards and Wallington Industries* (1990)).

(d) The Surplus Arising from the Proceeds of Local Events such as Jumble Sales and Raffles

This source of the association's funds presents the least difficulty. In fact, as made clear in *Re Bucks Constabulary Fund (No 2)* (1979), there are two reasons why the resulting trust option should be excluded. First, the people paying for jumble and raffle tickets, etc., are entering into a purchase contract with the association for items of jumble or raffle tickets and they obtain all they are entitled to when that contract is carried out. The 'donors' have no claim on any surplus assets, having received their full contractual entitlement. Second, and in any event, it is not the donor's money which goes to the association but the profit from the jumble sale or raffle after deduction of expenses. Consequently, any surpluses derived from these activities cannot go by way of resulting trust and normally will be treated as an accretion to the general funds of the association to be used by the members individually, subject to their contract *inter se* (*Re Recher's Trust* (1972)). The surplus may be distributed according to the rules of the association as before.

(e) The Surplus Deriving from Money Placed in Collection Boxes

Once again, there is a difficulty here because the identity of the donors may be impossible to establish and, indeed, they are likely to have given in such small amounts that no claim to surplus will be made. Thus, the resulting trust option seems impractical and absurd. However, as Harman J recognised in *Re Gillingham Bus Disaster Fund* (1958), this could be the logical solution, as the donor might well have intended that the money be used for the purposes of the association alone. Why else would he put money in a collection box? However, in *Re West Sussex Constabulary Widows Fund* (1971), Goff J was of the opinion that money derived from street collections was given 'out and out' by the donors, thus depriving them of any future claim to it. In that case, Goff J went further and held that even the members of the Benevolent Fund had no claim to the property because the association was not designed for their benefit, being 'outward looking'. Thus, the surplus fell to the Crown as *bona vacantia*. Further, although this is a rather unattractive solution, and something of a last resort, *Westdeutsche v Islington LBC* confirmed that the existence of a resulting trust depended on the donor having an intention to recover his property. Consequently, where there is no such intention, there can be no possibility of a resulting trust. So, in our case, the Over Village Association may also be described as 'outward looking' and it is possible that both the resulting trust (lack of intention) and gift to members (not consistent with the purpose of the original donation) will be excluded.

This is the picture on the eve of the dissolution of the Over Village Association. Obviously, much depends on the reason why the various donations to the association were valid in the first place and the nature of the contract between the members (that is, the rules of the association). The treasurer should ensure that he or she is acquainted with those rules and the fact that it is possible for the appropriate surplus assets to be distributed to those members in existence at the date of dissolution. Failing that, the property may fall to the Crown as *bona vacantia*. Finally, any surplus derived from property which was subject to a primary trust will result to the donors.

QUESTION 21

Consider the ownership of the equitable interests in the relevant properties, in respect of each of the dispositions made by Alfred of properties which he originally owned absolutely:

(a)   A transfer of 10,000 shares in British Telecom plc to his wife, Beryl, subject to an option, exercisable by their son, Charles, at any time within the next five years, to repurchase 5,000 of the shares. The shares have been duly registered in Beryl's name and she pays 50 per cent of the dividends received to Alfred.

(b)   A transfer of £70,000 to the trustees of his daughter's marriage settlement: 'Upon trust to pay the income to my daughter, Danielle, so long as she does not have an abortion and on her death, to her husband, Ernest, and on his death to pay the capital and income to their children in equal shares.' Five years after the transfer Danielle has an abortion. Ten years after the transfer, Danielle, Ernest and their only child, Frederick, die in a fire.

How to Read this Question

This two part question on resulting trusts requires you to identify the ownership of the equitable interest in the shares, option and the cash fund. It is crucial to identify the location of the legal titles to the various properties and evaluate the conduct of the parties to determine whether the presumption of resulting trust has been rebutted.

How to Answer this Question

In answering this question students should focus on the existence of the presumption of resulting trusts and consider the existence of rebuttal evidence, if any. In addition, public policy issues, the doctrine of acceleration of postponed interests and *commorientes* need to be considered.

Up for Debate

The rationale for the resulting trusts is the subject of debate as analysed by W Swadling, 'A new role for resulting trusts' (1996) 16 Legal Studies 110; P Millett, 'Restitution and constructive trusts' (1998) LQR 399; Lord Browne-Wilkinson's judgment in *Westdeutsche Landesbank Girozentrale v Islington Borough Council* (1996).

Answer Plan

❖ Presumption of a resulting trust (RT) and evidence in rebuttal.
❖ Automatic resulting trusts or 'out and out' gifts.
❖ Limitation restricted by public policy.
❖ Acceleration of postponed interests.
❖ Doctrine of *commorientes*.

Answer Structure

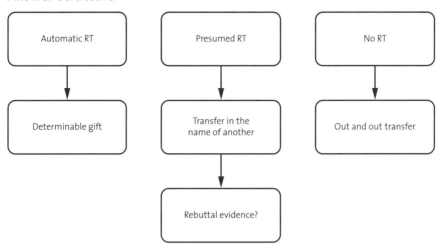

This diagram highlights the principles that are applicable in order to clarify the interests of the various parties.

ANSWER

In each of these transactions the location of the equitable interest is prima facie unclear. One solution adopted by the courts over the centuries is the institution of the resulting trust – automatic and presumed. The relevance of such a trust will be considered in respect of each transaction.[6]

(a) A Transfer of 10,000 Shares in British Telecom plc to his Wife, Beryl

We are told that the legal title to the BT shares has been vested in the name of Alfred's wife, Beryl. This involved a voluntary transfer of the legal title to property by a husband to his wife. There has been no indication as to the destination of the equitable interest in the shares. The prima facie solution adopted by the courts involves a presumption of a resulting trust in favour of Alfred (before the passing of the **Equality Act 2010** a presumption of advancement (gift) would have arisen in favour of Beryl as Alfred's wife). Thus, as a starting point Beryl is presumed to be a trustee of the equitable interest in 10,000 shares in favour of the transferor, Alfred. The existence of the resulting trust is a reference to the incidence of the onus of proof, i.e. Beryl bears the burden of rebutting the presumption.

6 The last resort nature of identifying interests under resulting trusts.

Has the presumption been rebutted? The presumption of resulting trust is an artificial rule for allocating the equitable interest in property when this is unclear. The presumption may be rebutted by evidence that establishes the true intentions of the parties. Such evidence may take the form of oral or written statements as well as the conduct of the parties. However, there are two principles that are applied by the courts in this context – whether the evidence is admissible and, if so, the weight to be attached to such evidence. We are told that Beryl pays 50 per cent of the dividends to Alfred. In the absence of oral or written evidence, this is evidence of conduct that is prejudicial to Beryl in the sense that it may indicate an acknowledgment from Beryl that 50 per cent of the equitable interest belongs to Alfred. Has she consistently paid this amount of the dividends to Alfred? Did she feel obliged to do so? Does Alfred expect to receive this amount when the dividends are paid to Beryl? Are there any mitigating factors that exist in favour of Beryl?[7] These are issues that are connected to the weight of the evidence. Issues of weight are for the tribunal of fact. If the court is convinced that Beryl's conduct acknowledges the interest of Alfred, the presumption of resulting trust will not be rebutted as to 50 per cent of the shares. There does not appear to be any evidence of the conduct of the parties regarding the remaining 50 per cent of the shares. On this basis Alfred will be presumed to retain the equitable interest in these shares as well and the presumption may not be rebutted. The effect would be that Beryl holds 50 per cent of the shares (capital) on resulting trust for Alfred, subject to the terms of the initial transfer. Alternatively, if the presumption is rebutted, Beryl will be entitled to the shares in equity but subject to the terms of the initial transfer.

An additional complication is that the initial transfer of the shares by Alfred to Beryl was subject to an option exercisable by Charles to repurchase 50 per cent of the shares within five years. Thus, the legal right to exercise the option was vested in Charles. This much is clear. The question in issue concerns the location of the equitable interest in the option. This is a voluntary transfer of property rights and accordingly gives rise to a presumption of resulting trust (prior to the **Equality Act 2010** a transfer of property by a father to his son would have given rise to a presumption of advancement). The effect is that, prima facie, Charles holds the legal right to the option in favour of Alfred. We have not been given any evidence that could be used in rebuttal of this presumption of resulting trust. Accordingly, Alfred may maintain his equitable interest in the option.

(b) A Transfer of £70,000 to the Trustees of his Daughter's Marriage Settlement

There are several issues in this problem. The terms of the trust indicate that the income is payable to Danielle until her death, subject to a restriction that she does not have an abortion. Five years after the transfer Danielle has an abortion. The first issue is whether this clause is void on the ground of public policy. It is not a positive requirement that Danielle must have an abortion (which might be void), but it is a negative prohibition that she does not have an abortion. On this basis it is likely that the clause is valid. The next issue concerns the effect of the abortion that Danielle arranged. In particular, would this

---

7   Identification of issues of fact.

condition trigger the termination of Danielle's interest? If the court decides that a condition subsequently has taken place and that this brings Danielle's interest to an end, the next issue is the destination of the equitable interest. Ernest, the next in line, is entitled to the income on the death of Danielle, and not merely on the termination of her interest. The issue is whether a resulting trust arises or, alternatively, that Ernest's interest is accelerated after Danielle has an abortion. The doctrine of acceleration of a postponed interest is based on the notion that if a prior interest under a trust fails so that the reason for the postponement disappears, a subsequent interest may be brought forward and be enjoyed immediately. The gap in ownership may be filled by an acceleration of a subsequent interest. There is no room for a resulting trust in order to delay the enjoyment of the subsequent interest. Such complications often take place where a draftsman of a trust or will fails to foresee a contingency which has in fact taken place. The court will construe the trust instrument or will in order to ascertain whether there is a gap in ownership and whether the doctrine of acceleration is capable of filling that gap: see *Re Cochrane* (1955). Applying the test to the facts of this case, it appears that no provision is made in the trust for the equitable interest in the events that have taken place. In such an event the court may apply the doctrine of acceleration and bring forward Ernest's life interest after Danielle's interest lapses.

All three parties die in a car crash. For the purposes of inheritance it may be necessary to ascertain the order in which the parties died. If there is no medical evidence to determine the order of death, the doctrine of *commorientes* (endorsed in **s 184** of the **Law of Property Act 1925**) may be adopted to identify when the deaths are deemed to take place. This rule stipulates that the order of deaths is based on the seniority of the individuals. Thus, Frederick is presumed to be the last to die and the property may be distributed to Frederick's heirs.

6 Constructive Trusts 1: The Duty Not to Make a Profit from the Trust and Co-ownership Trusts

INTRODUCTION

In the following two chapters we will turn our attention to one of the most versatile of all the forms of the trust concept: the constructive trust. Indeed, so versatile is this concept in the modern law that there really are several types of constructive trusts, all of which bear the same name, but which do not necessarily share the same characteristics or serve the same purposes, save only that they all arise by operation of law consequent upon some defect of conscience on the part of the constructive trustee. In this particular chapter, we will consider two specific kinds of constructive trust. First, there is the constructive trust that is imposed on a trustee or other fiduciary as a consequence of that person using his or her position to make a personal profit or gain. In essence, this constructive trust requires the trustee or fiduciary to account for any such profits on trust for the beneficiaries or persons to whom the fiduciary duties are owed: see *Crown Dilmun Ltd v Sutton* (2004). It is in the nature both of a remedy against the trustee/fiduciary for unauthorised activities and a safeguard that ensures that she acts for the benefit of the trust and not for herself. This is essentially a personal obligation imposed on the trustees or other fiduciaries not to profit from the exercise of their fiduciary duties and the remedy may involve an account of such profits. Second, we shall consider the particular principles applicable to the acquisition of interests in land where a person claims a share in a matrimonial or quasi-matrimonial home belonging in law to another. This species of constructive trust is in the nature of a remedy against the legal owner of property, against whom the constructive trust is deployed, in order to achieve equity between the parties.

At the outset, it should be noted that it is notoriously difficult to define with precision the exact circumstances in which a constructive trust may arise. Yet, perhaps that is just as it should be. If there is a common thread that links all types of constructive trust (and that is debatable), it is that they are used to prevent and rectify inequitable conduct. Consequently, some of the material considered in this chapter may well overlap with material considered elsewhere.

QUESTION 22

Discuss the trusts issues raised in each of the situations below and advise the parties concerned:

(a) Sgt Jim Tow was until recently a British member of the UN peacekeeping force in Utopia. He was in charge of the security of food depots. He has accumulated a sum of £50,000 in a London bank account. This money came from bribes he received from some civilian workers of a large aid agency working in Utopia who were illegally selling UN food supplies to private food shops. These facts have now been exposed by a Sunday newspaper.

(b) Peter is the company secretary of two companies, namely X Co Ltd and Y Co plc. Six months ago he passed on to his friend, James, special company information on the two companies. James subsequently sold the information to a third company for £100,000, which he shared with Peter.

Aim Higher

A fiduciary will be required to disgorge any unauthorised profits he makes in breach of his fiduciary duties. This may be achieved by a constructive trust of the profits or he will be personally liable to account in favour of the innocent party. The remedies that are available vary with the circumstances of each case. In particular, relevant issues include whether the contract with the third party has been performed or not and whether the fiduciary still has the property under his control.

How to Read this Question

This two part question concerns the duty to account that is imposed on a trustee or fiduciary. Specifically the issues involve the law with respect to fiduciaries receiving bribes and strangers to a trust receiving trust property or assisting in a fraudulent breach of trust.

How to Answer this Question

In answering this question you are required to deal with the following material issues – who is a fiduciary? The status of bribes received by fiduciaries, the effect of a trustee or fiduciary putting himself in a position of conflict of duty and interest, the status of key information concerning the trust and the liability of strangers to a trust intermeddling with trust property.

Up for Debate

Students are advised to consider the issue of whether a breach of fiduciary duty is related to a personal or proprietary claim by the innocent party. On this issue see C Conte, 'No proprietary relief for breach of fiduciary duty' (2012) LQR 184 and S Elliott and C Mitchell, 'Remedies for dishonest assistance' (2004) 64 MLR 16.

Answer Plan

❖ Conflict of duty and interest.

❖ Duty to account for bribes received.

❖ Whether trust information may be treated as trust property.

❖ Knowingly receiving trust property.

Answer Structure

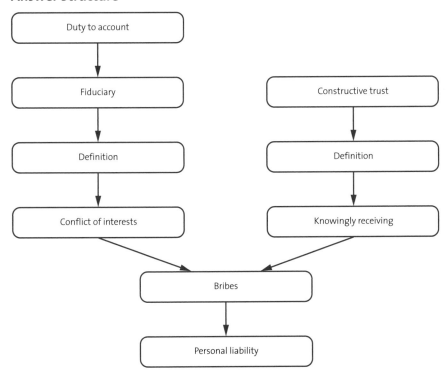

This diagram highlights the personal liability to account for breach of trust and the liability as constructive trustee.

ANSWER

(a) Sgt Tow

Jim Tow has accumulated £50,000 from bribes by illegally selling UN food supplies to private shops. The question is whether he is accountable to the UN agency for these bribes.[1] The general rule is that a person occupying a position of confidence (such as a trustee or fiduciary) is prohibited from deriving any personal benefit by availing himself of his position, in the absence of authority from the beneficiaries, trust instrument or the court. In other words, the trustee or fiduciary should not place himself in the position where his duties may conflict with his personal interest. If such a conflict occurs and the

1   Elements of liability for knowingly receiving claim.

trustee obtains a benefit or profit, he is accountable to the claimants as if he is a construc-tive trustee. This is known as the rule in *Keech v Sandford* (1726).

The ingredients of the claim are:[2]

(1) the defendant holds a fiduciary position towards the claimant; and
(2) the defendant obtained a benefit; and
(3) there is a causal connection between the relationship and the benefit.

Failure to establish all of these conditions would lead to a failure in the proceedings. The first issue is whether Sgt Tow is a fiduciary. This is a question of law. The concept was defined by Millett LJ in *Bristol and West Building Society v Mothew* (1996) as someone who has undertaken to act for or on behalf of another in circumstances which give rise to a rela-tionship of trust and confidence. Millett LJ went on to lay down the duties imposed on a fiduciary and added that he is prohibited from making an unauthorised profit. On the facts of the problem Sgt Tow was a member of the UN peacekeeping force in Utopia. He acts on behalf of an international agency. It would appear that Sgt Tow, as a security officer, is undoubtedly a fiduciary and owes fiduciary duties to the claimant; see *Reading v Attorney General* (1951). The next issue is whether he had obtained a profit. This is a question of fact and we are told that he has accumulated £50,000 in a London bank account. Did he receive this sum in his capacity as a fiduciary? This is also a question of fact and requires a causal link to be found between the receipt of the sum and his fiduciary capacity. We are told that the £50,000 was received as bribes for the illegal sales to private shops. This is conclusive evidence that, in effect, he abused his position as a security officer and consciously and deliberately released the food to unauthorised persons in return for remuneration. On the question of accountability for the bribes, the clear rule is that the defendant is required to pay back the bribes that he received: see *Lister & Co v Stubbs* (1890), *Sinclair Investments v Versailles Ltd* (2011) and contrast *Attorney General for Hong Kong v Reid* (1994). But if the defendant had invested the bribes and received a profit, a more complicated question is involved, namely, whether he is accountable only for the bribes and whether in addition to the bribes he is accountable for the profits derived from the bribes. The solution adopted by the Court of Appeal in *Lister v Stubbs* was that on receipt of the bribe a relationship of debtor and creditor is created. This did not involve the trust notion. However, the Privy Council in *Attorney General for Hong Kong v Reid* refused to follow *Lister* and decided that both the bribe and the additional profit are held upon trust for the persons to whom the duty is owed. On receipt of the bribe, the fiduciary becomes a trustee of the sum for the benefit of the innocent party and is liable to account for this property and any derivative profits. If the bribe is used to purchase other property which decreases in value, the fiduciary is required to account for the difference between the bribe and the undervalue. Alternatively, if the prop-erty has increased in value, the innocent party is entitled to claim the surplus, because the fiduciary is not entitled to profit from a breach of his duties. The reason for this rule is that when the bribe is received, it is required to be paid immediately to the claimant; principle – equity considers as done that which ought to be done. Thus, a constructive trust is attached

2 Uncertain nature of degrees of knowledge.

to the bribe. The effect is that the £50,000 in the bank account may be the subject of a constructive trust in favour of the claimant. More recently the Court of Appeal in *Sinclair v Versailles* (2011) refused to follow the Privy Council decision in *Reid* and instead endorsed the *Lister* principle. In similar vein the Supreme Court in *Williams v Central Bank of Nigeria* (2014), decided that a claim for dishonest assistance was a claim *in personam* and subject to the limitation period of six years. The effect is that an agent or other fiduciary who receives a bribe has a personal liability to account to the principal for the amount of the bribe as a debtor. The claim is personal and not proprietary and therefore the claimant does not acquire an interest in investments acquired with the proceeds of the bribe.

(b) Peter

Peter, a company secretary, is an officer of the companies X Co Ltd and Y Co plc and is clearly a fiduciary in respect of those companies. He discloses sensitive information concerning the companies to James. On the basis of the analysis in (a) above he is in breach of his duties as a fiduciary in both unlawfully disclosing the information and receiving a profit as a result of the disclosure. He has allowed his duties to conflict with his interest: see *Industrial Developments v Cooley* (1972) and *Regal (Hastings) Ltd v Gulliver* (1942). In *Boardman v Phipps* (1967) an argument was raised as to whether information was capable of being treated as trust property. The House of Lords, by a majority, decided that confidential information was capable of being trust property. On the facts of this problem Peter has used trust property (information) to derive an unauthorised profit and is therefore accountable as a constructive trustee.[3]

Peter's accomplice, James, may also be liable as a constructive trustee and be under a duty to account to the claimants for the profits that he made by selling confidential information (trust property). The nature of liability would depend on whether James still has the property in traceable form or not. The test of liability under this head, as laid down by Hoffmann LJ in *El Ajou v Dollar Land Holdings plc* (1994), is whether:

- ❖ James received trust property,
- ❖ in breach of trust; and
- ❖ knows that the information is trust property; and
- ❖ acts in a way inconsistent with the trust.[4]

On the first issue the court decided in *Boardman v Phipps* that confidential information is capable of being trust property (see above). With regard to the problem there was clearly a breach of trust in that the companies did not authorise the disclosure of the information. Does James have knowledge that the information is trust property? 'Knowledge' for these purposes had been classified by Peter Gibson J in *Re Baden Delvaux* (1983) as including subjective and objective knowledge. This is a question of degree. Since James does not repay the proceeds of sale to the companies, he acts inconsistently with the trust. Accordingly, a court order may be attached to the £100,000 received by James.

---

3   Attempting to identify the basis of liability for knowingly receiving claims.
4   Liability to account but no constructive trust.

Alternatively, in *Re Montagu Settlement Trust* (1987) and more recently in *BCCI v Akindele* (2000) the court decided that the basis of liability when a stranger receives trust property for his own benefit is unconscionability, i.e. whether it would be unconscionable for the defendant to retain the property. The court also decided that the test is subjective awareness.

If James did not receive the trust property but merely assisted Peter dishonestly in a fraudulent design, he (James) will be accountable as if he was a constructive trustee. This was the test laid down in the definitive case of *Royal Brunei Airlines v Tan* (1995). The basis of liability is dishonestly assisting in a fraudulent scheme. In *Twinsectra v Yardley* (2002) the House of Lords decided that the test for dishonesty is the combination test that exists in criminal law, i.e. the defendant's conduct is dishonest by reference to the ordinary standards of reasonable and honest people *and* that he himself realised that his conduct was dishonest by those standards. This is both an objective and subjective test. Further, in *Barlow Clowes International Ltd v Eurotrust* (2006), the Privy Council decided that an inquiry into the defendant's views about standards of honesty was not required. The standard by which dishonesty is judged is objective. In *Abou-Ramah v Abacha* (2006) and *Starglade v Nash* (2011), the Court of Appeal endorsed the approach that was adopted in *Barlow Clowes* (2006) and confirmed that the standard for dishonesty is objective.

Common Pitfalls

Students sometimes fail to appreciate the distinction between breaches of duties by trustees and breaches of fiduciary duties by trustees. Breaches of fiduciary duties only occur when the fiduciary does not act with the beneficiary's best interests in mind.

QUESTION 23

A trustee must not place herself in a position where her interest and duty conflict.

▶ **Discuss, with reference to decided cases.**

How to Read this Question

This is a descriptive question on the duty of the trustee not to place herself in a position where her duty and interest conflict and is a case based discussion of the principle. It is also necessary to state the occasions when a benefit received by a trustee may be retained by her.

How to Answer this Question

In answering this question it is necessary to state the justification for this inflexible rule of law and illustrate the principle and relevant exceptions to the rule through case law.

Up for Debate

This is a rigid duty that is imposed on trustees and fiduciaries. A good understanding of the notion of fiduciary accountability will be enhanced by analysing the issues explored by J Edelman, 'When do fiduciary duties arise?' (2010) 126 LQR 302.

Answer Plan

❖ The duty to account is imposed on persons already in a fiduciary position in order to ensure that any profit made by virtue of that position is not retained.

❖ The trustee's duties are owed to the trust and any unauthorised benefit received by the trustee is claimable by the trust.

❖ Examples of various circumstances in which this liability can arise.

❖ Occasions when certain benefits may be authorised by law.

Answer Structure

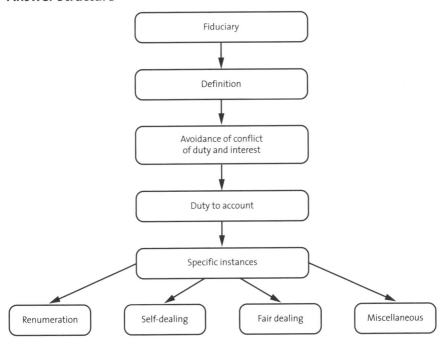

This diagram illustrates the extent of the fiduciary duty to account.

ANSWER

The essence of the trust or fiduciary relationship is that the fiduciary owes clear and strict duties to administer the trust property or other assets for the benefit of those entitled in equity to that property or assets. In order to ensure that these duties are honoured in full, there is a virtually absolute bar against the trustee using her position for any personal gain. Such is the strictness of this rule that a duty to account for any benefit received will be imposed on a trustee or other fiduciary irrespective of any intentional deceit, recklessness or negligence on her part (*Regal (Hastings) Ltd v Gulliver* (1942)).[5] It is enough if the trustee or fiduciary has simply placed herself in a position where her duty to the trust has conflicted with her own interest. In *Crown Dilmun Ltd v Sutton* (2004), the court decided that a fiduciary

5 Clear basis of liability in dishonest assistance cases.

who concealed information from his employer concerning the opportunity to redevelop property in order to benefit himself, was accountable to the claimant for the profits received.

This overriding principle of equity is of general application, and it is now recognised that there are a number of identifiable situations where the court will intervene to impose a duty to account on a trustee or fiduciary.

First, as a matter of principle, trustees are under a duty to act without remuneration: trusteeship is essentially gratuitous. The trustee's obligation is to ensure the most efficient running of the trust, without the self-interest of creating unwarranted work for which they could be paid (*Robinson v Pett* (1734)). Any remuneration so received will presumptively be payable to the beneficiaries unless authorised by law including the trust instrument. The **Trustee Act 2000** contains general provisions authorising the payment of remuneration or stipulating the circumstances in which remuneration can be paid (ss 28–30). They will provide remuneration for nearly all professional trustees, subject to any express terms of the trust instrument. Other means by which the trustee may properly claim to keep any remuneration arise from the existence of a contract to that effect with the beneficiary (although a promise to fulfil existing duties is not good consideration), under certain statutory provisions (for example, s 42 of the **Trustee Act 1942**; **Judicial Trustee Act 1896**), under the special rules relating to solicitor trustees (*Cradock v Piper* (1850)) and where the payment is earned during administration of assets abroad (*Re Northcote's Will Trusts* (1949)).

Second, there is a rule that a trustee may not purchase for herself certain types of property, in particular rights in property which should properly be purchased for the beneficiaries. So, a renewal of a trust lease in favour of the fiduciary will be held on constructive trust for the beneficiaries (*Keech v Sandford* (1726)). This will be so even if it is clear that the landlord would not have renewed the lease in favour of the beneficiaries. The trustee's duty is to act in the best interests of the beneficiaries, not in her own, and there is an irrebuttable presumption of law that a trustee cannot take the benefit of the lease for herself (*Re Biss* (1903) and *Popat v Shonchhatra* (1997)).

Third, as explained in *Tito v Waddell (No 2)* (1977), a trustee is unable to purchase the trust property itself. Simply put, the trustee cannot be both vendor (as trustee) and purchaser of property which she is holding for the benefit of another (*Ex p Lacey* (1802)). This is known as the 'self-dealing' rule, although it should be emphasised that, in some circumstances, a trustee will be permitted to retain her purchase if the reasons for the self-dealing rule are not present,[6] see *Holder v Holder* (1966).

Fourth, and in similar vein, the 'fair dealing' rule makes it clear that a trustee may only purchase the interest of the beneficiary if the transaction was at full market value and the trustee disclosed all material facts (*Dougan v Macpherson* (1902)).

Fifth, there are a number of cases, involving different factual backgrounds, where the court has imposed a constructive trust on a fiduciary because of a conflict of interest and duty in a

---

6   Initial confusion as to the meaning of dishonesty.

business context. For example, it has been held that any fees paid to company directors who hold those directorships because of their legal ownership of trust shares must be held on trust for the beneficiaries (*Re Francis* (1905); *Re Macadam* (1946)). As mentioned before, the essence of the matter is that such directors will have received fees only because they were trustees, although if their appointments were not due to their holding trust shares, the fees may be retained (*Re Dover Coalfield Extension* (1908)). Again, in *Williams v Barton* (1927), a trustee who persuaded the trust to employ a firm of stockbrokers from whom he received a commission was held to hold that commission on constructive trust for the beneficiaries, and in *Boardman v Phipps* (1967), a solicitor who made a profit from the purchase of shares, having gained important information while acting as a fiduciary, was required to hold that profit on trust. A further example is provided by *Reading v Attorney General* (1951), where an army sergeant was held to be a constructive trustee of monies received for escorting vehicles unsearched through army checkpoints, although in *Regal (Hastings) Ltd v Gulliver* (1942) it was emphasised that neither fraud nor absence of bona fides was necessary to trigger the imposition of the constructive trust in these circumstances (see, also, *LSE v Pearson* (2000)). The presence of a good motive may mean, as in *Boardman*, that a fiduciary is entitled to receive equitable remuneration for her skill in achieving a profit, even though the profit itself must be held on trust for the beneficiaries. Obviously, however, this jurisdiction will not be exercised in favour of a fiduciary who is *mala fides* or whose fiduciary duties positively prohibit personal gain (*Guinness plc v Saunders* (1990)).

Clearly the equitable principle that a trustee must not place herself in a position where her interest and duty conflict has many applications. However, it must not be thought that the types of liability discussed above are exhaustive, or that every case of a conflict of interest and duty can be neatly pigeonholed into one of these categories. By way of example, in *Attorney General for Hong Kong v Reid* (1994), the Privy Council has held that a bribe accepted by a person in a fiduciary position will be held on constructive trust for the person(s) to whom the fiduciary duty is owed, so disapproving of *Lister & Co v Stubbs* (1890), which for many years had decided that no constructive trust could exist in these circumstances. However, in *Sinclair Investments v Versailles Ltd* (2011) the Court of Appeal refused to follow *Reid* and decided that the recipient of a bribe owes a personal duty to account to the principal for the amount of the bribe and this principle does not extend to assets purchased with the proceeds of the bribe. More recently in *Williams v Central Bank of Nigeria* (2014) the Supreme Court approved the principle laid down in *Sinclair*.

QUESTION 24

The **Trustee Act 2000** contains widely drawn statutory authority permitting professional trustees to charge for their services. This is a very desirable reform of the pre-existing law.

▶ Discuss.

How to Read this Question

This is a descriptive question that focuses on the justification of the principles laid down in the **Trustee Act 2000** authorising professional trustees to be paid for their services. The effect of acting for the trust without authority to be paid should also be dealt with.

How to Answer this Question

A good answer would include the justification for the general rule requiring trustees to avoid a conflict of duty and interest. The inadequacies of the pre-2000 law ought to be highlighted but the main focus of the answer will be the methods by which the **Trustee Act 2000** has dealt with the problem.

Up for Debate

The requirement of compensation for breach of fiduciary loyalty was explored by M Conaglen, 'Equitable compensation for breach of fiduciary duties' (2003) 119 LQR1. It is recommended that you analyse this article thoroughly.

Answer Plan

❖ Discuss inadequacies in the old law.
❖ Outline **Trustee Act 2000** provisions on trustee remuneration.

Answer Structure

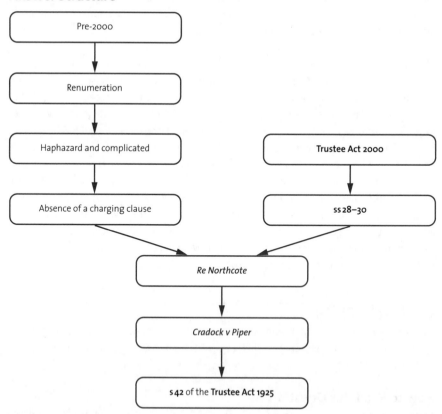

This diagram highlights the changes made by the **Trustee Act 2000** authorising trustees to be paid for their services.

ANSWER

The office of trusteeship is inherently gratuitous, springing from the fundamental principle that a trustee must not place himself in a position where his interest and duty conflict (*Bray v Ford* (1896)). Consequently, before the **Trustee Act 2000**, it was clear both in principle and practice that a trustee should act without remuneration (that is, payment for services rendered), unless there was some specific rule of law or equity under which the trustee could charge.[7] The overriding fear was that the trustee might be tempted to generate income for himself by creating work, thus unnecessarily overloading the trust and acting in his own interest instead of that of the beneficiaries (*Robinson v Pett* (1734)). Of course, it was also true that the gratuitous nature of trusteeship could itself cause problems. For complicated trusts, it is essential that the beneficiaries are able to rely on experienced and professional advisers, but these are unlikely to be willing to act without payment. Even in smaller trusts, the amount of time and effort devoted to the trust's administration may reflect lack of payment and, instead of preventing the overloading of the trust, the absence of payment might result in too little attention being paid to its affairs; a balance needs to be struck.

Prior to the Act, the balance was adopted by acceptance of the principle that there was nothing unlawful in a trustee receiving payment for fulfilling his duties, provided that this could be justified by reference to some specific provision in the trust instrument or a general rule of law. Unfortunately, as discussed below, it is clear that these pre-**Trustee Act 2000** principles indicating when a trustee could receive remuneration were haphazard, complicated and altogether unsatisfactory.[8]

By far the most common method by which trustees could have established – and still can establish – a right to receive remuneration is by relying on an express clause in the trust instrument authorising the trustees to be paid (*Willis v Kibble* (1839)). This method will continue to be common for professionally drafted trusts, especially for trusts that employ professional trustees such as banks and investment managers.[9] Such a charging clause can be drafted widely so as to give appropriate recompense to trustees acting in a professional capacity. In addition, under **s 28** of the **Trustee Act 2000**, where such a clause exists and the trustee is a trust corporation or is a trustee acting in a professional capacity, the trustee is entitled to receive such remuneration even if the services rendered could have been provided by a lay (that is, non-professional) trustee. This effectively reverses the old law with respect to 'charging clauses', which were always construed strictly against a trustee and prevented charging for work that could be regarded as not within the professional ambit of the trustee. In this sense, the **Trustee Act 2000** supports and enhances the efficacy of charging clauses in trusts (see, also, **s 28(4)(a)**: signature of a witness to the will does not invalidate a charging clause in the will in favour of that witness). It is a welcome change to the law and releases trust law from the scope of rules developed at a time when trusts were largely private matters undertaken for private tasks.

---

7 Specific identification of the elements of the claim.
8 Structured discussion of the cases.
9 Statement of liability including the remedy.

In the absence of a charging clause in a trust, the law prior to the **Trustee Act 2000** made it difficult for a trustee to claim remuneration. So, although the court had (and probably still has) an inherent jurisdiction to order the payment of remuneration, including authorising payment for the first time or varying an existing charging clause (*Re Duke of Norfolk's Settlement Trusts* (1981); *Foster v Spence* (1996)), the power was limited. The court would not authorise remuneration simply for the benefit of the trustee, but only if the payment of remuneration would be for the better administration of the trust. When deciding whether to exercise its discretion, the court would consider every aspect of the case, including how the administration of the trust would be improved, the need to protect beneficiaries from unscrupulous trustees and the essentially gratuitous nature of trusteeship, and only if there was a demonstrable need for professional trustees or if the trustees could not undertake the proper administration of the trust without devoting more of their own time, would remuneration be awarded.[10]

Second, although it was possible for a trustee to establish a right to remuneration through the conclusion of a contract to that effect with the beneficiaries, the courts looked with scepticism at such arrangements. For example, the trustee might have been forced into an unfavourable contract (or any contract) by a threat from the trustee to abandon his duties under the trust. Consequently, such contracts were rare (*Ayliffe v Murray* (1740)) and, in any event, the trustee must have offered consideration for the beneficiaries' promise to pay, which could not be the promise to carry out the duties under the trust which the trustee is already obliged to perform.

Third, there remain several (relatively limited) statutory provisions that authorise the payment of remuneration to certain types of trustees. It must be emphasised, however, that these provisions do not authorise the payment of trustees generally, but rather are designed to ensure that specific trustees appointed for specific purposes can be paid (for example, under s 42 of the **Trustee Act 1925**). A trust corporation appointed by the court may be authorised to charge the trust for administering it, and similar provisions exist in respect of the judicial trustee, the public trustee and persons appointed as custodian trustees (s 1(5) of the **Judicial Trustee Act 1896**; ss 4(3) and 9 of the **Public Trustee Act 1906**).

Fourth, it remains the case that a trustee may be entitled to retain any remuneration received as a result of administering assets abroad, provided that these are received involuntarily (*Re Northcote's Will Trusts* (1949)). This exception is of limited importance and is born more of convenience than of principle. The essence of the matter seems to be that the court regards the payment of remuneration from outside its jurisdiction as presumptively outside its control, unless it is in the nature of a bribe or is otherwise inequitable. Finally, a solicitor trustee has a unique right to receive remuneration for work undertaken on behalf of the trust, provided that these 'profit costs' relate to work undertaken on behalf of the trust generally (and not in respect of his trusteeship alone) and are no greater than those that 'could have been incurred if the solicitor had not been a trustee' (*Cradock v Piper* (1850)). Again, this is a limited exception to the general pre-**Trustee Act 2000** principles and is akin to the solicitor trustee being paid for work which is in addition to his normal duties as trustee.[10]

....

10 Factors relevant in exercising the court's discretion.

Obviously, apart from the use of the charging clause, which is now made more effica-cious by the **2000 Act**, there was limited scope for a trustee to claim remuneration. The absence of such a clause meant that a trustee had little hope of claiming remuneration unless one of the limited exceptions applied. It was in order to meet this deficiency that the **Trustee Act 2000** now provides, in s 29, methods by which different types of trus-tees may claim remuneration. First, under **s 29(1)**, a trustee who is a trust corporation (not being a trustee of a charity) 'is entitled to receive reasonable remuneration out of the trust funds for any services that the trust corporation provides', provided that no such remuneration is provided for in the trust instrument or by any other statutory pro-vision. Second, under **s 29(2)** a trustee who acts in a professional capacity (not being a trust corporation, sole trustee or trustee of a charity) is entitled to receive reasonable remuneration if every other trustee has agreed in writing to such payment, again pro-vided that no such remuneration is provided for in the trust instrument or by any other statutory provision. In addition, under **s 30** of the **Trustee Act 2000**, regulations may be made concerning the provision of remuneration to trustees of charities who are trust corporations or who act in a professional capacity.

These are wide powers, with **ss 29** and **30** providing, for the first time, a general right for trust corporations, trustees acting in a professional capacity (not being sole trus-tees) and trustees of charitable trusts to be paid for work done on behalf of the trust. It seems now that it is only sole trustees (not being a trust corporation or charitable trustee) that have no general statutory right to remuneration. This is entirely appropri-ate in an age where the trust has developed beyond the 'family' trust so common in many of the earlier cases.

Note
Questions 23 and 24 addressed the wider issue of when a trustee must avoid a situation where his interest and duty conflict and this raises some issues about remuneration.

QUESTION 25
Cassandra is the registered proprietor of a large house in London. In 2008 she met Donald, a young merchant banker, and soon she had invited him to live with her. Donald willingly accepted, not least because he was about to be evicted from his own flat through his inability to pay the rent. At first, Donald insisted that he shared the expenses of running the house, but it soon became clear to him that Cassandra had more money than sense, and he accepted her generosity without complaint. After some time, Cassan-dra began talking about 'the future', and although he was not entirely committed to the relationship, Donald played along, especially as Cassandra had told him that the house was as good as his own now that they were together. This slice of luck encouraged Donald to abandon even what little financial caution he possessed, and he had soon spent nearly all of his savings on various luxury, but unnecessary, items of furniture for the house and far too many visits to the casino. By this time, Cassandra was becoming a little annoyed at Donald's behaviour, and after one terrible row, in which she had told him to leave, Donald promised to mend his ways. Subsequently, he became altogether more

responsible and even began to redecorate the house at his own expense and overhaul the garden. Unfortunately for him, this had come too late for Cassandra, and now she has decided to throw Donald out of the house.

Donald is devastated and comes to you for advice as to whether he can claim a share in the house.

How to Read this Question

This question concerns the acquisition of beneficial interests in property belonging to another through the medium of constructive trusts. In concrete terms, the problem revolves around a contest between the legal owner of the property – Cassandra – and the person who may be able to claim an interest in the property under a constructive trust – Donald. If he is successful, Cassandra will hold the legal title on trust for both of them, in such shares as the court determines.

How to Answer this Question

You need to state and apply the general principles of acquisition of equitable interests in the family home through the advent of the remedial constructive trust. It is crucial to identify in whom the legal ownership of the property is vested. The prima facie rule is that equity follows the law. The burden of poof will rest on the party without the legal title claiming an equitable interest in the property. State the essential elements of a common intention constructive trust. The quantification of the share of the equitable interest is determined by reference to the intentions of the parties as construed by the courts.

Up for Debate

The seminal decisions of the House of Lords in *Stack v Dowden* and *Jones v Kernott* have attracted a great deal of academic debate as to the merits and limits of the remedial constructive trust of the family home. Prominent articles on the subject include J Mee, '*Jones v Kernott*: inferring and imputing in Essex' (2012) Conv PL 167; M Pawlowski, 'Imputed intention and joint ownership: a return to common sense: *Jones v Kernott*' (2012) Conv PL 149; J Roche, '*Kernott, Stack* and *Oxley* made simple: a practitioner's view' (2011) Conv PL 123.

Aim Higher

The answer to this question illustrates the danger of becoming too rigid in the use of constructive trusts. The question requires knowledge of the relevant law but also an understanding of the role and purpose of constructive trusts in these types of cases. As will be apparent, the general theory of trusts put forward in *Westdeutsche Landesbank Girozentrale v Islington LBC* (1996) is very important.

Answer Plan

- ❖ General principles of acquisition of beneficial interests through constructive trusts, *Stack v Dowden* (2007), *Jones v Kernott* (2011).
- ❖ The legal owner as constructive trustee.
- ❖ The need for a promise, reliance and detriment, *Lloyds Bank v Rosset* (1991).
- ❖ Quantifying the share.
- ❖ Whether a remedy can be refused on general equitable principles.

Answer Structure

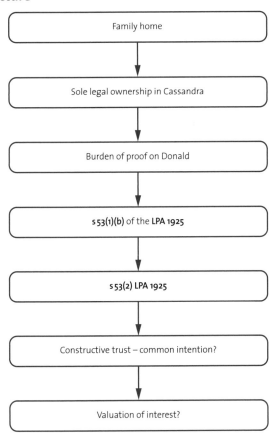

This diagram illustrates the application of the relevant principles in determining the respective interests of the parties in the family home.

ANSWER

On the facts as stated, it seems clear that when Donald met Cassandra, Cassandra was sole legal owner of the property and that it was not subject to any mortgage. The property belonged to Cassandra absolutely and had already been paid for. In *Stack v Dowden* (2007) the House of Lords decided that as a starting point the maxim 'equity follows the law' was applicable, i.e. the beneficial interest will prima facie be enjoyed by the party with the legal title, namely Cassandra. The burden of proof will therefore lie on Donald to establish an equitable interest by way of a constructive trust. He must plead a promise or oral assurance plus detrimental reliance in order to establish that it would be inequitable for Cassandra to deny him a share in the property. There are a number of factors to consider here.

In *Stack v Dowden* and *Jones v Kernott* the court introduced the single regime of the constructive trust as a means of resolving disputes between parties as to the equitable interests in the family home. There are two hurdles for Donald to overcome in order to succeed in his claim to an interest in the house. First, to discharge a burden to prove that Cassandra intended him to have a beneficial interest in the property. This question is determined objectively by the courts. The significant facts have already been identified. It may be doubtful whether Donald may discharge this burden, but if he does, the second issue involves the evaluation of that interest. The courts will consider all the material facts in order to determine what would be fair to the parties: see *Oxley v Hiscock* (2004).

First, it is clear that Donald readily moved into the house at Cassandra's instigation. However, there is no suggestion at this stage that Cassandra has made any promise or assurance in relation to ownership of the property. As Lord Bridge made clear in *Lloyds Bank v Rosset* (1991), the obligations of common or shared *occupation* of property are not identical with the *obligations* of shared ownership and consequently it is extremely unlikely that a court would be prepared to divine a promise of shared ownership from facts such as ours. Indeed, because in *Rosset* Lord Bridge went so far as to suggest that it was virtually impossible *as a matter of principle* to infer a promise from conduct per se, there seems little upon which Donald can base a claim at this stage. Even if by some intellectual gymnastics it is possible to discover a promise made to Donald, there is no evidence of detrimental reliance. Although Donald does vacate his current residence, and even though such action has, in the past, been held to constitute detriment (*Tanner v Tanner* (1975)), it is clear that his actions are prompted by his own circumstances and have little to do with whatever Cassandra may or may not have promised.

Second, there is little chance that Donald may claim an interest just because he has insisted on paying household expenses. The payment of household expenses is not equivalent to payment of the purchase price of property (*Burns v Burns* (1984)) and (as above) there is no oral assurance to which this expenditure can be linked as detrimental reliance. Indeed, such statements that Cassandra does make (see below) are made *after* Donald spends money. In other words, these monetary payments are not made to the acquisition of the property, nor are they in reliance on a promise. There is no interest to be found on these facts (*Burns v Burns* (1984) and *Lloyds Bank v Rosset* (1991)).

Finally, however, it appears that Cassandra does make a promise of sorts to Donald and it is a matter of construction whether this is sufficient to raise an interest in his favour by way of a constructive trust. First, a problem exists with intention: does Cassandra intend to grant Donald a share in the property by her references to 'the future' and her apparent statement that the house is 'as good as' his? In our case, we do not know what Cassandra actually meant, but may a reasonable person in Donald's position conclude that this was an assurance about the ownership of the shared home? This issue is determined by reference to an objective standard. Such a principle is clearly supported by *Midland Bank v Cooke* (1995) which, although distinguishable because in that case there were some payments towards the purchase price, suggests that the court will take a generous view of what the parties 'intended'. The same principle was applied in *Stack v Dowden* (2007) and *Jones v Kernott* (2011). Consequently, Cassandra may find herself in some difficulty having assured Donald that he had a share in the property, even if this was not actually her intention (see, for example, *Eves v Eves* (1975), where the real intention was to deny an interest). Furthermore, it seems clear from the facts that Donald has relied on this assurance in that he has spent his savings on various items of furniture and visits to the casino.

With reference to the alleged detriment, Cassandra might claim that this kind of detrimental reliance is insufficient to found an interest by way of a constructive trust because it was unrelated to the property (money spent at the casino) and part was not necessary for the use and enjoyment of the property (luxury furniture). Indeed, certain cases, such as *Gissing* and *Christian v Christian* (1981), suggest that the detriment suffered as a result of the promise or assurance must be related to the property over which the interest is claimed; for example, spending money on improvements. However, an alternative view is that all that is required is detriment which has been caused by the promise, the nature of such detriment being immaterial. This second approach has much to commend it, especially since it is consistent with the theory that the essence of the constructive trust in these cases is the fact of a promise made and then inequitably denied. The detriment is, on this view, merely the trigger for the trust, not the reason for its existence in the first place. So, following this approach, Donald appears to have a reasonably strong claim to an equitable interest in Cassandra's property. He can show an assurance, reliance and detriment. This means that Cassandra's subsequent attempt to evict him – which may be seen as an attempt to withdraw the promise – comes too late (*Turton v Turton* (1987)). By that time, the equity may have been raised in his favour.[11]

Finally, however, as adviser to Donald, one must issue a word of caution. In some cases, constructive trusts appear to treat morally innocent people harshly, but only then in order to do equity to another person who has a greater claim. Yet, what constructive trusts will not be used for is to enable an undeserving litigant to gain a windfall which is not merited: the trust fixes on the conscience of the legal owner of property; it will not be imposed mechanically to assist the undeserving (*Westdeutsche Landesbank Girozentrale v Islington LBC* (1996)). The very essence of the constructive trust is that it is not rigid in application and does not have hard and fast rules. This much was stated by Lord Diplock in *Gissing v Gissing* (1971) and is a feature of the use of constructive trusts in later cases, including those cases difficult to reconcile with each other such as *Lloyds Bank v Rosset* (1990) on the one hand and *Midland Bank v Cooke* (1995), *Stack v Dowden* and *Jones v Kernott* on the other side of the spectrum. Thus, if the constructive trust is rightly to be regarded as a means of remedying inequitable conduct in circumstances where the conscience of the legal owner is affected, a court may well take the view that Donald should not be able to rely on it to claim a benefit which he appears not to deserve.[11]

---

11   Application of the principles of law to the facts.

Common Pitfalls

Questions concerning interests in the family home are regularly asked in land law examinations and occasionally in examinations on trusts law. Students ought to be encouraged to reconcile the principles laid down in the leading judgments in the five House of Lords decisions in *Pettitt v Pettitt*, *Gissing v Gissing*, *Lloyds Bank v Rosset*, *Stack v Dowden* and *Jones v Kernott*. Note that in *Stack*, Lord Neuberger arrived at the same conclusion as Baroness Hale but by a different route.

7 Constructive Trusts 2: The Liability of Strangers to the Trust

INTRODUCTION

We have seen already in previous chapters that to accept the office of trustee is to open oneself and one's conduct to the closest scrutiny. Not only is the trustee expected to behave at all times with the utmost propriety, but there are also circumstances when even the morally innocent fiduciary may find himself subject to the coercive jurisdiction of the court. Furthermore, it is not only trustees proper who may find themselves in this position, for the reach of a court of equity is both long and powerful. As we shall see in this and the following chapters, third parties may all too easily become embroiled in the trust's affairs and, as far as the various remedies of the beneficiaries are concerned, it is often irrelevant whether these 'strangers to the trust' are innocent, negligent or downright dishonest.

The problems considered in this chapter relate to the liability of a person who is a stranger to the trust – broadly defined as a person who was not originally appointed a trustee or to a fiduciary position. In very general terms, any person who interferes with the operation of the trust or who assists the trustee in a breach of his trust duties may find himself fixed with a constructive trust and answerable to the court and the beneficiaries for any misapplication of the trust property. Of course, it is not in every situation that a stranger to the trust is held liable to the beneficiaries as a constructive trustee. Yet in appropriate cases, when the conditions established by the case law are fulfilled, the constructive trust swings into operation and provides a most powerful remedy.

In simple terms, a stranger to the trust may become accountable to the beneficiaries or be treated as a constructive trustee in four situations:

(a) by dishonestly assisting the trustee in a breach of trust;
(b) by receiving trust property for his own use in the knowledge that it was transferred in breach of trust;
(c) after having received trust property in conformity with the terms of the trust, by knowingly dealing with that property in breach of the terms of the trust; and
(d) by inducing the trustee to commit a breach of trust.

Together, these different examples of accounting as a constructive trustee give the beneficiary some hope of redress in the event of a breach of trust, even if the trustee has escaped the clutches of the court or no longer has the trust property. One note of caution ought to be mentioned. Millett LJ in *Paragon Finance v Thakerar* (1999) opined that the liability of an accessory is strictly not as a constructive trustee because he does not acquire the trust property. His liability is to account to the beneficiaries for any benefits received. This is a 'personal' liability to account rather than an *in rem* liability. Once again, as with so much in the law of trusts, the 'rules' are to be found in case law, although there is some doubt whether the growing volume of case law actually has done anything to clarify the law.

QUESTION 26

Analyse, with reference to decided cases, the circumstances in which a 'stranger' may be liable as a constructive trustee for intermeddling with the management of a trust.

How to Read this Question

This essay question requires you to deal with the rationale for the liability of strangers to a trust to account to the beneficiaries and to identify, by reference to decided cases, the elements of such liability.

How to Answer this Question

Points to raise in answer to this question are the distinctions between liability as a constructive trustee and the duty to account. The focus of this question involves the nature of the liability of a stranger as a trustee *de son tort*, knowingly receiving or dealing with trust property and dishonest assistance in a fraudulent scheme.

Up for Debate

The law is in a state of flux and is uncertain as to its practical application (even if the principles are clear) in the context of the liability of strangers to a trust to account. Instructive reading include S Gardner, 'Knowing assistance and knowing receipt: taking stock' (1996) 112 LQR 56 and P Millett, 'Restitution and constructive trusts' (1998) 114 LQR 399.

Aim Higher

In *Royal Brunei Airlines v Tan* (1995) Lord Nicholls laid down the test for dishonesty as subjective, in that it requires the accessory to know the facts which to a reasonable person would indicate that he was participating in a breach of trust. But the standard of judging dishonesty was objective in the sense that it is determined, not by the defendant, but by the views of honest and reasonable people. This view was clarified by the Privy Council in *Barlow Clowes v Eurotrust* (2006) and endorsed by the Court of Appeal decisions in *Abou-Ramah v Abacha* (2006) and *Starglade v Nash* (2010). In *Twinsectra v Yardley* (2002), it is arguable that Lord Hutton (who gave the leading judgment) confused this test when he adopted the *R v Ghosh* (1982) 'combined' objective and subjective test for dishonesty in criminal law.

Answer Plan

❖   The nature of a stranger's liability as constructive trustee and its justification.
❖   Trustee *de son tort*.
❖   Knowing receipt or dealing.
❖   Dishonest assistance.
❖   Lack of clarity: position of principle.

Answer Structure

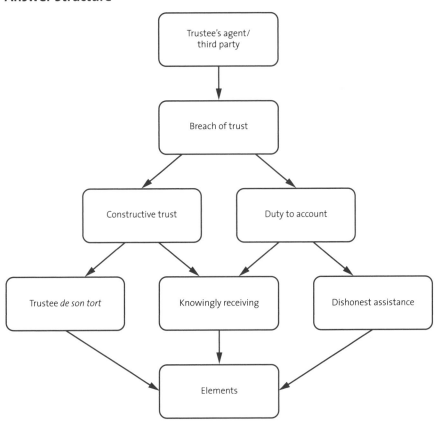

This diagram illustrates the heads of liability of strangers to a trust.

ANSWER

First, a stranger to the trust may become a constructive trustee because he or she has assumed the duties of a trustee. In other words, if a stranger takes it upon himself to meddle with the trust property as if he were a trustee, equity will treat him as such a trustee (*Mara v Browne* (1896)). This is trusteeship *de son tort* and the essential point is that the person fixed with liability as a constructive trustee has stepped into the shoes of the original trustees or fiduciaries, as in *James v Williams* (1999). It is effectively self-appointed trusteeship, see *Dubai Aluminium Co v Salaam* (2002).

Second, equity will impose a constructive trust on a stranger who has received trust property for his own benefit in breach of the terms of the trust. This form of liability is often referred to as 'knowing receipt or dealing' with the trust property (*Baden Delvaux and Lecuit v Société Générale pour Favouriser le Développement du Commerce et de l'Industrie en France SA* (1983); *Houghton v Fayers* (2000)).

It seems, then, that there are three primary conditions for the imposition of this liability: *Houghton v Fayers*.[1] First, and obviously, there must be disposal of assets in breach of trust or breach of fiduciary duty. Second, the stranger must either have lawfully received property and thereafter applied it for his own purposes in a manner inconsistent with the terms of the trust (inconsistent dealing: *Karak Rubber v Burden* (1972)) or, in the alternative, have received trust property for his own benefit (knowing receipt: *International Sales Ltd v Marcus* (1982)). Third, it seems that the transferee must have some degree of knowledge or notice of the fact that the transfer (or inconsistent dealing) was in breach of trust (*Polly Peck International plc v Nadir (No 2)* (1992); *Westdeutsche Landesbank Girozentrale v Islington LBC* (1996)).

Unfortunately, the precise degree of knowledge required for liability for knowing receipt/inconsistent dealing is uncertain.[2] On the one hand, it has been suggested that, before liability can arise, the recipient must either know or be reckless as to whether the transfer to him or subsequent use of property is in breach of trust. This degree of knowledge equates to the first three of Peter Gibson LJ's infamous categories of knowledge in *Baden Delvaux* (1983) and necessarily has the effect of restricting the circumstances in which a stranger may be liable. It has been applied in cases such as *Carl Zeiss Stiftung v Herbert Smith & Co (No 2)* (1969), *Re Montague* (1987) and, in a commercial context, in *Cowan de Groot Properties v Eagle Trust plc* (1992), *Eagle Trust v SBC Securities (No 2)* (1992). Alternatively, other cases suggest that liability should exist if the stranger is subjectively aware of or is simply negligent with regard to the facts of a breach of trust. This ensures that liability will arise when *any* of the five categories of knowledge in *Baden Delvaux* exists. Cases such as *International Sales Ltd v Marcus* (1982), *Belmont Finance Corporation v Williams Furniture (No 2)* (1980) and the closely argued judgment of Millet J at first instance in *AGIP (Africa) Ltd v Jackson* (1992) support this view. It is implicit in the recent judgment of Ferris J in *Box v Barclays Bank* (1998). Indeed, if it is true that the essence of liability for knowing receipt/inconsistent dealing is that the stranger has received property for his own benefit to which he was not entitled, then (in the absence of a pure 'no fault' restitutionary liability) it is quite appropriate that he should be obliged to return it unless he was innocent of all participation in a breach of trust and it should make no difference whether the alleged transaction in breach arose out of a 'commercial' or 'private' trust.[3] Of course, what a 'reasonable' person should have known or enquired about may vary according to the circumstances – and the nature of the transaction may affect this – with strangers acting commercially being under a lesser duty to enquire and hence a lesser chance of liability (*El Ajou v Dollar Land Holdings plc* (1994) (first instance)). Yet, in principle, negligence should not be a defence to a claim by a person with a

---

1   Elements of liability for knowingly receiving claim.
2   Uncertain nature of degrees of knowledge.
3   Attempting to identify the basis of liability for knowingly receiving claims.

better title. In *BCCI v Akindele* (2000), the Court of Appeal tried to overcome these difficulties by noting that the state of knowledge 'must be such as to make it unconscionable' for the recipient to retain the benefit. This reformulation by Nourse LJ clearly is intended to avoid the controversy surrounding the '*Baden* categories' and the uncertainties produced by the 'knowledge/notice' distinction. However, it is not certain that 'unconscionability' is any less opaque than previous attempts to identify the 'core' reason for liability.

Moving now to examine the liability of a stranger for dishonestly assisting another to commit a breach of trust (*Barnes v Addy* (1874); *Royal Brunei Airlines v Tan* (1995)). It is important to realise here that, unlike knowing receipt/inconsistent dealing, the stranger may never receive the trust property and, even if he does, it is not for his own benefit. Consequently, this is a form of secondary liability, usually resorted to when for some reason the trustee who has committed the fraudulent breach of trust cannot be found or has insufficient funds to satisfy the claims of the beneficiaries. In addition, the stranger's liability is to account for the profits. Strictly he is not a constructive trustee, for he does not receive the trust property but merely assists in a breach of trust: see Millett LJ in *Paragon Finance v Thakerar* (1999).[4]

However, the liability belongs to the stranger alone, hence it is no longer true that the stranger can be liable only if the trustee himself has behaved fraudulently. This was established by the Privy Council in *Tan*. Of course, it remains true that the stranger must himself be culpable. In *Tan*, however, Lord Nicholls, for the Privy Council, made it clear that what was required was for the assistor to be 'dishonest'. He indicated that an objective standard was required but added that the experience and knowledge of the defendant may be taken into account.

In *Twinsectra v Yardley* (2002), the majority of the House of Lords adopted the criminal law test for dishonesty (as laid down by Lord Lane CJ in *R v Ghosh* (1982)) namely, the defendant's conduct is dishonest by reference to the ordinary standards of reasonable and honest people *and* that he himself realised that his conduct was dishonest by those standards. This involves both objective and subjective questions. In *Barlow Clowes International Ltd (in liquidation) v Eurotrust International Ltd and others* (2006), the Privy Council decided that no inquiry is required to be made as to the defendant's view about standards of dishonesty. Consciousness of dishonesty involved consciousness of those elements of the transaction which made participation transgress ordinary standards of honest behaviour. It did not also require the defendant to have thought about what those standards were. In short, the standard by which the defendant's dishonesty is judged is purely objective. In *Abou-Ramah v Abacha* (2006), the Court of Appeal reaffirmed the notion that the test of dishonesty is objective and requires the court to decide that the defendant knows of the elements of the transaction which makes it dishonest according to the normally accepted standards of behaviour. The objective standard for dishonesty was further clarified by the Court of Appeal in *Starglade Ltd v Nash* (2010). The objective test is decided by the court by reference to the defendant's knowledge and experience.

....

4   Liability to account but no constructive trust.

Further, there are significant issues concerning the standard of proof required for dishonesty. In *Jyske Bank v Heinl* (1999) it was held that the standard of proof involved a high level of probability greater than a 'balance of probabilities' and the inability of the claimants to meet this meant that the 'assistance' claim in *Akindele* was unsuccessful. However, in *Statek Corp v Alford* (2008), the High Court decided that the standard of proof of dishonesty is the traditional civil standard of a balance of probabilities.

An alternative view was put forward by Lord Nicholls writing extra-judicially. A person can be made liable to account for intermeddling with trust property whenever this is necessary to reverse an unjust enrichment, having regard to the defendant's status as a bona fide purchaser for value or any defence of change of position.

Note

A general answer to such a question is sufficient, provided that there is ample reference to case law.

Common Pitfalls

Under the heading 'knowingly receiving or dealing', students fail to distinguish whether the liability of the third party is proprietary or personal. Liability is proprietary where the third party unlawfully receives the trust property for his benefit and still has the property, or its traceable proceeds, under his control. On the other hand, liability is personal where the third party knowingly receives the trust property for his own benefit, but no longer retains the property or its traceable proceeds. The courts initially referred to the latter liability as one of constructive trusteeship. Today it is recognised that this is a personal liability to account.

QUESTION 27

The liability of a stranger for meddling with trust property should be strict. Then, subject only to the defence of change of position, the courts could determine in all the circumstances whether the defendant should return property to the beneficiaries without having to agonise about the defendant's state of mind.

▶ Discuss.

How to Read this Question

This is an essay question that requires you to identify and analyse the rationale for liability of an intermeddling stranger to a trust.

How to Answer this Question

A good answer will identify the basis of liability for dishonest assistance and knowing receipt. The issue is whether liability should be based on restitution, fault or whether liability should be strict. There are eminent advocates who support each of these views.

Up for Debate

This question reflects the academic debate which is raging over the scope of, and proper conditions for, the granting of equitable remedies consequent on a breach of 'trustee-like' duties imposed on strangers. It is a large issue. The following articles are instructive: Lord Clark, 'Claims against professionals: negligence, dishonesty and fraud' (2006) 22 Professional Negligence 70 and T Hibbert, 'Dishonesty and knowledge of accessories and recipients' (2000) JIBL 138.

Aim Higher

The test of personal liability based on unconscionability as laid down by Nourse LJ in *BCCI v Akindele* (2000) was earlier rejected as meaningless by Lord Nicholls giving judgment in the Privy Council in *Royal Brunei Airlines v Tan* (1994). At the same time Nourse LJ gave little or no guidance as to how this elusive principle would be approached.

Answer Plan

- ❖ Basis of liability for dishonest assistance and knowing receipt.
- ❖ Confirmation that some degree of fault is required: *Royal Brunei Airlines v Tan* (1995), *Westdeutsche Landesbank Girozentrale v Islington LBC* (1996).
- ❖ The restitution angle and the change of position defence.
- ❖ Confusion of language: the problem of semantics.
- ❖ Confusion of facts: receipt or assistance.
- ❖ The application of law to facts – a recipe for different interpretations of the law.

Answer Structure

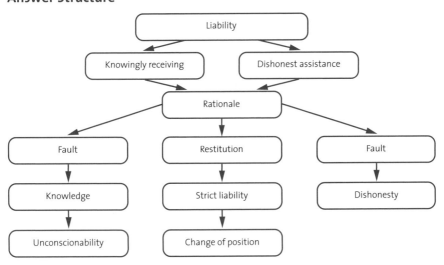

This diagram constructs the essential elements of liability of strangers to a trust and suggested reforms.

ANSWER

Liability in 'assistance'-type cases is to account to the beneficiaries as though the defendant is a constructive trustee: see *Paragon Finance v Thakerar* (1999).[5] The property has not been received by the stranger for his own benefit (*Barnes v Addy* (1874)). Consequently, it is apparent that such liability should never be triggered by simple factual assistance, but only where such assistance is tainted by personal fault. Further, as is made clear by the Privy Council in *Royal Brunei Airlines v Tan* (1995), the stranger may be liable only where he is 'dishonest': mere negligence, or a deliberate but honest assistance, is not sufficient to found liability (see, for example, *Ferrotex v Banque Français de l'Orient* (2000)). The dishonesty test now replaces the old tests of knowledge based on the *Baden* categories for assistance liability. However, although *apparently* simpler, there were difficulties initially as to what amounts to dishonesty, or how it is proven.[6] *Brinks v Abu-Saleh (No 3)* (1995) suggests that dishonesty implies some knowledge on the part of the stranger, but it was not clear whether this concerns the existence of a trust, or of the fact of breach, or of the fact that the property is another's, or if it has some other meaning. The test today for dishonesty was laid down by Lord Nicholls in *Royal Brunei Airlines v Tan* (1995). It means that the defendant had acted with a lack of probity or simply not acted as an honest man in the circumstances of the case. This definition was construed by Lord Hutton in *Twinsectra v Yardley* (2002) as involving the criminal law test for dishonesty (as laid down by Lord Lane CJ in *R v Ghosh* (1982)). This test incorporates a combined objective and subjective standard. The defendant's conduct is dishonest by reference to the ordinary standards of reasonable and honest people *and* that he himself realised that his conduct was dishonest by those standards. However, in *Barlow Clowes International Ltd (in liquidation) v Eurotrust International Ltd and others* (2006), the Privy Council decided that no inquiry is required to be made of the defendant's view about standards of dishonesty. Consciousness of dishonesty involved consciousness of those elements of the transaction which made participation transgress ordinary standards of honest behaviour. It did not also require the defendant to have thought about what those standards were. The standard applicable here is objective. In *Abou-Ramah v Abacha* (2006), the Court of Appeal affirmed that the standard is objective and it is unnecessary to show 'subjective dishonesty' in the sense of consciousness on the part of the defendant that the transaction was dishonest. It will be sufficient if the defendant knows of the elements of the transaction which makes it dishonest in accordance with the normally acceptable standards of behaviour. Thus, the standard by which the defendant is judged is objective but with a subjective element. This approach was endorsed by the CA in *Starglade Ltd v Nash* (2010). In reversing the decision of the trial judge, the CA decided that the test is whether the judge is convinced that the defendant's behaviour is or is not within the ordinary standards of honest commercial behaviour.

Turning then to 'knowing receipt', it seems clear that the essence of the liability of the stranger in these cases is that he has received trust property for his own benefit: per

5   Clear basis of liability in dishonest assistance cases.
6   Initial confusion as to the meaning of dishonesty.

Millet J in *AGIP (Africa) Ltd v Jackson* (1992). Liability comprises an obligation to return the property or account for it out of his own resources. Consequently, the liability is primarily restitutionary: to return property which belongs to another. With this in mind, the crucial question is whether the stranger, who has received the property for his own benefit, will be liable only when he was at 'fault' (that is, had some degree of 'knowledge') or whether the liability is strict – so that even an innocent defendant can be liable – subject to a defence of change of position. At present, it seems that liability is fault based: see Lord Browne-Wilkinson (*obiter*) in *Westdeutsche Landesbank Girozentrale v Islington LBC* (1996) and, firmly, the Court of Appeal in *BCCI v Akindele*. Yet, as noted below, this has been challenged, although there is little unanimity among the cases for what degree of knowledge is required. It has been suggested in cases such as *Carl Zeiss Stiftung v Herbert Smith & Co (No 2)* (1969), *Re Montague* (1987) and *Cowan de Groot Properties v Eagle Trust plc* (1992) that liability arises only when the stranger had 'want of probity', probably meaning intention or recklessness as to whether the property was transferred in breach of trust, and some case law suggests that mere negligence might be too low a standard in so-called 'commercial' cases where the strangers are professional advisers merely executing the wishes of the trustee (*Cowan de Groot Properties v Eagle Trust plc* (1992); *Polly Peck International plc v Nadir (No 2)* (1992)). Alternatively, other cases suggest that liability should exist if the stranger is simply negligent with regard to the terms of the trust: in other words, if he should have known that the transfer of trust funds or his own subsequent dealings with them were in breach of trust. This ensures that liability will arise when *any* of the five categories of knowledge in *Baden Delvaux* exists (subjective and objective knowledge). Judgments in cases such as *International Sales Ltd v Marcus* (1982), *Belmont Finance Corporation v Williams Furniture (No 2)* (1980), at first instance in *AGIP (Africa) Ltd v Jackson* (1992) and *Box v Barclays Bank* (1998) support this view. Different again is the approach in *Akindele*, where Nourse LJ seeks to avoid this past confusion by saying that the recipient must act 'unconscionably' before liability can arise. How this differs from 'knowledge' or 'notice' is unclear, although it seems certain that it does presuppose some element of fault.

This doubt about the practical application of the test of 'fault' required to fix a stranger with liability for 'knowing receipt' raises a more fundamental point: namely, whether liability should depend on any fault at all. After all, if liability is triggered by receipt and the obligation is to account for its value (or return it if still held), then should not merely innocent recipients also be liable? Of course, recipients would need a defence, as every circumstance in which X might receive Y's property could not find liability (for example, if X were a bona fide purchaser for value). This approach – generally thought to be purely restitutionary – is indicated by the House of Lords in *Lipkin Gorman v Karpnale* (1991) and has been argued forcefully academically by Lord Nicholls writing extra-judicially. Certainly, that was the position with the claim at law and many would argue that there is no reason for any difference merely because the beneficiaries of a trust are pursuing a claim in equity. Lest this is thought to be unfair to the innocent stranger, it is balanced by the recognition of a general defence – 'change of position'. This would be available to any stranger to defeat the imposition of a constructive trust, if the court thought fit, depending on whether the stranger has changed his position in reliance on receipt of the money.

As is evident, this introduces an element of discretion into the fixing of receipt liability, but it is not at all clear whether the 'knowledge' based test really is any more objective.

Common Pitfalls

The notion of strict liability to be imposed on third parties who intermeddle with trust property was advocated extra-judicially by Lords Nicholls and Millett but rejected by Nourse LJ in *BCCI v Akindele*. The strict liability approach is based on the notion that unless the defendant is forced to disgorge the benefit received he would otherwise be unjustly enriched. Thus, his liability should not be based on knowledge, but merely that he would be enriched at the claimant's expense. The defendant, however, may be able to raise the defence of 'bona fide change of position' in appropriate cases.

QUESTION 28

Arnold is the agent of Tarquin, the trustee of a settlement in favour of 'the children of Sarah'. Tarquin instructs Arnold to pay £5,000 to Len, who, Tarquin says, is the illegitimate child of Sarah and himself. Tarquin also instructs Arnold to invest £10,000 in the stock exchange in Tarquin Enterprises Ltd, to buy £5,000 worth of tickets in the national lottery (all of which lose) and to transfer £10,000 to Clarence as payment for services rendered to the trust. One year later, Tarquin goes missing with the remaining trust fund monies. Moreover, it transpires that Len is in fact the child of Tarquin and Emily (Arnold's sister) and that the money has all been spent. Tarquin Enterprises have gone bust due to a dramatic withdrawal of cash from their bank account.

Advise the children of Sarah as to their remedies, if any, against Arnold and Clarence.

How to Read this Question

This question requires you to deal with breaches of trust and the liability of Tarquin, the trustee, and Arnold and Clarence, strangers to the trust. The claims of the beneficiaries may include wrongful distribution, knowingly receiving trust property and dishonestly assisting in a fraudulent breach of trust.

How to Answer this Question

In our particular case, it seems that 'the children of Sarah' – the beneficiaries of the trust – would be unable to pursue an action in breach of trust against Tarquin (their trustee) because he has disappeared. Consequently, they must resort to alternative remedies, which, in this case, means attempting to establish that strangers to the trust are fixed with constructive trusteeship because of their interference or involvement with the activities which have caused loss to the trust estate. Importantly, it must be remembered that the liability of the strangers – Arnold and Clarence – can exist only if *inter alia* there has actually been a breach of trust: *Brown v Bennett* (1998). The familiar liability of 'dishonest assistance' and 'knowing receipt' can arise only if the dealings with the trust property disclose a breach of the terms of the trust.

Up for Debate

The proper rationale for the liability of strangers to a trust has been the subject of academic discussion. Articles that have explored the elements of liability include S Gardner, 'Knowing assistance and knowing receipt: taking stock' (1996) 112 LQR 56 and C Mitchell, 'Dishonest assistance, knowing receipt and the law of limitation' (2008) Conv 226.

Answer Plan

❖   Liability as a constructive trustee for knowing receipt and dishonest assistance.
❖   Level of knowledge or dishonesty required: whether satisfied.
❖   Profits.

Answer Structure

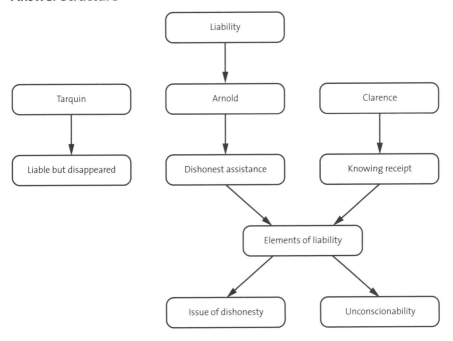

This diagram identifies the nature of the liabilities of Tarquin, Arnold and Clarence for breaches of trust.

ANSWER

As far as the wrongful distribution of the £5,000 of trust monies to Len is concerned, it is a clear breach of the terms of the trust (*Re Hulkes* (1886)). If any liability exists, it will lie in 'dishonest assistance', for clearly Arnold has participated in Tarquin's breach of trust. In order to maintain a successful action against Arnold on this ground, two essential conditions must be fulfilled.[7] First, it must be established that Arnold has assisted Tarquin in a breach of trust. This is a factual matter. Assistance implies positive help although, in this case, it is not difficult to establish. *Royal Brunei Airlines v Tan* (1995) makes it clear that the liability is the stranger's and the state of mind of the trustee cannot colour it. A 'simple' breach of trust is enough. Second, *Tan* also makes it clear that the stranger's assistance must be coloured by his own 'dishonesty' before liability can arise. In *Twinsectra v Yardley* (2002), the majority of the House of Lords adopted the criminal law test for dishonesty (as laid down by Lord Lane CJ in *R v Ghosh* (1982)). This involves both objective and subjective questions. Controversy surrounded the *Twinsectra* test. In *Barlow Clowes v Eurotrust* (2006), the Privy Council decided that dishonesty was to be judged by reference to an objective standard. The test was whether the defendant was conscious of those elements of the transaction that made his participation transgress the ordinary standards of honest behaviour. In *Abou-Ramah v Abacha* (2006), the Court of Appeal endorsed the decision in *Barlow Clowes* and decided that the test of dishonesty is predominantly objective but with a subjective element and that *Barlow Clowes* does not involve a departure from the *Twinsectra* case. The Court of Appeal decided that the test for dishonesty will be satisfied if the defendant *knows* of the elements of the transaction which make it dishonest in accordance with the normally acceptable standards of honest behaviour. In *Starglade Ltd v Nash* (2010), the CA decided that the test for dishonesty was the principle stated by the Privy Council in *Barlow Clowes* and involved an objective standard. The judge will then consider the conduct, experience and knowledge of the defendant to determine whether his conduct may be characterised as dishonest.

Moreover, there is controversy in respect of the standard of proof of dishonesty. In *Jyske Bank v Heinl* (1999) it was decided by the Court of Appeal that the claimant bears a high standard of proof exceeding the traditional civil standard, but not as high as the criminal standard of proof. However, in the more recent case, *Statek Corp v Alford* (2008), the High Court reverted back to the traditional civil standard of proof of a balance of probabilities. No doubt each case will be unique to its own facts.[8]

In our case, we do not know with certainty Arnold's state of mind or motives, but it might be significant that Len's mother is Arnold's sister. While not conclusive, this does suggest some participation in Tarquin's fraud and, if this is true, Arnold will be accountable and ordered to repay the £5,000 to the trust fund which Len has now dissipated.

Much the same considerations apply to the two further 'investments' made by Arnold on Tarquin's instructions except that, in both cases, there is no clear evidence of a breach of trust. This makes it impossible to be certain whether the strangers will be accountable for dishonestly assisting Tarquin in his activities. Of course, as above, the possibility that a breach of trust has occurred can be inferred from the nature of the investments ordered

....

7   Specific identification of the elements of the claim.
8   Structured discussion of the cases.

by Tarquin, as it is hardly likely that the trust deed authorises investment in one of the trustee's own companies or in a purely speculative lottery and such investments may well be outside **ss 3** and **4** of the **Trustee Act 2000**. Yet this is only a rebuttable presumption. With that in mind, it is again necessary to assess Arnold's state of mind in order to determine whether the beneficiaries have a remedy in a dishonest assistance claim concerning these lost trust funds. Unfortunately, there is nothing in the facts of the problem to help us here and, as we have seen, the fact that no reasonable person would have acted as Arnold did (that is, Arnold was negligent) is not enough to trigger the powerful duty to account in assistance cases (*Tan*). In the absence of further evidence, the matter must rest there.

The third stage of the beneficiaries' proceedings against the 'strangers' will be an attempt to fix Clarence with constructive trusteeship or the duty to account, this time on the basis of 'knowing receipt'. If this liability is successfully established, Clarence will be required to return the £10,000 to the trust and any profit that it has generated while in his hands (*English v Dedham Vale Properties* (1978)).[9] As a first step, it is apparent that Clarence has received the £10,000 for his own use and benefit, thus establishing clearly that this is a case of 'receipt' (*AGIP (Africa) Ltd v Jackson* (1992); *BCCI v Akindele* (2000)). Yet, before Clarence can be liable, it must be established both that the transfer to Clarence was in breach of trust and that Clarence had sufficient awareness or 'knowledge' of this to make him liable or that it is unconscionable for him to retain the benefit (*Akindele*). In fact, although these are separate criteria, it often happens that they are interwoven, as they are in this case. So, if it is true that Clarence has rendered services to the trust, the payment of £10,000 may well be legitimate (that is, there is no breach) – **s 14** of the **Trustee Act 2000** – and, even if the payment is not legitimate per se, Clarence could easily be a bona fide purchaser for value (having 'paid' for the money with his services) and thus not be liable. On the other hand, if the transfer to Clarence was in breach of trust – perhaps as part of a scheme to defraud the beneficiaries – Clarence's position must come under much closer scrutiny. If a breach has occurred, Clarence will be liable if he had 'knowledge' of the relevant facts. There is no agreement in the case law as to which level of knowledge is required for 'receipt' liability. Some cases (for example, *Cowan de Groot Properties v Eagle Trust plc* (1992)) suggest that either 'actual knowledge' or 'recklessness' must exist in order to establish liability. In *Re Montague* (1987), Megarry VC also argues powerfully in favour of a minimum standard of 'want of probity'. On the other hand, other cases (*International Sales Ltd v Marcus* (1982); *Belmont Finance Corporation v Williams Furniture (No 2)* (1980); *Box v Barclays Bank* (1998)) indicate plainly that receipt liability can be triggered by mere negligence, and this was also the view of Millet J in his very thorough judgment in *AGIP (Africa) Ltd v Jackson* (1992). Possibly, it is the meaning to be given to the 'unconscionability' test put forward in *Akindele*, but this remains to be seen. In our case, it is not clear whether Clarence has any knowledge of the breach of trust; he may be innocent. An enquiry must be made as to Clarence's understanding of Tarquin's actions and, it is

---

9 Statement of liability including the remedy.

submitted, the better view is that he will be liable as constructive trustee if he was merely negligent or worse: that is, if any of the five categories of knowledge identified in *Baden Delvaux and Lecuit v Société Générale pour Favouriser le Développement du Commerce et de l'Industrie en France SA* (1983) are present.

Note

This problem question is quite general and one should not shy from stating that the precise answer depends on facts which are not made apparent in the question. Of course, this means that the answer requires a discussion of the principles behind the rules.

8

The Law of Tracing

INTRODUCTION

One of the most effective remedies available to a beneficiary who has been deprived of the trust property as a result of a breach of trust by the trustee is to be found in the law of tracing. 'Tracing' of trust property – either 'at law' or 'in equity' – enables a claimant to identify his ownership of property into whosoever's hands that property falls and to recover it to the extent that the defendant still possesses it. Most importantly, it is clear that a claimant who relies on the tracing process is tracing his or her ownership of the property irrespective of the form the property has taken in the hands of the defendant. In *Foskett v McKeown* (2000), Lord Millett drew a distinction between 'following' and 'tracing'. Both processes involve exercises in locating the assets of the claimant. 'Following' is the process of identifying the *same* asset as it moves from hand to hand. 'Tracing' is the process of identifying a *new* asset as a substitute for the old. For example, if the trustee wrongly distributes trust property – being cash – to X, and X uses that cash to purchase a car, the claimant may 'trace' his ownership through the cash into the car and recover it from X. It should also be noted at this early stage that the remedies attached to the process of tracing and the liability of a stranger as constructive trustee (Chapter 7) are frequently complementary. So, a third party who has received trust property with 'knowledge' that there has been a breach of trust may be a constructive trustee and subject to the tracing process. In the former case (that is, that of constructive trusteeship), he must hold the trust property for the beneficiaries *and* be subject to a personal liability. As we shall see in the case of successful tracing, the defendant may be entirely innocent but must still return the property in its present form to the rightful owners.

In addition, it is reasonably clear that tracing in equity is a 'proprietary' institution in the sense that a successful claimant asserts his right to the property per se: hence, if the defendant is bankrupt, the claimant may recover 'his' property (assuming it exists and is identifiable) and he is not treated as a general creditor and does not have to take only a share of the defendant's assets. It is a matter of 'hard-nosed property rights': *Foskett v McKeown* (2000). Obviously, such a powerful remedy cannot go unchecked and it should come as no surprise that the availability of the remedies attached to tracing in equity is restricted to certain situations. Unfortunately, the precise circumstances in which tracing is available are not universally agreed – either academically or judicially – nor, indeed, is there agreement as to whether tracing 'at law' and tracing 'in equity' are as similar as they first appear. These issues, as well as problem questions testing an awareness of how tracing works in practice, are the staple of examinations.

As inferred already, there are two forms of tracing: tracing 'at law' (common law tracing) and tracing 'in equity'. Tracing at law is available to any person who has legal title to property and its primary purpose is to identify the person who the legal owner should sue, that being the person into whose hands the property has passed. Once the defendant has been identified, the claimant may then sue on a variety of causes of action as circumstances dictate. These are the action for 'money had and received', being appropriate where the property traced is money, and an action in conversion or for wrongful interference, where the property consists of goods or other kinds of property. We should note, however, that recent case law has tended to 'deconstruct' claims in tracing – especially at law – and to regard the claim as an example of a general restitutionary liability, whereby the defendant should return property to the claimant if the defendant has been unjustly enriched at the claimant's expense, to the extent of the unjust enrichment, in circumstances where there is no defence of change of position (*Trustee of the property of FC Jones v Jones* (1996)). In addition, as we shall see, there is one serious limitation on the effectiveness of tracing at law, for it is impossible to trace at law if the original property has been mixed with any other property (as opposed to having been exchanged for any other), although, again, this may be changing.

Fortunately, tracing into a 'mixed fund' is perfectly possible in equity. Moreover, given that tracing at law requires the claimant to have *legal* title to property, it is clearly not available to a beneficiary under a trust who, after all, has only an equitable title. Consequently, most of the issues examined in this chapter will focus on tracing in equity, that being the remedy available to a beneficiary under a trust and that being the remedy that *does* permit a claim to be made even though the trust property has been mixed with some other, even with that of the trustee himself: *Foskett*. Finally, we shall see that another aspect of the proprietary nature of tracing in equity is that it entitles the claimant both to the property which the defendant has in his possession and to any increase in its value that it may have acquired in the meantime (*Foskett*: entitled to benefits of life insurance because premiums were paid with beneficiaries' money). Until recently, this has not been possible in law, but, once again, the move to a generally restitutionary approach may make even this possible (*Trustee of the property of FC Jones v Jones*).

QUESTION 29

What are the essential requirements for a successful tracing claim at law and in equity?

Aim Higher

The courts have drawn a distinction between 'following' and 'tracing'. 'Following' the assets in the hands of the defendant involves the process of identifying the same asset (but not in its substituted form, such as the proceeds of a sale) with the effect that the claimant may attach an order on to the property. 'Tracing' is the process whereby the claimant identifies and protects his interest in the asset, even in a substituted form.

In *Westdeutsche* (1996), Lord Browne-Wilkinson indicated that a thief holds stolen property on constructive trust for the rightful owner as the thief's conscience necessarily is bound. This means that the owner could trace the property through the hands of the thief into the hands of the ultimate recipient. It is an example of the 'act in breach' giving rise to both the claim and the fiduciary relationship necessary to support it. Clearly, this wide view would do much to reduce the practical obstacle placed in the way of tracing by the need to establish the fiduciary relationship. However, in *Shalson v Russo* (2003), Rimer J doubted Lord Browne-Wilkinson's view and stated that a thief has no title to property that he steals and thus cannot become a trustee of it. The true owner retains the legal and beneficial titles to the property. Perhaps the better view is that the thief does acquire title through his act of taking possession, but he does not acquire a better title than his victim.

In *Boscawen v Bajawa* (1995), the Court of Appeal indicated that equitable tracing should be regarded as a route to a defendant for all manner of remedies. So, in that case, once the defendant had been identified as having received the claimant's money (transferred in breach of trust), the claimant was subrogated to (that is, placed in the position of) the mortgagee whom the defendant had paid off with the money. So, it appears that equitable tracing – just like its counterpart at law – is developing a new restitutionary cloak.

How to Read this Question

This is a broad based essay question on tracing at law and in equity. It would be appropriate to establish the rationale and requirements of tracing in each jurisdiction and highlight the limitations applicable to each.

How to Answer this Question

It is often difficult to describe and analyse the law of tracing in the abstract. The concept of following or tracing the ownership of property is metaphysical, but nevertheless very powerful if one happens to be the defendant in a tracing claim. The 'big' question is whether tracing at law and tracing in equity will survive as distinct classes of action in the face of the new restitutionary approach. Following *Foskett v McKeown*, it seems that they will for some time to come. However, in essays such as this, examples are always useful to illustrate difficult concepts.

Up for Debate

The law of tracing is still being refined in equity. Articles that highlight some of these refinements include R Grantham and C Rickett, 'Tracing and property rights: the categorical truth' (2000) MLR 905 and P Oliver, 'The extent of equitable tracing' (1995) 9 Tru LI 78.

Answer Plan

❖ The purpose of a tracing claim, both at law and in equity.
❖ Conditions for both claims.

❖ Advantages of a tracing claim
❖ Differences between them: in establishing the remedy and in respect of the defences available to a defendant.

Answer Structure

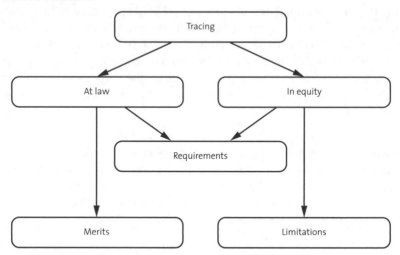

This diagram illustrates the process of tracing at law and in equity.

ANSWER

Common law tracing is a means of following legal title to property through successive persons until the property (or its present equivalent) is identified in the hands of the defendant. In essence, it is a means to an end, not the end itself (*AGIP (Africa) Ltd v Jackson* (1992); *Trustee of the property of FC Jones v Jones* (1996)). When the present possessor of the property in which the claimant's legal title subsists is identified, the claimant has a choice of remedies against that possessor. If the property is money, then the action will be against the present recipient for 'money had and received' (*Lipkin Gorman v Karpnale* (1991)), whereas if the property is a specific item, then the action will lie in tort for wrongful interference with goods or conversion. In the former case, the amount of the money 'had and received' by the defendant will be returned to the claimant and, in the latter case, the defendant will pay damages representing the value of the item or, in exceptional cases, the item itself may be returned at the discretion of the court.[1]

In the first place, tracing at law (and in equity) requires the property to be in identifiable form. If it has been destroyed, or money has been dissipated, then tracing is of no use: the property and the *legal* title to it are extinct. Second, tracing at law requires the claimant to have had legal title to property. Therefore, as a matter of principle, it is not

---

1 Multitude of remedies to complement the tracing process.

available to a beneficiary under a trust who is, of course, a person with a pure equitable title. Moreover, it must be clear that the claimant has retained legal title to the property. Given that title to money usually passes with possession, it is often easy to defeat a claim at law, see *Box v Barclays Bank* (1998). Third, the personal nature of tracing at law may cause problems if the defendant has gone bankrupt because, in theory, the personal claim of the tracer will rank equally with other personal claims made on the bankrupt's estate. Fourth, although there has been much debate, it seems that tracing at law is not available if the claimant's property has been mixed with that of another person and then passed on. The essence of the matter is that mixing at law renders the legal title to the property unidentifiable, in much the same way as if the property had actually been destroyed. Fifth, being traditionally regarded as a personal claim, an innocent defendant in an action supported by common law tracing should not normally be required to disgorge profits made by use of the property wrongfully received. The claim is for the value of the property, not *the* property (compare tracing in equity). However, in *Jones v Jones* (1996), the Court of Appeal held, on general restitutionary principles, that if the defendant had no title to the money she had received, then she had no title to the profits she made by using it. Finally, it may now be the case that a defendant may be able to plead 'change of position' as a defence to an action triggered by common law tracing (*Lipkin Gorman v Karpnale* (1991)). For example, it may well provide a defence to a claim in money 'had and received' for a person who is a bona fide purchaser for value of the claimant's property and to other persons who, in all innocence, have received the claimant's property in circumstances where the court thinks they should not be held personally liable.[2]

Tracing in equity does not suffer from the practical limitations of common tracing and consequently is much more versatile. Importantly, tracing in equity is regarded as proprietary in nature, with the consequence that it attaches directly to the property in the hands of the possessor (no matter what its current form) and gives the claimant paramount rights to recover it, even if the defendant is bankrupt. The defendant has no right to the claimant's property and so it forms no part of the defendant's assets. Furthermore, the proprietary nature of the claim means that the claimant is entitled to any increase in the value of 'his' property while it has been out of his possession, as where shares are purchased with trust money and they rise in value (*Re Tilley* (1967); *Foskett* (2000)). The remedies in equity include a charge over property in the defendant's hands if it represents the claimant's original ownership, or an order for the return of specific assets, or a charge over specific funds, or a charge over a specific portion of the property or funds.[3]

The trigger for a claim of equitable tracing is that the claimant must have an equitable proprietary interest in property and *only* an equitable proprietary interest (*Re Diplock* (1948)). Consequently, a beneficiary under a trust may trace in equity, but a trustee (legal title only) and an absolute owner may not. Second, unlike the position at law, it seems

---

2   Limitations as to tracing at law.
3   Broader approach to tracing in equity.

that tracing in equity can occur only if there was in existence a fiduciary relationship between the equitable owner and some other person before the events giving rise to the tracing claim occurred (*Sinclair v Brougham* (1914); *AGIP (Africa) Ltd v Jackson* (1992); and confirmed in *Westdeutsche Landesbank Girozentrale v Islington LBC* (1996)). This will always be the case where the claim arises out of a trust and it is clear that courts may do their utmost to find the required fiduciary relationship in order to facilitate the tracing claim (*Chase Manhattan Bank v Israel-British Bank* (1981)).

Third, it is inherent in the equitable tracing claim that the property of the beneficiaries must have been transferred to another person wrongfully. Otherwise, the equitable owner has no right or reason to claim its return. Fourth, being a claim in equity, equitable tracing is not possible against a person who is a bona fide purchaser of the legal estate for value without notice, although it may still be possible to trace against the person who has sold the trust property to the purchaser (*Re Diplock* (1948)). Likewise, it appears that the court has a discretion to disallow tracing against an innocent volunteer (that is, a person who gives no value for the trust property but is innocent of wrongdoing), if to do otherwise would be inequitable in all the circumstances. It is felt that this discretionary limitation in *Re Diplock* is now subsumed in the developing defence of change of position advocated by Lord Goff in *Lipkin Gorman* (1991). Similarly, the defence will not be available to a wrongdoer, such as a defendant who has acted in breach of his fiduciary duties. In any event, the mere fact that the defendant has spent the money in whole or in part, in the ordinary course of things, does not, of itself, render it inequitable that he should be called upon to repay the claimant. However, if the defendant has spent the claimant's money on a venture which would not have been undertaken but for the gift, such conduct would be capable of being construed as a change of position. In *Niru Battery Manufacturing Co v Milestone Trading Ltd (No 2)* (2004), the Court of Appeal decided that good faith was the touchstone of the defence of change of position and that this concept was incapable of definition.

In conclusion, it is apparent that both tracing in law and tracing in equity can be powerful tools in the hands of persons wrongfully deprived of their property. At present, the conditions for the application of each are different and some would argue that they are fundamentally different in purpose. However, the object of tracing is quite limited: it is to restore to the claimant that which he has been wrongfully deprived, often in breach of trust.

Common Pitfalls

Some students attempting this type of question have a tendency to write all they know of the details of cases without a structure and neglecting the policy considerations behind some of the decisions. This essay does not require discussion of the particular rules of equitable tracing (for example, *Re Hallett* (1880), *Re Oatway* (1903), *Clayton's Case* (1816), etc.).

QUESTION 30

Charles was the trustee of a large private trust fund. He cashed a cheque for £26,000 drawn on the trust fund and gave the money to James, the trust's financial adviser, with directions to use half to purchase shares for the trust and to use half to invest in antique furniture. James used £7,000 of the money to purchase shares in X Co in the name of the trust, and he delivered the share certificates to Charles as promised. However, he used a further £10,000 to purchase shares in Y Co in his own name, although he has now given these to his daughter as a birthday present, much to her surprise. James puts a further £5,000 in his own bank account, in which he already has some £4,000 of his own money. Out of this account, he purchases shares in Z Co to the value of £3,000, and gives them to his son. He spends the rest of the money from this bank account on a family holiday. The final £4,000 of the trust money was used to purchase antique furniture at a local auction.

The shares in X Co have slumped in value; those in Y Co have remained constant; but those in Z Co have trebled in value. Unfortunately, James has disappeared, and the furniture turns out to be fake and is worthless. Advise Charles of any action he might take to recoup the losses to the trust fund.

How to Read this Question

This is a problem question on breach of trust and tracing at law and in equity. This is evident in the question because we are told that one of the parties, James, in possible breach of trust has disappeared. It would not be possible to pursue James personally for breach of trust. Instead the claim of the trust fund is to advise the claimants on recouping the loss.

How to Answer this Question

In answering this question it would be advisable to state and apply the principles of law concerning the breach(es) of trust and the process of tracing at law subject to the possible defences available to the defendants. Once the trust property becomes mixed with the fiduciary's funds we would be required to consider the merits of tracing in equity, indicating the advantages and limitations of doing so.

Up for Debate

In *Lipkin Gorman v Karpnale* (1991), the House of Lords introduced the defence of change of position but indicated that the details are to be determined on a case by case basis. An instructive article on the subject is M Halliwell, 'Restitutionary claims: a change of position defence' (1992) Conv 124.

Aim Higher

In theory, because the question asks one to advise the trustee, it might be possible not to consider equitable tracing at all – because, on one view, the trustee has no equitable title to trace. However, this would not be good *practical* advice given that a partially effective remedy in equitable tracing is available to the beneficiaries.

Answer Plan

❖ Tracing at law: existence of legal title and continuance of that title.
❖ Appropriate remedy and defences, if any.
❖ The need to trace in equity: the beneficiaries.
❖ Increase in value of trust property.
❖ New restitutionary approaches.

Answer Structure

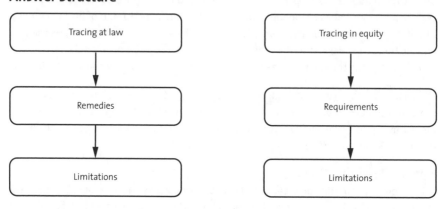

This diagram depicts the nature of tracing both at law and in equity.

ANSWER

This problem raises a number of issues concerning the remedies available to a trustee (Charles) and the beneficiaries for whom he holds the trust property when the trust property is misapplied in breach of trust. However, perhaps the first piece of advice that one may offer to Charles is to warn him of the possibility that he may be sued personally for breach of trust by the beneficiaries. Of course, the acts in breach were committed by James – Charles's agent – but it is clear that Charles might be held personally liable for losses to the trust estate through James's action if Charles did not fulfil his duties in respect of agents under ss1, 21 and 22 of the **Trustee Act 2000**, or otherwise delegated a function which he should have exercised personally (see s11 of the **Trustee Act 2000**).[4] Similarly, there is no doubt that James would have been liable for breaching his contract of agency and probably also as constructive trustee for knowingly dealing inconsistently with trust property (*Karak Rubber v Burden* (1972)). In this regard, it is worth noting that the £7,000 worth of shares purchased in X Co in the name of the trust are safe and that the furniture purchased by James, according to his instructions, is also part of the trust estate, even though it is worth very little.

If at all possible, Charles should be advised initially to seek to trace the missing trust funds at *law*. The advantages of this approach are, first, that there is no need to prove

4 Nature of the liability of Charles and James.

an initial fiduciary relationship (although this would not be a problem for the beneficiaries); second, that an action to recover the property can be made against any persons who have received it, regardless of their state of mind or whether any of them still retains it (*AGIP (Africa) Ltd v Jackson* (1992)); and third, that the defences available to the recipient of the property are fairly limited in scope, even though a change of position defence to a claim at law may now be accepted as valid (*Lipkin Gorman v Karpnale* (1991)).[5] If Charles can establish that he – as trustee – retained legal title to the £10,000 which was transferred to James, and which James improperly invested in Y Co, he may be able to maintain a tracing claim at law against these assets which now lie in the hands of James's daughter. In this connection, Charles will have to establish that he has a legal right of ownership which has survived the transfers to James and subsequently to his daughter. This would not appear to be a problem in this case, especially since James received the money as agent (see *Lipkin Gorman v Karpnale* (1991)). Thereafter, James could not transfer the shares beneficially to his daughter under the equitable maxim *nemo dat quod non habet*. In addition, there is no doubt that a claim to trace at law will survive changes in the nature of the property, providing that it is not mixed with any other property (*Taylor v Plummer* (1815)). Thus, Charles will be able to trace his legal title to the property through James to his daughter. Charles will be able to maintain an action against James's daughter personally for wrongful interference with goods and can expect damages to the value of the property she has received. This liability will persist even if she has disposed of the shares and may be defeated only if she can rely on the defence of 'change of position', recognised in *Lipkin Gorman v Karpnale* (1991) and applied in *Bank Tejaret v HKSB* (1995). This is unlikely in the circumstances as there is no evidence that James's daughter has in any way acted to her own detriment in innocent reliance on her receipt of the shares.

The next issue concerns the £5,000 which James places in his own bank account, where there is £4,000 of his own money. James has mixed the trust money with his own money before purchasing the shares and giving them to his son. This is fatal to a claim of tracing at law against James's son because, as far as the common law is concerned, the mixing of property before it is passed to the recipient makes it unidentifiable (*AGIP (Africa) Ltd v Jackson* (1992)).[6] It is possible that Charles could argue that James became a constructive trustee for *him* on the basis that James must have known that he was behaving in breach of trust and so became a trustee on the basis of conscience, following *dicta* in *Westdeutsche Landesbank Girozentrale v Islington LBC* (1996). This would trigger a claim in equity by Charles – the trustee and now beneficiary: *Twinsectra v Yardley* (2002). However, perhaps the best advice is that if the trust fund is to have a good chance of recovering the £5,000, the beneficiaries must be persuaded to pursue a tracing claim in equity against the shares now in the possession of James's son. In fact, there is every chance that an equitable tracing claim would be successful, at least in so far as the trust fund monies remain identifiable. For example, there is an initial fiduciary relationship and the beneficiaries undoubtedly have an equitable

---

5   Advantages of tracing at law compared with tracing in equity.
6   Limitations on tracing at law.

proprietary interest (*Re Diplock* (1948)). Moreover, as noted above, so long as the beneficiaries' equitable proprietary interest is identifiable, it is irrelevant that the property is no longer in its original form or that it has been mixed with other property (*Re Hallett* (1880); *Re Oatway* (1903)). The beneficiaries may trace the trust fund money into James's bank account and, following the rule in *Re Oatway* (1903), James will be presumed to have spent £3,000 of the trust money on the shares in Z Co (not following *Re Hallett* (1880) because there are no monies left in the bank account which could satisfy the beneficiaries' claim). Given that James's son is not a bona fide purchaser for value, he cannot resist the tracing claim against the shares. But if the circumstances had warranted it, he may have been entitled to the defence of change of position: see Lord Goff in *Lipkin Gorman*. In the present case James's son still retains the shares in Z Co and there is no evidence that he has changed his position. Thus, he may not have a defence to a claim to recover the shares in equity. It should also be noted that the beneficiaries are entitled to the increase in the value of Z Co's shares because tracing in equity gives the claimants a proprietary right to property and any increase in its value (*Foskett*).

Finally, as noted above and as *Re Diplock* (1948) makes clear, equitable tracing is unavailable when the property ceases to be identifiable. The money spent by James on a family holiday is lost and, following the traditional approach, the beneficiaries will be forced to rely on personal remedies (if any) against the trustee in order to recover the outstanding £2,000.

For the sake of completeness, it should also be noted that both James's daughter and son may incur the additional liabilities of constructive trusteeship if they have knowingly received trust property in breach of trust and, furthermore, the bank which cashed Charles's cheque could, in theory, be liable for assisting Charles in a breach of trust, provided they were dishonest (*Royal Brunei Airlines v Tan* (1995)). Again, both are unlikely on the facts as given (see *Lipkin Gorman v Karpnale* (1991)).

Common Pitfalls

Students do not always appreciate that tracing at law is simply a means of identifying the defendant, who is then subject to a specific remedy, because the liability of the defendant is personal, not proprietary. In other words, the person identified as the defendant through common law tracing is personally liable to the claimant for either money had and received or wrongful interference with goods, and must, therefore, pay the claimant, whether or not he still retains the property in question.

QUESTION 31

Zebedee is the trustee of a trust fund, holding a sum of money on trust for Dougal and Florence. At the same branch of the bank at which the trust account is held, Zebedee has his own current account which stands in credit at £500. The following events occur:

(a)   Zebedee pays £6,000 of the trust fund into his own account;

(b)   he then draws out £500 which he invests in the Roundabout Property Co;

(c)   he draws a further £3,000 from his account and gives it to his son, Brian, an antique dealer, who uses his skill to make a very successful purchase of a painting at auction;

(d)   he draws out a further £1,000, £500 of which he spends on making improvements to his house and the other £500 he gives to his daughter, Ermentrude, so that she can pay off her debt to Loanshark Co;

(e)   he pays £500 to the local hospital appeal, which has used the money to purchase some much needed equipment; and

(f)   he pays £500 into the current account of the Springboard Trust, of which he is also a trustee and which is in credit at £400. He then buys shares in Magic Co for £700 and entertains his family to dinner with the remainder.

Zebedee has gone bankrupt and the shares in Roundabout Property Co have halved in value. The painting is worth £10,000 and the shares in Magic Co have trebled in value. Advise Dougal, Florence and the Springboard Trust as to their remedies, if any.

How to Read this Question

It is evident that this is a tracing question by reference to the various breaches of trust committed by the trustee before his bankruptcy. It is also clear that since there has been a mixture of funds that tracing at law would not be possible but tracing in equity will have to be considered.

How to Answer this Question

In answering this question it is necessary to first identify the breach(es) of trust and set out the elements of a tracing claim in equity. In addition, the limits of tracing in equity, including a change of position defence is relevant to the question.

Up for Debate

The rules concerning the process of tracing may overlap with the doctrine of subrogation. It is instructive to read the following article on the subject, P Birks, 'Tracing, subrogation and change of position' (1996) 9 Tru LI 124.

Answer Plan

- ❖   Breach of trust action is the first resort.
- ❖   In the event of an unsatisfied claim, tracing may be available.
- ❖   Loss of the remedy – change of position.
- ❖   Mixed funds: two trusts.
- ❖   Replacement of trust funds.
- ❖   Innocent volunteers.

Answer Structure

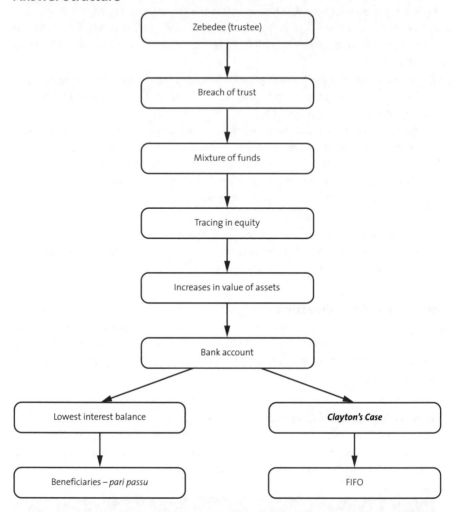

This diagram indicates the nature of the tracing process in respect of the various properties.

ANSWER

Although it is not absolutely clear from the facts of the problem, it is highly likely that Zebedee, the trustee, has committed a series of breaches of trust when disposing of the trust fund monies in the way indicated. Certainly, his mixing of the trust monies with his own may well be a breach of trust and it is highly unlikely that the trust instrument authorises him to make gifts to his children or other causes.[7] However, Zebedee is bankrupt, and personal claims against him will have to be abated in Zebedee's bankruptcy along with the claims of other creditors. In such circumstances, the beneficiaries will wish

7   Consideration of a breach of trust.

to pursue such proprietary remedies as they might have, as this will give them a right to their property per se in priority to those who are 'merely' creditors. Tracing in equity may well prove to be the route to the most effective remedy.[8]

Fortunately, there is no doubt that Dougal and Florence are entitled to pursue equitable tracing. It is possible in equity to trace ownership into, through and out of a mixed fund, so the fact that the trustee has mixed the £5,000 of trust money with that of his own will not defeat the tracing claim.

When Zebedee transfers the trust money into his account, it is likely that he is committing a breach of trust. First, there is the £500 withdrawn from the mixed account and used to purchase shares in Roundabout Co Ltd. The change in nature of the beneficiaries' equitable interest – from money into shares – is not an obstacle to equitable tracing, provided that the shares can be said to have been purchased with the beneficiaries' money in the first place, bearing in mind that Zebedee has £500 of his own money in the mixed bank account.[9] In this regard, *Re Hallett* (1880) decides that a trustee making purchases from a bank account in which funds are mixed must be presumed to have spent his own money first, as there is always a presumption against a breach of trust. Yet, in our case, this would mean that the shares in Roundabout belonged to Zebedee, even though, after all the events have taken place, there is no money left in the account to return to the beneficiaries. In these circumstances, when, in effect, there is nothing in the bank account to trace to, *Re Oatway* (1903) makes it clear that the beneficiaries can turn to property purchased out of the mixed fund as being the embodiment of their equitable interest, even if, at the time it was purchased, there was enough money to satisfy their claim.[10] Consequently, the Roundabout shares will belong in equity to Dougal and Florence, although the fact that the shares are now worth only half their original value means that they will have to rely on their personal claim against Zebedee to recover the balance.

In principle, the same considerations apply to the £3,000 which Zebedee then withdraws and pays to his son; this is trust money and capable of being traced. Again, the fact that it was then used to purchase an antique painting will not destroy the tracing claim. Moreover, the added complication that the property (as money, and then a chattel) is in the hands of Brian, a third party, is no bar. Brian is not a bona fide purchaser for value, although there is no indication that he knew the money was transferred to him in breach of trust and is unlikely to be a constructive trustee (*Westdeutsche Landesbank Girozentrale v Islington LBC* (1996)). *Re Diplock* (1948) makes it clear that equitable tracing is perfectly possible against an innocent volunteer where the property is identifiable. The court is most likely to order the return of the painting itself as this is where the beneficiaries' equitable interest is to be found, especially since the proprietary remedy carries with it any increase in the value of the property (*Re Tilley* (1967); *Foskett v McKeown* (2000)).

....

8 Primacy of tracing in equity.

9 Distinction between following and tracing.

10 Significance of presumptions in respect of tracing claims in equity.

The issue of the identifiable nature of the trust property is quite pertinent when considering the next £1,000 which Zebedee withdraws, half of which he gives to his daughter and half of which he spends on his own house. In *Re Diplock*, the House of Lords was of the view that it was impossible to trace money that had been used to pay off a debt, both because the creditor could be regarded as a purchaser for value and because the money effectively ceased to exist as independent property. Consequently, at first, unless Zebedee's daughter (or Loanshark Co) has taken the money with knowledge of the breach of trust, and is thereby a constructive trustee, there appears to be no route to a successful recovery of this £500. By way of contrast, however, the Court of Appeal, in *Boscawen v Bajawa* (1995), allowed the claimant a remedy against a defendant who had used monies traced to him to pay off a mortgage. In *Boscawen*, the claimant was subrogated to the creditor who had been paid off.[11] So, in our case, if we follow *Boscawen*, and similar reasoning adopted by the House of Lords in *Banque Financière de la Cité v Parc (Battersea) Ltd* (1998), the claimants will be subrogated to Loanshark Co, and may be able to recover the money by enforcing the debt against Ermentrude as creditors.

Turning to the £500 spent by Zebedee on his house, this might be recovered. It is perfectly possible to levy a charge for a specific amount on property owned by another if this would enable the beneficiaries' interest to be protected. Indeed, there is no such objection to levying a charge on the property of the trustee who has actually committed the breach of trust.

Conversely, however, there are doubts whether the £500 paid to the local hospital can be recovered by the beneficiaries. There is no doubt that the property is traceable per se; the facts suggest that the money has been used to purchase identifiable equipment. It is clear that the court has a general discretion to deny tracing where it would be inequitable to permit it and this may prevent recovery from the hospital.

The mixing of the final £500 with the £400 of the Springboard Trust raises the question of the ability to trace to an asset (the shares in Magic Co) when all claimants to it (Dougal, Florence and the beneficiaries of Springboard Trust) are innocent. In principle, unless the rule in *Clayton's Case* (1816) applies, the two sets of claimants will be able to trace and claim the shares in Magic Co in proportion to their money in the mixed bank account before the purchase took place: that is, in the ratio 5:4 (£500:£400). As before, both parties will be able to retain any increase in the value of their portion of the shares (*Re Tilley* (1967); *Foskett v McKeown* (2000)). The balance in the account would be shared on a similar basis. If, on the other hand, *Clayton's Case* does apply, then the beneficiaries of the Springboard Trust will be able to claim that the first £400 worth of Magic Co shares belongs to them, on a 'first in, first out' basis.[12] However, even if it is clear that Zebedee's account is an 'active' bank account within the *Clayton* rule, *Barlow Clowes International Ltd (In Liquidation) v Vaughan* (1992) establishes that *Clayton's* rule is one of convenience only and should not be applied either where the property of the respective claimants is identifiable or where it would achieve an inequitable result. A similar view was echoed in

---

11 Complementary nature of the doctrine of subrogation.
12 Alternative but unpopular solution in *Clayton's Case*.

Commerzbank Aktiengesellschaft v IMB Morgan (2004). It is suggested, therefore, that the proportionate share rule (*pari passu*, 5:4) should prevail.

Any sums which the beneficiaries cannot claim, and where they still suffer a loss, can be recovered only in a personal action against Zebedee or against any of the third parties who may have had such an awareness of the material facts as to make them liable as constructive trustees.

QUESTION 32

By his will, Terrence appointed Edward and Edwina as his executors and trustees and bequeathed £500,000 to Lucy and £300,000 for the charitable purposes of the War Veterans Association. Edward and Edwina took all proper steps to prove the will and, after making all proper enquiries, paid over the monies to Lucy and the charity. However, Terrence had provided for David and Dee, as his residuary legatees, and they claimed successfully that the will should be set aside on the grounds of Lucy's undue influence over Terrence. Likewise, it appears that the War Veterans Association is not entitled to charitable status, being merely a non-charitable association. It also transpires that Rack, a creditor of Terrence who had been abroad at the time of Terrence's death, is owed a large sum of money, and he now claims £300,000.

Unfortunately, the strain of this was too much for both Edward and Edwina: they turned to gambling and both are now bankrupt. Lucy, however, has spent £100,000 on completely renovating her house, £150,000 on shares in the stock market and £50,000 on a year of high living. The War Veterans Association has spent all the money on providing pensions for disabled servicemen.

▶ **Advise David, Dee and Rack as to their rights, if any, in Terrence's estate.**

How to Read this Question

This problem question includes the liability of trustees for possibly innocent breaches of trust, claims for knowingly receiving trust property for the defendant's benefit, the tracing process and the *in personam* claim of unpaid or underpaid creditors or next of kin within the *Re Diplock* rules.

How to Answer this Question

In answering this question you are required to discuss the following: the action for damages for breach of trust, the imposition of a constructive trust, the law of equitable tracing and the specialised *Re Diplock in personam* action are perhaps the most widely used.

Up for Debate

The restrictions imposed on the claims of the unpaid or underpaid creditors or next of kin as laid down in *Re Diplock* were considered in an article written by J Martin, 'Recipient liability after Westdeutsche' (1998) Conv 13. It is advisable to read this article carefully.

Answer Plan

- ❖ Loss of the remedy.
- ❖ Innocent and culpable defendants.
- ❖ *Re Diplock in personam* remedy – strict liability.
- ❖ Defence of change of position.

Answer Structure

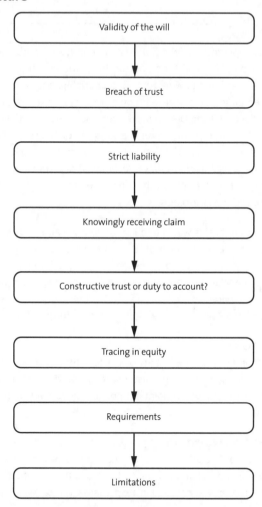

```
┌─────────────────────────────────────┐
│          Validity of the will         │
└─────────────────────────────────────┘
                   │
                   ▼
┌─────────────────────────────────────┐
│            Breach of trust            │
└─────────────────────────────────────┘
                   │
                   ▼
┌─────────────────────────────────────┐
│            Strict liability           │
└─────────────────────────────────────┘
                   │
                   ▼
┌─────────────────────────────────────┐
│        Knowingly receiving claim       │
└─────────────────────────────────────┘
                   │
                   ▼
┌─────────────────────────────────────┐
│   Constructive trust or duty to account?  │
└─────────────────────────────────────┘
                   │
                   ▼
┌─────────────────────────────────────┐
│           Tracing in equity           │
└─────────────────────────────────────┘
                   │
                   ▼
┌─────────────────────────────────────┐
│             Requirements              │
└─────────────────────────────────────┘
                   │
                   ▼
┌─────────────────────────────────────┐
│             Limitations               │
└─────────────────────────────────────┘
```

This diagram highlights a claim for breach of trust and the liabilities of strangers as constructive trustees or for accounting.

ANSWER

It is clear that even innocent and honest trustees may be liable in damages for breach of trust if they have failed to carry out the terms of the trust or fulfil their fiduciary duties

(*Tito v Waddell (No 2)* (1977)). Unfortunately for Edward and Edwina, it seems that they may have committed breaches of trust in paying the trust money to Lucy and the War Veterans Association, even though this may have been due to an understandable mistake as to law or facts (see, for example, *Re Diplock* itself).[13] It may well be that the two trustees could mount a successful defence to such an action – perhaps under **s 61** of the **Trustee Act 1925** on the grounds that they have behaved honestly and reasonably and ought fairly to be excused (*Williams v Byron* (1901)). In any event, we are told that they are now bankrupt and so are unlikely to be able to satisfy the large claims of David and Dee for their losses of £800,000, even assuming they had no defence to the action. This means that the two claimants must seek alternative remedies.

As a first choice, it may be that David and Dee will wish to establish that Lucy should be regarded as a constructive trustee of the £500,000 she has received. If this proves to be the case, Lucy will be personally liable for this entire amount, whether or not she retains any of it. Of course, such liability is not easily established, and David and Dee will have to assert that Lucy has knowingly received trust property in breach of trust within the principles discussed in *International Sales Ltd v Marcus* (1982), *AGIP (Africa) Ltd v Jackson* (1992) and *BCCI v Akindele* (2000).[14] Undoubtedly, the transfer was in breach of trust – because of the finding of undue influence – and Lucy has received the property for her own benefit, as witnessed by her subsequent use of it. The crucial question then remains whether she has a sufficient degree of knowledge to fix her with liability. Fortunately, whatever doubts there are as to the required degree of knowledge for knowing receipt – intention/recklessness and/or negligence (*Baden Delvaux and Lecuit v Société Générale pour Favouriser le Développement du Commerce et de l'Industrie en France SA* (1983)) or (if different) 'unconscionability' see *BCCI v Akindele* – the finding that Lucy procured the will by her undue influence is enough to establish her knowledge of the relevant facts. She will be a constructive trustee of the money she has received. As noted above, this imposes on her a personal liability to repay the £500,000. Of course, it is quite likely that she will be unable to find this amount of money and we are told that she has spent at least £300,000 on specific projects. In such circumstances, while David and Dee may well be able to recover the unspent £200,000 and perhaps even some of the balance out of Lucy's other assets, the beneficiaries would be well advised to resort to the proprietary remedy of tracing.

There is no doubt that David and Dee would be able to satisfy the preconditions for tracing in equity identified in *Re Diplock* (1948): as residuary legatees they have an equitable proprietary interest and there is a clear fiduciary relationship between them and Edward and Edwina. Moreover, *Re Diplock* does indicate that recovery of property through tracing in equity might be refused if the property has been so mixed with that of an innocent volunteer that a successful action would be inequitable (now regarded as a change of position defence: see *Lipkin Gorman v Karpnale* (1991)). Lucy is not 'innocent' and, therefore, there is every chance that David and Dee would be granted a charge over Lucy's house, either to the value of the money spent on it (£100,000) or in the proportion that

---

13 The strict nature of liability for breach of trust.
14 Knowingly receiving trust property or unconscionability.

£100,000 represents of the house's value after improvement (*Re Tilley* (1967); *Foskett v McKeown* (2000)). To some extent, whether the court chooses the fixed charge (£100,000) or the proportionate charge may depend on the value of the house and whether the court feels that the two claimants should benefit from any windfall profit arising from an increase in the house's value. The same considerations apply, *mutatis mutandis*, to Lucy's investment in the stock market. Finally, it is unfortunately quite likely that the £50,000 spent on 'high living' will be untraceable, having been dissipated on uni-dentifiable purchases. This amount will have to be the subject of the personal claim against Lucy and/or the trustees.

David and Dee may also be able to maintain a tracing claim against the assets spent by the War Veterans Association. As before, there is no doubt about the nature of David's and Dee's equitable interest or the existence of their proprietary rights. Moreover, it is inherent in a tracing claim that the funds sought to be recovered have been transferred to the recipient in breach of trust; otherwise there is no ground of recovery. In this case, it is clear that the property should never have been distributed to the Association, since it is not a charity. The trust was for a non-charitable purpose, and therefore void, with the money resulting to the residuary legatees under the beneficiary principle (*Re Endacott* (1960)). In fact, these are similar facts to *Re Diplock* itself. Unfortunately, however, like *Re Diplock*, this tracing claim may run into difficulties. As noted above, *Re Diplock* suggests that tracing will not be permitted where it would be inequitable to force the return of the property from an innocent volunteer.

However, that is not the end of the matter. In *Re Diplock*, the House of Lords expressly accepted the existence of a limited *in personam* action, available against the recipients of property, at the suit of unpaid or underpaid creditors or next of kin arising out of a wrongly administered testamentary estate.[15] In our case, given that the estate of Terrence has been wrongly administered, David and Dee and Rack (the creditor) will have a personal action against Lucy and against the officers of the War Veterans Association, all of whom have received funds from the executors and trustees. Importantly because the action is personal (*in personam*), it is irrelevant that the recipients no longer have the property and they must satisfy the claims of the three claimants out of their own funds. As is clear, this is a powerful remedy and this is one reason why currently it exists only in the context of a wrongly admin-istered testamentary estate (and possibly after a wrongful distribution of the assets of a defunct company – *Re Leslie Engineers Co Ltd* (1976)). It is also true that the claimants must exhaust their personal actions against the executors before they can proceed further, although that is not a problem in our case. Finally it is likely, following *Lipkin Gorman v Karp-nale* (1991), that the officers of the War Veterans Association might be able to plead 'change of position' to minimise or deny their liability. This defence does, however, lie in the discre-tion of the court, and it may well be that, in the light of the bankruptcy of the executors, the court will admit the claim of Rack (who has little chance of a tracing claim being a 'mere' contractual debtor: *Box v Barclays Bank* (1998)), and perhaps David and Dee to the extent that they have not recovered the funds from other sources.

....

15 Significance of the personal action by the unpaid creditors or next of kin.

Note

These three problem questions show the diverse range of issues that can arise in the law of tracing. Note how useful *Re Diplock* can be: it is authority for nearly every aspect of tracing in equity. Consider also the powerful nature of the *Re Diplock in personam* remedy. This is an invention of equity, limited in nature, but potentially ruinous for the innocent recipients of wrongly distributed funds. It remains to be seen whether *Lipkin Gorman* is authority for the existence of a general, strict liability restitutionary remedy – subject, as always, to the change of position defence.

9

Breach of Trust

INTRODUCTION

It is perhaps surprising that the last of the beneficiary's remedies to be considered is the personal action for breach of trust. After all, the attempt to fix a stranger with a duty to account or constructive trust (Chapter 7) and the remedy of tracing (Chapter 8) are triggered by an initial breach of trust by the trustee. Moreover, even in situations where these other remedies are available, if the trustee responsible for the breach is able to satisfy the claims of the beneficiaries in full, a personal action for damages for breach of trust will be the normal course of action and the court may insist that it is pursued before other avenues are followed. As we have seen, the duty to account and the constructive trust and the remedy of tracing are used principally against third parties, being persons who have meddled with the trust or who have come into possession of the trust property subsequent to the trustee. In contrast, the action for breach of trust is personal to the trustee in two senses. First, only those trustees who are responsible for the breach of trust may be sued for damages, although the extent of the 'personal responsibility' of a trustee for breach of trust is quite wide. Second, the action for breach of trust itself is a personal action and the successful claimant (usually the beneficiary) will become a normal judgment creditor. Consequently, in the event of the trustee's bankruptcy or death, the beneficiary will have to take her chance along with all of the other creditors and claimants and may not receive all of the damages awarded in the breach of trust action. This is why the proprietary remedies discussed in the two previous chapters are so useful when specific trust property is still identifiable.

It would be a mistake to believe that the action for breach of trust is not important. It is the first weapon of the wronged beneficiary and one whose net can be cast particularly widely. In general terms, there are four areas of concern to the student although, as ever, this is a somewhat arbitrary classification. First, questions arise as to what actually constitutes a breach of trust and who is responsible for it. This is tied to the standard of care required of trustees and the measure of compensation for a proven breach. Second, there is much case law concerning the circumstances in which a trustee may be liable for breach of trust even though the 'act in breach' was committed by another person, such as an agent or co-trustee. This can be easily confused or interwoven with issues in the first category. Third, the relationship of trustees with each other consequent upon a breach of trust can seem confusing, hence questions concerning the liability of trustees *inter se* and any remedies they may have against each other are often asked in examinations. Fourth, and perhaps less difficult, the student must have an awareness of the trustee's possible defences to an action for breach of trust. Once again, in all of these issues, case law is important although various provisions of the **Trustee Act 1925** and the **Trustee Act 2000** are relevant and must be examined with some care.

QUESTION 33
In what circumstances may a trustee successfully plead a defence to an established breach of trust?

How to Read this Question
This essay question requires you to discuss the variety of defences or means of mitigation available to trustees who are sued for breach of trust. Ever so often with breach of trust questions students fail to consider the possible defences available to trustees.

How to Answer this Question
There are a wide variety of defences available to trustees both at common law and by statutory provisions. Certain defences are available only against certain claimant beneficiaries such as participant beneficiaries or those granting trustees informed consent to the alleged breaches of trust, see *Re Pauling*, indemnity of trustees *Chillingworth v Chambers*, s 62 of the **Trustee Act 1925**. In addition there are occasions when a claim may not succeed against the trustees in breach, see s 61 of the **Trustee Act 1925**, claims brought outside the limitation period and claims barred by virtue of exemption clauses.

Up for Debate

The effect of exclusion clauses in relieving liability of the trustees for a proven breach was considered by the Court of Appeal in *Armitage v Nurse*. The court made a point of encouraging Parliament to intervene to limit their effect. But the 2006 Law Commission Report recommended that the provision of exclusion clauses in settlements ought to be self-regulated by the trust industry's professional bodies. It is worth reading the judgment of the Court of Appeal and the Law Commission Report.

Answer Plan
❖   Release/acquiescence by the beneficiary.
❖   Participation/consent to a breach of trust by the beneficiary.
❖   **Sections 61 and 62 of the Trustee Act 1925**.
❖   Statutory limitation and laches.
❖   The joint and several liability of trustees: although a trustee may be liable, an indemnity may be obtained from co-trustees who are more culpable.

Aim Higher

Students ought to be aware that the nature of the defences and reliefs available to trustees fall into three categories. These are defences available against particular beneficiaries, those available against all beneficiaries and those 'quasi-defences' available to one trustee against another.

Applying the Law

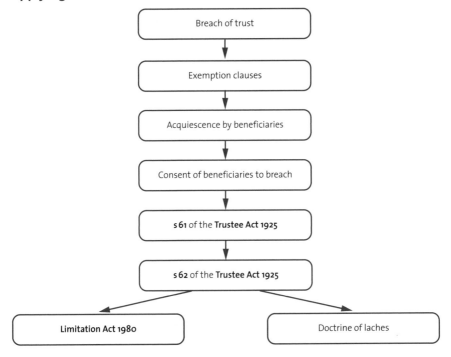

This diagram lists the possible defences that may be raised by a trustee in proceedings for breach of trust.

ANSWER

The defences available to trustees may be found in both statute and common law. First, a trustee may rely on the principle that a beneficiary who *participates* in, or *consents* to, a breach of trust by the trustee will thereafter be barred from bringing an action for breach of trust (*Life Association of Scotland v Siddal* (1861)). The essence of the matter is that that particular beneficiary has so involved himself with the breach that he should not thereafter be able to deny it and, consequently, it is irrelevant whether the beneficiary actually benefits from the breach or not (*Fletcher v Collis* (1905)).[1] Whether the beneficiary has become so involved will be a question of fact, although it is clear that the beneficiary must be aware of all the relevant facts and understand fully the nature of the transaction which is proposed (*Re Pauling* (1964)). Similarly, the consent must be freely given and it has been said that a beneficiary who consents or participates without independent advice may not be so aware of what is proposed as to bar him from a later action for breach of trust (*Holder v Holder* (1966)). Again, the personal nature of this defence, operating as it does against particular beneficiaries, means that the trustee may still face claims arising from his activities from other beneficiaries not implicated in the breach.

1   Justification for the defence.

In similar vein, a beneficiary's conduct after the breach may be such as to amount either to a *release* of the trustee or *acquiescence* in the breach sufficient to protect the trustee from later suit by that beneficiary (*Farrant v Blanchford* (1863); *Stafford v Stafford* (1857)). The essential point here is that the beneficiary's conduct after the breach has occurred may be such that it amounts to a personal bar against pursuing an action. As with cases of consent, whether there has been a release or acquiescence is a question of fact and, again, the state of knowledge of the beneficiary is decisive. For cases of release, the classic judgment in *Farrant v Blanchford* emphasises that a release is effective only if the beneficiary was of full age and capacity and had full knowledge of all the circumstances and of his claims against the trustee. This seems to suppose that, unlike cases of consent (and possibly *ex post facto* acquiescence), a release can be effective only if the beneficiary realised he was releasing a trustee from a breach of trust. At first, this seems quite logical yet cases of prior consent require knowledge of the facts and circumstances, but not that they amount to a breach, and this is sometimes said to be the position with *ex post facto* acquiescence as well (*Holder v Holder* (1966)). It would be unfortunate if there was a distinction between consent/acquiescence on the one hand and release on the other and so it is submitted that the general test put forward in *Re Pauling* should be adopted.

There are circumstances when beneficiaries may be compelled to use their beneficial interests to indemnify the trustees for monies paid out in restoration of a breach of trust. Although the trustee is under a personal obligation to make restoration for loss flowing from the breach of trust, he may recover all or part of that sum from certain beneficiaries. This may be achieved in either of two ways. First, a court of equity has an inherent and discretionary jurisdiction to impound (that is, confiscate) a beneficiary's equitable interest in order to indemnify the trustee when the beneficiary has instigated or requested a trustee to commit a breach of trust (*Chillingworth v Chambers* (1896)) or when the beneficiary had consented to a breach of trust out of which he had received a personal benefit, such confiscation being limited to the benefit received (*Fletcher v Collis* (1905)). Second, this equitable jurisdiction has been extended by s 62 of the **Trustee Act 1925** which gives the court a discretionary power to indemnify a trustee out of the beneficiary's interest if the breach of trust was committed 'at the instigation or request or with the consent in writing' of the beneficiary. Once again, the court will not exercise its statutory discretion unless the beneficiary knew and understood all the relevant facts which thereafter amounted to a breach of trust (*Re Somerset* (1894)), although it is only in respect of consent that the trustees' claim to indemnity under s 62 must be supported by writing.

In addition, a 'stand-alone' defence is available to the trustees irrespective of the actions of individual beneficiaries and which can afford a defence to an action by them all. According to s 61 of the **Trustee Act 1925**, the court has a discretionary power to relieve a trustee from liability for breach of trust, in whole or in part, if it appears that the trustee 'has acted honestly, reasonably, and ought fairly to be excused'. It is clear that, despite the general words of this section, this is not a statutory modification of the strict liability of trustees. The statute does not give the court a general power to exempt all honest trustees but is for those exceptional occasions when there is simply no justification in conscience for the imposition of liability despite the fact that a breach has occurred (*Williams v Byron* (1901)). Moreover, the elements of the defence are to be read conjunctively so that a trustee must establish that he has acted honestly and reasonably and ought fairly to be excused (*Davis v Hutchings* (1907)).

In the recent case, *Lloyds Bank plc v Markandan and Uddin* (2012) EWCA 65, the CA refused to grant relief under s 61 of the **Trustee Act 1925** to a firm of solicitors on the ground that the defendants did not act reasonably.

Finally, mention must be made of three further matters. First, the general principles of limitation of actions applies to the action for breach of trust in much the same way as to other personal actions.[2] Thus, except in the case of fraud or where the trustee has possession of trust property or had possession of trust property and converted it to his own use (s 21(1)(a) and **(b)** of the **Limitation Act 1980**; and see *Armitage v Nurse* (1997)), no action for breach of trust can be brought after six years have expired from the date the action accrued. There is no period of limitation for cases within s 21(1)(a) and (b), and liability for dishonesty endures without limitation of time (*Armitage*). Second, the liability of trustees *inter se* may be adjusted by a claim for a contribution by those trustees who have been required to make entire restoration against those who have not paid or who are more culpable. This jurisdiction now resides primarily in the **Civil Liability (Contribution) Act 1978** (see, for example, *Dubai Aluminium Co v Salaam* (2002)), although there are three situations outside the Act where one trustee may be made to indemnify completely any others who have actually made restoration to the beneficiaries: where a trustee has received trust money and made use of it (*Bahin v Hughes* (1886)); where the trustee at fault was a solicitor trustee on whose advice the other trustees relied (*Re Linsley* (1904)); and where a trustee is also a beneficiary of the trust (*Chillingworth v Chambers* (1896)). Third, a trustee in breach may escape liability by relying on an exemption clause. These are popular with professional trustees as they mitigate the strict liability of trusteeship. Further, as *Armitage v Nurse* (1997) illustrates, an exemption clause can be effective to exclude liability for negligence and 'equitable fraud' (that is, deliberate but honest breaches believed to be in the interests of beneficiaries), although it cannot exclude liability for dishonesty.

Common Pitfalls

This type of question may appear on an examination paper as either an essay or a problem. Students are advised to adopt a structured approach to their answers by first dealing with the possible breaches of trust committed by the trustees and, if appropriate, identifying which trustees have been responsible for these breaches, before considering whether there is a right of contribution or defence available to some of the trustees. Too often, students confuse the various issues, with disappointing consequences.

QUESTION 34

'A trustee may be liable to pay compensation for his own breach of trust and in some cases for those committed by others.'

▶ Analyse the concept of 'a breach of trust' and assess whether the above is an accurate statement of the law relating to liability for breach of trust.

2　Importance of limitation periods and laches.

How to Read this Question

This question requires you to identify action on the part of the trustee that may amount to a breach of trust. In addition you are required to consider the extent to which a trustee is required to make compensation for the loss suffered by the trust as well as the consequences of imposing joint and several liability on the trustees as a whole.

How to Answer this Question

In answering this question you are required to consider the following:

- ❖ What constitutes a breach of trust?
- ❖ The scope of liability for breach of trust.
- ❖ The prominence of exclusion clauses.
- ❖ The test for compensating the trust for the loss suffered by the breach.
- ❖ The distinction between primary and vicarious liability under the **Trustee Act 2000**.
- ❖ The scope of the principle of joint and several liability of trustees.
- ❖ Contributions and indemnities between trustees.

Up for Debate

The flexible nature of equitable compensation for breach of trust, as distinct from the common law notion of the measure of damages, was explored by J Edelman and S Elliott, 'Money remedies against trustees' (2004) 18 Tru LI 116, which you are urged to read. In addition was Lord Browne-Wilkinson justified in suggesting in *Target Holdings v Redfern* that the rules on causation and breach could be applied differently in 'commercial' and 'traditional' trust cases.

Applying the Law

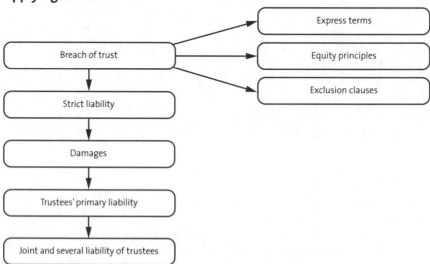

This diagram specifies the sources and extent of liability of the trustees for breach of trust.

ANSWER

The liability for breach of trust is generally strict in the sense that it is enough that the trustee has committed the act or omission which amounts to a breach of trust.[3] For liability purposes it is irrelevant whether the trustee knew he was committing the breach and did so for his own benefit, or was reckless as to the possibility of a breach occurring or was negligent of the same or was entirely innocent and honest. Thus, it remains a breach of trust for even if he believed he was acting in conformity with the terms of the trust (as in *Re Diplock* (1948)) and did so in the belief that his action was in the best interests of the beneficiaries (*Harrison v Randall* (1852)).

The all encompassing nature of this liability is the main reason why professional trustees insist on the inclusion, in the trust instrument, of a clause excluding liability for certain types of breach of trust. As *Armitage v Nurse* (1997) illustrates, an exemption clause can be effective to exclude liability for negligence and 'equitable fraud' (that is, deliberate and honest breaches believed to be in the interests of beneficiaries), although it cannot exclude liability for dishonesty. Despite some fierce criticism of *Armitage v Nurse*, the **Trustee Act 2000** leaves the existing law on exclusion clauses untouched and, further, permits the exclusion of the statutory duty of care imported by **s1** (see **Sch 1** and **s7** of the **Trustee Act 2000**).[4]

Once the liability of a trustee for breach of trust is established, the trustee is under an obligation to make good such loss as flows from the breach of trust, although the loss is not limited to that which is reasonably foreseeable (*Target Holdings Ltd v Redferns* (1996)). In this sense, the essential quality of the trustee's obligation is compensatory, but not being limited by considerations of foreseeability and remoteness of damage (see, for example, *Re Dawson (Decd)* (1966)), can be more extensive than damages for breach of contract or those which lie in tort. Of course, that does not mean that the trustee is liable for all loss that flows directly or indirectly from his breach of trust, for there must still be a causal link between the breach of trust and the loss to the claimant (*Swindle v Harrison* (1997)). The essential question is, then, whether it could be shown that the loss would not have occurred but for the breach (*Target Holdings*) and no liability for the total loss will arise if the trustee can show that the loss, or part of it, would have occurred in any event – as where the beneficiaries lose money because of a fall in the value of property rather than because of the admitted misapplication of trust funds (*Target Holdings*), or where the claimant would have acted in the same way had the breach not occurred (*Swindle*).

Finally in this survey of the nature of liability for breach of trust, two further supplementary rules may be noted. First, if there is no loss, or no provable loss (*Nestlé v National Westminster Bank* (1992)), the trustee's liability is limited to account for any profits he has received (*Vyse v Foster* (1874)). Second, in general, the losses occasioned by a breach of trust in one transaction cannot be set off against any profits made by them in another

---

3 Good point to make that liability is strict.
4 Important to state the justification for trustees' defences.

(*Dimes v Scott* (1828)), save in the exceptional case where the loss making transaction and the profit making transaction can be regarded as essential ingredients of the same activity (*Bartlett v Barclays Bank Trust Co (No 2)* (1980)).

It is also important to appreciate that it is inherent in the concept of breach of trust, as with other forms of liability, that only those trustees responsible in law for the breach will be liable to the beneficiaries.[5] This is self-evident. However, because it is perfectly possible for a trustee to commit a breach of trust through omission as well as commission, the extent of a trustee's personal responsibility for breach is more extensive than might first be imagined. In simple terms, a trustee will be liable for a breach of trust in the following situations, even though some other person may have committed the acts or omissions that constitute the *actus reus* of the breach.

First, and most obviously, a trustee will be liable for a breach of trust where he has actually committed the acts in breach, as where a trustee pays money to the wrong persons (*Re Diplock*) or makes off with the trust fund. Second, a trustee may be liable for failing to perform a duty imposed on him by the trust instrument or general law, as where a trustee fails to safeguard the trust's assets. Third, a trustee (A) may be liable for a breach of trust even if the act or omission in breach was committed by a co-trustee (B), but only if A can be said to have failed in his duty to supervise the trust's affairs, which failure facilitated the breach of trust by B: see, for example, *Bahin v Hughes* (1886). This is not liability for B's actions (it is not vicarious), but rather A's primary liability because of his failure to monitor the trust in accordance with his own duty. This duty may spring from the common law, or constitute an aspect of the statutory duty of care imposed on trustees in respect of their powers under the **Trustee Act 2000** (**s 1** and **Sch 1**). An example is where a co-trustee pays away money to the wrong beneficiaries and was allowed to do so by the inattention of his colleagues. Fourth, a trustee may be liable even if the act or omission in breach of trust was committed by an agent employed to act on the trust's behalf, but only if it can be shown that the trustee failed in his duty in one of two ways: (a) by falling below the standard of care required by trustees in the appointment of agents, etc. (for example, stockbrokers): **s 1** and **Pt IV** of the **Trustee Act 2000**; or (b) by failing to review the exercise of the delegable functions of agents as required by **s 22** of the **Trustee Act 2000**.

Finally, it should be noted that once the liability of particular trustees for a breach of trust has been established, that liability is, between them, joint and several. Of course, in practice, one liable trustee may be more culpable than another and, as a matter of principle, it is unfair that only one of the trustees should be made to bear the entire liability. Consequently, a contribution may be sought from other liable trustees under the **Civil Liability (Contribution) Act 1978**. Further, in limited circumstances, a liable trustee may be required to pay a complete indemnity to the trustee who has been required to make restitution to the beneficiaries under the principle of joint and several liability. This occurs where the indemnifying trustee was a solicitor on whose advice the other trustees relied (*Re Linsley* (1904)), where the trustee has committed fraud (*Re Smith* (1896)), where the

5   Liability of the trustee is personal. This is an integral part of the question.

trustee has received the trust property and made use of it for his personal benefit (*Bahin v Hughes* (1886)) and where the trustee is also a beneficiary (*Chillingworth v Chambers* (1896)). Reference may also be made to the potential liability of a trustee who retires: first, for a breach of trust committed while he was a trustee; and, second, for breach of trust committed by his successors, if the retirement was designed to facilitate such a breach (*Head v Gould* (1898)). The **Trustee Act 2000** has, at last, brought some clarity and certainty to this area of the law.

10 The Office of Trustee and its Powers and Duties

INTRODUCTION

This chapter represents something of a 'sweeping up' of several issues that have not been dealt with so far. Necessarily, in the subjects considered in previous chapters, much has been said about the responsibilities of trustees, their duties towards the beneficiaries and the powers they enjoy in respect of the trust property. Many of these responsibilities are of a general nature – such as the duty to respect the terms of the trust and the power to choose beneficiaries under a discretionary trust – and they should not be forgotten in any general discussion of the nature of trusteeship and the extent of the trustee's powers and duties. In particular, in Chapter 6, we examined the trustee's duty not to make a profit from the trust and this forms an integral part of any discussion of trustee's duties. Thus, it must not be thought that the specific matters considered in this chapter are the only attributes of trusteeship; nor, indeed, should it be assumed that there is any essential thread that ties together the matters dealt with below in a way that excludes consideration of other issues.

The questions considered in this chapter cover several areas: first, the trustee's duty not to delegate any of his essential responsibilities under the trust; second, the appointment and removal of trustees; third, the trustee's power of maintenance and advancement; fourth, the trustee's power of investment; and, fifth, the variation of trusts, being the extent to which the duty to carry out the terms of the trust as originally conceived can be altered by application to the court.

The duty not to delegate is another example of the powerful nature of the trust obligation. It is for the trustee to discharge his specific duties and to exercise any discretionary powers. Any unauthorised delegation of these responsibilities is itself a breach of trust. Indeed, even if a trustee legitimately delegates some administrative function connected with the trust (such as the purchase of shares), that trustee still may be liable for breach of trust even though the act which gives rise to the breach was committed by the person to whom the task was entrusted. Second, although the appointment and removal of trustees may seem a technical matter, it is of considerable practical importance. Trustees die, retire or simply desire to have nothing more to do with the trust and it is imperative that the good administration of the trust fund does not suffer because of a lack of new or suitably qualified trustees. The relevant principles are to be found primarily in statute, albeit supplemented by case law. Third the power of maintenance and advancement refers to an attribute enjoyed by trustees of certain kinds of trust. In outline, such powers allow the trustee either to use the income from trust property for the benefit of an infant beneficiary before the infant is actually entitled to it (power of maintenance) or to pay a proportion of the trust's capital sum to a potential beneficiary before he or she becomes absolutely entitled to it (power of advancement). These powers may be either expressly included in the trust instrument or implied under ss 31 and 32 of the **Trustee Act 1925**. Fourth, the investment of trust property is one of the most important of the trustees' responsibilities, for it ensures that the trust fund generates the maximum benefit for all the beneficiaries. Consequently, it is vital that the trustees invest the capital monies lawfully, securely and competently, bearing in mind the need to provide a good income for those immediately entitled and to preserve the capital value of the fund for those entitled in remainder. Most professionally drafted trusts include express powers of investment but a trustee may also take advantage of the provisions of the **Trustee Act 2000**. Finally, the court's power to sanction a change in the nature or extent of the powers and duties of a trustee (and, indeed, other aspects of the trust) falls within the general law on variation of trusts. As we shall see, this jurisdiction is both inherent and statutory although, because it often involves amending the settlor's or testator's original intentions, the court exercises its power with considerable care and in limited circumstances only. This is particularly so where it is not only the trustees' powers and duties that may be varied but also the nature and extent of the beneficiaries' equitable interests.

QUESTION 35

Explain the circumstances when a court may sanction a variation of the terms of a trust.

Aim Higher

It is important to appreciate that in this type of question the student takes a broad view of the various administrative and dispositive provisions that exist to vary the terms of the trust. A detailed examination of the principles under the **Variation of Trusts Act 1958** alone is not advisable.

How to Read this Question

This essay question requires you to collect and comment on the occasions when the trustees may seek approval to depart from the terms of the trust. The departure may be justified both administratively and dispositively under the inherent jurisdiction of the court or by statute

How to Answer this Question

In answer to this question you are required to state the justification to vary the terms of the trust and the position where the beneficiary's consent may not be obtained. The limitations regarding the inherent jurisdiction of the court are required to be noted before embarking on the various statutory provisions authorising transactions for the benefit of the trust.

Up for Debate

The nature of 'benefits' within the **Variation of Trusts Act 1958** was reviewed by the Court of Appeal in *Goulding v James* (1997) and noted by P Luxton, 'Variation of trusts: settlor's intention and the consent principle in *Saunders v Vautier*' (1997) 60 MLR 719. It is recommended that you read Mummery LJ's judgment before the article.

Answer Plan

- ❖ The need for a power to vary trusts.
- ❖ Intervention of the court where consents cannot be obtained.
- ❖ Inherent jurisdiction of the court.
- ❖ **Section 57** of the **Trustee Act 1925**.
- ❖ **Section 53** of the **Trustee Act 1925**.
- ❖ **Section 64** of the **Settled Land Act 1925**.
- ❖ **Variation of Trusts Act 1958**.

Answer Structure

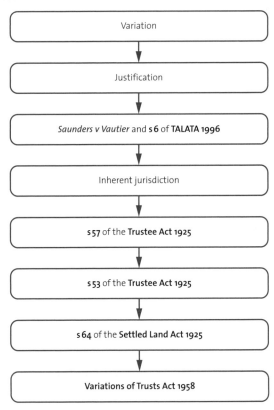

This diagram lists the various tests by the courts and statutes in order to modify the terms of the trust.

ANSWER

It is intrinsic in the nature of a trust that the trustees are under an obligation to carry out the terms of the trust according to the trust instrument, as modified or superseded by the general law. However, there may be many reasons why the details of the trust, the powers and duties of the trustees, or even the nature and extent of the beneficiaries' interests as originally specified, prove impossible to implement in practice. Likewise, the testator or settlor cannot be expected to foresee all possible future contingencies and no amount of expansive or open-ended drafting can hope to cover all possibilities. Therefore there must be some method by which the terms of a trust may be varied, in detail and in substance.[1] Today, the great majority of proposed variations of trust arise because of a desire to minimise the tax liabilities of the trust (see *Re Weston* (1969)), although applications to vary can have other, more altruistic motives, such as a desire to protect the trust property from wayward beneficiaries (*Hambro v Duke of Marlborough* (1994)).

As a matter of principle, it is open to all of the beneficiaries under a trust, providing they are of full age and capacity, to consent to any proposed reordering of the trust (*Saunders v Vautier* (1841) and related powers under **s6** of the **Trusts of Land and Appointment of Trustees Act (TOLATA) 1996**).[2] However, many of the trusts where a variation would be most beneficial are precisely those where the beneficiaries are either unwilling or unable to consent – for example, because they are infants or members of a hypothetical class, such as future children. In these cases, a variation of the terms of the trust can be achieved only with the aid of the court exercising its inherent or statutory jurisdiction.

The court's inherent jurisdiction to order a variation of trust on the application of either the trustees or interested beneficiaries was examined in detail by the House of Lords in *Chapman v Chapman* (1954). Effectively, this decision limited the court's power to approve a variation in cases of genuine emergency or necessity caused by unforeseen events which the proposed transaction is designed to remedy, see *Re New* (1910).[3] Such was the concern at the restrictive nature of the inherent jurisdiction revealed in *Chapman* and the limited nature of the existing statutory jurisdiction, that the Law Reform Committee proposed the enactment of a general statute granting the court a greater jurisdiction to authorise variation of trusts. The result was the **Variation of Trusts Act 1958**.

Before considering the **Variation of Trusts Act (VTA) 1958** in detail, brief mention should be made of three other forms of statutory jurisdiction to vary trusts. Under **s57(1)** of the **Trustee Act 1925**, the court is given the jurisdiction to vary the powers of the trustees so as to enable them to achieve transactions connected with the administration of the trust that would otherwise be impermissible. Importantly, this jurisdiction is limited to varying the *administrative* powers of the trustees (such as the power of investment) and does not enable the court to sanction a change in the nature or extent of the beneficiaries' equitable interests (*Re Downshire* (1953); *Mason v Fairbrother* (1983)). Second, the court has a limited jurisdiction to

---

1   The justification in order to modify the terms of the trust.
2   Adjustment of the terms under general principles of law.
3   Justification for the **VTA 1958**.

authorise certain otherwise impermissible transactions under **s 53** of the **Trustee Act 1925** in cases where this is necessary to provide for 'the maintenance, education or benefit' of any infant beneficially entitled to trust property (*Re Gower* (1934)), and this can include making the trust more tax efficient (*Re Meux* (1958)). Third, and of real significance, **s 64** of the **Settled Land Act 1925** gives the court power to authorise the tenant for life to undertake any transaction affecting settled land which 'in the opinion of the court would be for the benefit of the settled land, or any part thereof'. Obviously, this jurisdiction applies only to land within a settlement, and no new settlements may be created after 1 January 1997 (**s 7** of **TOLATA**), but it does permit the court to vary both the administrative provisions of the trust and the beneficial entitlements of the equitable owners (*Re Downshire* (1953)). Indeed, as *Hambro v Duke of Marlborough* (1994) illustrates, **s 64** may be used to alter the beneficial entitlements of an equitable owner against his wishes and may even result in the transfer of the land to completely new trusts (see, also, *Raikes v Lygon* (1988)).[4]

The **Variation of Trusts Act 1958** also allows changes to be made to both the administrative powers of trustees and the beneficial interests of the equitable owners, although the court's jurisdiction under this statute is of a general and wide-ranging nature and was entirely novel (*Re Steed* (1960)). However, the Act does not simply empower the court to authorise any variation to the terms of a trust as it thinks fit. Rather, the Act builds upon the *Saunders v Vautier* principle that all of the beneficiaries, if of full age and capacity, can consent to a variation of their trust. Thus, under **s 1**, the court is empowered to give its consent to a variation or arrangement of the trust on behalf of any of four classes of person who are incapable of consenting for themselves. These are:

(a)   infants with a vested or contingent interest (**s 1(1)(a)**);
(b)   persons who may become entitled to an interest as being a member of a specified class on the happening of a future event, except if that person would be a member of the class if the future event happened on the date of application to the court (**s 1(1)(b)**);
(c)   persons unborn (**s 1(1)(c)**); and
(d)   persons with an interest under a discretionary trust arising in consequence of a protective trust, where the interest of the principal beneficiary has not failed (**s 1(1)(d)**).

Although these provisions appear complicated (and **s 1(1)(b)** has caused difficulties – see *Knocker v Youle* (1986)), the essential point is that the court will consent for these people (who may be adults or infants respectively) but may only do so if it is satisfied (for classes (a), (b) and (c)) that the variation is for those persons' benefit. Moreover, although the 'benefit' will usually be financial in the form of fiscal advantages (*Re Sainsbury* (1967); *Re Robertson* (1960)), the court can consent to a variation that is of moral or social benefit to the beneficiaries (*Re Weston* (1969); *Re CL* (1969)), and, in exceptional circumstances, this benefit can outweigh any financial disadvantage caused by the variation (*Re Holt* (1969)). In *D (a child) v O* (2004), the court accepted jurisdiction under the **VTA 1958** to increase the amount subject to the statutory power of advancement under **s 32** of the **Trustee Act 1925**. Likewise, the court will consider the proposed scheme as a whole and may even consent to a variation that contradicts the settlor's original intentions (*Re Remnant* (1970); but see, *contra, Re Steed*

....

4   Other forms of variation without resort to the **VTA 1958**.

(1960)). There is some doubt, however, whether a completely new scheme which undermines the essential basis of the trust can amount to a 'variation' or 'arrangement' that the court could approve, see *Re T* (1964), contrast *Re Ball* (1968).

Common Pitfalls

Case law is important when discussing the **Variation of Trusts Act** as it adds much-needed life to the bare bones of the statute. A similar question could ask the student to discuss the meaning of 'benefit' under the **VTA** when, obviously, considerable case law should be cited.

QUESTION 36

David is a solicitor to a trust. The trustees are Margaret and Norman and the beneficiaries Edward and Francis. The trust instrument contains a clause excluding the trustees from liability for any loss or damage to the income or capital of the fund 'unless such loss or damage shall be caused by their own actual fraud'. The assets of the trust included a painting which David wished to buy. David informed the trustees of his wish and, upon David's suggestion, the trustees approached a valuer, Tony, from whom they sought a valuation of the painting. David was aware that Tony had previously been convicted of an offence involving fraud but did not reveal that fact to the trustees. The trustees themselves made no inquiry as to Tony's character and merely accepted David's nomination of him.

Having been told by David of his wish to buy the painting, Tony puts its value at £100,000, approximately one half of its true market value, and David bought it from the trustees at that price. He has just sold it for £210,000.

▶ Discuss the possible liabilities of Margaret, Norman, David and Tony to the beneficiaries.

How to Read this Question

This problem question requires you to deal with the liabilities of express trustees, Margaret and Norman and third parties to the trust, David, the solicitor and Tony, a valuer. In addition you are required to consider the validity of an exclusion clause.

How to Answer this Question

In answering this question you are required to consider the duty of care imposed on express trustees, the degree of protection from liability in respect of the exclusion clause, the nature of fiduciary duties and the liability of strangers for knowingly receiving trust property and dishonest assistance in a fraudulent breach of trust (accessory liability).

Up for Debate

The nature of fiduciary accountability was considered by J Edelman, 'When do fiduciary duties arise?' (2010) 126 LQR 302, and M Conaglen, 'Nature and function of fiduciary loyalty' (2005) 121 LQR 452, which are worthy of study.

Answer Plan

- ❖ Trustees' duty of care.
- ❖ Extent of exclusion clause.
- ❖ Fiduciary duties.
- ❖ Knowingly receiving property for one's benefit.
- ❖ Accessory liability.

Answer Structure

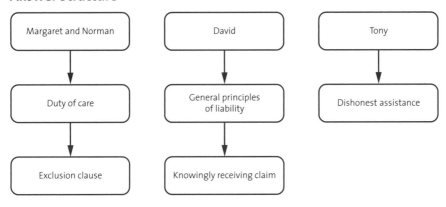

This diagram presents the possible claims that may be brought against the trustees and third parties.

ANSWER

Liability of Margaret and Norman

Margaret and Norman are the express trustees under the settlement. They are required to exercise a duty of care. The standard of care as laid down by s1 of the **Trustee Act 2000** is such care and skill as are reasonable in the circumstances:

(a) having regard to any special knowledge or experience he has or holds himself out as having; and

(b) if he acts as a trustee in the course of a business or profession, to any special knowledge or experience that it is reasonable to expect of a person acting in the course of that kind of business or profession.[5]

Thus, the section has created an objective/subjective test of the standard of care required from the trustees. The minimum degree of care and skill expected from a trustee is to be determined purely objectively by the court. But this standard of care may be increased by reference to the trustees' special knowledge or experience acquired personally or held out by them. **Schedule 1** to the **Trustee Act 2000** lists the occasions when the duty of care arises. This includes occasions when trustees enter into arrangements in order to dele-

5 Factors taken into consideration to determine whether the duty of care was complied with.

gate functions to agents, nominees and custodians as well as the review of their actions. On the facts of the problem, the trustees were aware that David, a fiduciary to the trust, wished to purchase the trust property, a sale was made to David, the trustees relied on David's recommendation of a valuer, Tony, and the trustees made no inquiries as to Tony's character; Tony turns out to have had a previous conviction for a crime involving fraud. Did the trustees review the actions of the agent, Tony, with any degree of care? These factors are strong indications that the trustees may not have exercised the appropriate degree of care necessary in the execution of their office.[6]

However, the trustees may be entitled to rely on the exclusion clause that exists in the trust instrument. Assuming that the clause had been validly inserted in the instrument, the issue concerns the extent to which such a clause may protect the trustees from a claim for breach of trust. Such clauses are not, without more, void on public policy grounds. Moreover, provided the clause does not purport to exclude the basic minimum duties of the trustees, it may not be construed as being void for repugnancy to the trust.[7] Some of the minimum duties which may not be excluded are the duties of honesty, good faith and acting for the benefit of the beneficiaries: see *Armitage v Nurse* (1997). In this case the court decided that the expression 'actual fraud' conjures up the notion of dishonesty and is not capable of protecting trustees. In the problem, breach of duties owing to actual fraud is not excluded by virtue of the clause, for such breach is expressly inserted in the proviso. In effect, the settlor intended to protect the trustees from breaches owing to 'constructive fraud' or breaches of fiduciary duties. On this basis the clause may be sufficient to protect the trustees from a claim by the beneficiaries.

David's Liability

First, David may not be able to claim protection from the exclusion clause, even as a constructive trustee. The clause is intended to protect express trustees and in any event there may be actual fraud involved in David's conduct.

In order to establish the liability of David, the beneficiaries are required to establish the following three cumulative propositions:

(a) the defendant holds a fiduciary position towards the claimant; and
(b) the defendant obtained a benefit; and
(c) a causal connection exists between the relationship and the benefit.[8]

A fiduciary is an individual who is aware that his judgment and confidence are relied on, and have been relied on, by the claimant, see *Bristol and West Building Society v Mothew* (1996), an overriding duty of loyalty is expected from him. In *Boardman v Phipps* (1967), a solicitor to a trust was treated as a fiduciary. In like circumstances, David is a solicitor to the trust and would be treated as a fiduciary.

6 Duty of care imposed on trustees.
7 Test to determine the validity of the exclusion clause.
8 Elements of liability of a fiduciary.

Has David obtained a benefit? This is a question of fact and the issue seems clear that he obtained a benefit, namely a profit of £110,000. Alternatively, he had obtained trust property, namely the painting valued at £200,000 approximately. Did he obtain this benefit as a result of his fiduciary relationship to the trust? Again, this is a question of fact. David informed the trustees of his desire to purchase the painting, he recommended a valuer who was unsuitable to give an independent valuation of the chattel, he failed to disclose material facts to the trustees. The cumulative effect of these facts suggests that David was in breach of his fiduciary duties to the beneficiaries.

There is an additional basis of liability as David purchased the trust property – has he knowingly received trust property for his own use? The basis of liability under this head is that a stranger who knows that a fund is trust property, transferred to him in breach of trust, cannot take control of the property for his own benefit, but is subject to the claims of the trust. He is not a bona fide transferee of the legal estate for value without notice. The elements of the cause of action were stated by Hoffmann LJ in *El Ajou v Dollar Land Holdings plc* (1994). These are that the claimant is required to prove first, a disposal of his assets in breach of fiduciary duties; second, the beneficial receipt of the assets or their traceable proceeds by the defendant; and, third, knowledge on the part of the defendant that the assets are traceable to a breach of fiduciary duty. The types of knowledge for these purposes were laid down in *Re Baden Delvaux* (1983) as encompassing all types of knowledge, including constructive knowledge.[9]

Alternatively, Megarry VC in *Re Montagu's Settlement* (1987) reviewed the basis of liability under this head and decided that the test is 'want of probity' which requires subjective knowledge of wrongdoing on the part of David. This view was affirmed by the Court of Appeal in *BCCI v Akindele* (2000) where Nourse LJ declared that the categories of knowledge are best forgotten and the test of liability is whether it would be unconscionable for David to retain the property. This is a question of law for the courts to decide. On the facts of the problem it is clear that David is aware that the painting is trust property transferred to him in breach of trust. He will therefore become a constructive trustee. As David has sold the painting to a third party, possibly a bona fide transferee of the legal estate for value without notice, the remedy available to the beneficiaries is to recover the profit from David.

Tony's Liability

Tony's liability may be based on the fact that he was an accessory in the breach of trust or dishonestly assisting in a fraudulent breach of trust. The liability here was stated in the classic case of *Royal Brunei Airlines v Tan* (1995) as fault based and involving a duty to account. Assistance involves any act (including an omission when there is a duty to act) effected by another which enables the defendant to commit a dishonest breach of trust.[10] In *Brinks Ltd v Abu-Saleh (No 3)* (1995), it was decided that a defendant is required to lend assistance in the knowledge of, or belief in, the existence of the trust, and the knowledge

---

9 Liability for knowingly receiving trust property.
10 Tony's liability as an accessory.

that his assistance will facilitate the breach of trust. Tony was introduced to the trustees by David in order to value the trust asset and significantly undervalued the painting. It is a question of fact whether this was done dishonestly, negligently or innocently. The test of dishonesty was stated by reference to the *Twinsectra* (2002)/*Eurotrust* (2006)/*Abacha* (2006)/ *Starglade* (2010) decisions as involving an objective standard but with a subjective element. On the facts of the problem it would appear that Tony was aware that he was undervaluing the property with a view to assisting David in acquiring the same at an undervalue. It would seem that the test of dishonesty is satisfied and he will become liable for a breach.

The final point concerns Tony's status. Millett LJ in *Paragon Finance v Thakerar* (1999) opined that the liability of an accessory is strictly not as a constructive trustee because he does not acquire the trust property. His liability is to account to the beneficiaries for any benefits received.

Prior to the **Judicature Acts 1873/75** the principles of equity evolved to redress the gaps created by the rigid application of principles of common law. The theoretical justification of equity's intervention was based on principles of natural justice, fairness and morality. This was apparent by reference to the equitable maxims. These are a set of principles which illustrate the way equity was applied. Following the nineteenth statutory reforms the creative nature of equity had subsided into structured principles which developed the law on a more consistent basis.

Questions on equity, as distinct from trusts, are not covered in some examinations and, if they are, they tend to be set on selected areas. You need to check with your tutor as to whether this aspect of the syllabus warrants your preparation for exams. This chapter puts together a selection of questions on equitable concepts.

QUESTION 37

'The guidelines laid down in the *American Cyanamid* case were designed to achieve more certainty in the law as well as re-asserting judicial discretion.'

▶ **Discuss.**

How to Read this Question

This question requires you to evaluate the contributions made by the 'sea-change' decision of *American Cyanamid* to the law of interim injunctions.

How to Answer this Question

In answering this question you are required to deal with the following issues:

- ❖ Definition of interim injunctions.
- ❖ The nature of the test applied by the courts before *Cyanamid*.
- ❖ The guidelines introduced by Lord Diplock in *Cyanamid*.
- ❖ Exceptions or limitations to *Cyanamid* guidelines.
- ❖ Perception of the guidelines in subsequent case law.

Up for Debate

The *Cyanamid* case has been heralded in some quarters as involving a significant improvement in the law on interim injunctions whereas the critics would argue that the increase in the exceptions to the rule indicate that it is doubtful whether Lord Diplock's objectives have been achieved. This theme was explored by A Keay, 'Whither American Cyanamid? Interim injunctions in the 21st century' (2004) CJQ 132.

Applying the law

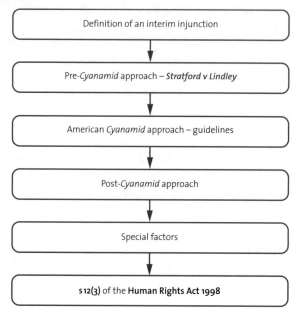

Definition of an interim injunction

Pre-*Cyanamid* approach – *Stratford v Lindley*

American *Cyanamid* approach – guidelines

Post-*Cyanamid* approach

Special factors

s 12(3) of the **Human Rights Act 1998**

This diagram outlines the main steps in the development of interim injunctions

ANSWER

An interim injunction is one made after the commencement of the proceedings but prior to the final determination of the court. The objective in obtaining such an injunction is to ensure that the status quo of the parties is maintained and that the claimant does not suffer additional loss before the substantive action is determined by the court.

The pre-*Cyanamid* approach of the courts to the grant of an interim injunction required the claimant to make out a strong prima facie case that he would succeed at the main trial, that damages would be an inadequate remedy and the balance of convenience favours the grant. This was the approach taken by the House of Lords in *Stratford v Lindley* (1965) and *Hoffman- La Roche v Secretary of State for Trade and Industry* (1975). In *Hubbard v Vosper* (1972), Lord Denning stated that the remedy of an injunction should remain flexible and that the court should take into account all the circumstances of the case.

In *American Cyanamid Co v Ethicon Ltd* (1975), the House of Lords, led by Lord Diplock, reviewed the principles regarding the grant of interim injunctions and was concerned that decisions at the interim stage were based, necessarily, on affidavit evidence alone and was not tested by cross-examination. It would be unrealistic to require the judge hearing the application for an interim injunction to spend the same time on the issue as the trial judge at the final hearing. Lord Diplock laid down guidelines that are required to be considered before the issue of an interim injunction. These are:

(1) There is a serious question to be tried, i.e. the claim is not frivolous or vexatious; whether damages would provide an adequate remedy for the claimant and is the defendant able to pay such sum? If the answer is yes the injunction would not be granted.

(2) Whether the undertaking as to damages provided by the claimant constitute adequate protection for the defendant and will the claimant be able to honour it? If the answer is yes, then the possibility of the defendant's success at the trial is no bar to the grant of the injunction.

(3) If there is doubt as to the adequacy of the remedy of damages, the court may consider the general balance of convenience. The factors that are taken into consideration vary from case to case. If the factors appear to be even balanced the court will preserve the status quo; where the court, having considered all of the above, is still unable to arrive at a decision it can take into account the relative strength of the parties' cases. The court should not embark on anything resembling a trial for the only evidence of the facts is in affidavit format. However where the strength of one party's case is disproportionate to the other this may be taken into account.

(4) Special factors may be taken into consideration in order to determine the balance of convenience. It does not give the court a licence to disregard the *Cyanamid* principles.

Clearly the central issue in *Cyanamid* is the balance of convenience as opposed to the strength of each party's case which comes lower down the order of issues to be considered. The policy was to maintain a balance between the parties so that the substantive matter may be tried at a later date.

The *Cyanamid* principles received a mixed response from the courts, although the bulk of the cases have endorsed the principles, there is a substantial number of cases that have sought to impose qualifications and create exceptions on the guidelines. In *Fellowes v Fisher* (1976), Lord Denning in the Court of Appeal found it impossible to reconcile the principles in *Cyanamid* with those laid down in *Stratford v Lindley* and felt that the old approach worked well. He had continued to consider the merits of the case as the central issue by treating these as 'special factors' that were separate from the 'balance of convenience' issue. Some courts, while endorsing the *Cyanamid* principles, have voiced a concern that there are cases where justice and the needs of the parties dictate a fuller hearing similar to that which existed before *Cyanamid*. Many judges have effectively created exceptions, expressly or impliedly, in order to navigate away from the principles in *Cyanamid*. In *NWL v Woods* (1979), the House of Lords recognised that the interim determination would be decisive and the matter would not go to a final hearing. In *Cambridge Nutrition Ltd v BBC* (1990), the Court of

Appeal recognised an exception in respect of the transmission of a television programme where time was all important. In similar vein are applications for mandatory injunctions, matters concerning industrial disputes, *AG v Punch Ltd* (2003). In some cases the courts have sought to avoid the *Cyanamid* principles by way of interpretation. In *R v Secretary of State for Transport, Ex p Factortame* (1990), the court decided that the case involved serious questions to be tried and points of law, thus avoiding *Cyanamid*.

In *Series 5 Software Ltd v Clarke* (1996), Laddie J suggested that Lord Diplock in *American Cyanamid* did not intend to exclude consideration of the relative strength of the parties' cases in most applications for interim injunctions. He suggested that what was intended was to avoid having to resolve difficult issues of fact or law on an interim application. The consideration of the relative strength of the parties' cases is thus not a matter of last resort but should be avoided in cases involving difficult disputes of fact or law.

The granting of interim injunctions has been affected primarily in the area of freedom of expression by the introduction of the **Human Rights Act 1998**. **Section 12(3)** enacts that no such relief (affecting the exercise of the right to freedom of expression) is to be granted so as to restrain the publication before trial *unless the court is satisfied that the applicant is likely to establish that publication should be allowed.* **Art 8** of the Convention involves the right to private or family life and **Art 10** declares the right to freedom of expression. In the overwhelming majority of cases the courts have declared that in the context of **s 12(3)** the *Cyanamid* principles are to be put on one side in favour of a consideration of the strength of each party's case. In *Douglas v Hello Ltd* (2001), the Court of Appeal stated that it was incumbent on the judge to consider the merits of the case. In *Cream Holdings v Banerjee* (2004), the House of Lords decided that the applicants had failed to show that they were more likely than not to succeed at trial in preventing the publication of the information.

QUESTION 38

'The two streams of jurisdiction (law and equity) though they run in the same channel run side by side and do not mingle their waters' W Ashburner, *Principles of Equity*, 1933, Butterworth & Co.

▶ Discuss.

How to Read this Question

This essay question requires you to examine the 'fusion' debate. The issue is whether **the Judicature Acts 1873/75** has fused the principles of law and equity or simply achieved an integration of the administration of law and equity?

How to Answer this Question

In answering this question you should define the meaning of the expression 'fusion' in this context. Briefly illustrate the dual system of law and equity before the **Judicature Acts** and consider the extent to which the two systems of rules have been integrated by reference to decided cases.

Up for Debate

This issue has generated a great deal of interest in English and Commonwealth juris-dictions. Prominent articles on the subject include A Mason, 'The place of equity and equitable remedies in the contemporary common law world' (1994) LQR 238 and J Martin, 'Fusion, fallacy and confusion: a comparative study' (1994) Conv. 13.

Applying the law

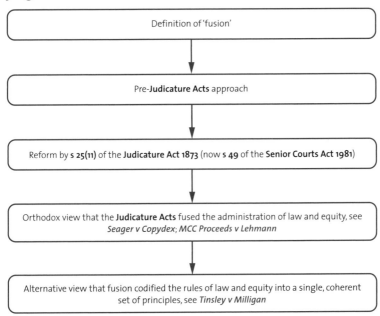

Definition of 'fusion'

Pre-**Judicature Acts** approach

Reform by s 25(11) of the **Judicature Act 1873** (now s 49 of the **Senior Courts Act 1981**)

Orthodox view that the **Judicature Acts** fused the administration of law and equity, see *Seager v Copydex*; *MCC Proceeds v Lehmann*

Alternative view that fusion codified the rules of law and equity into a single, coherent set of principles, see *Tinsley v Milligan*

This diagram sketches out the salient features in the 'fusion' debate.

ANSWER

The first issue to raise is the meaning of the word, 'fusion' in this context. The orthodox view is that the administration of law and equity has been fused by the **Judicature Acts** leaving law and equity free to develop by reference to the principles that existed before 1873/75. In short, no new cause of action or remedy has been created since the **Judicature Acts**. This is the view of Ashburner and the majority of judges and academics and will be explored shortly. An alternative meaning of the concept is that since the **Judicature Acts** the distinctions between legal and equitable estates or interests and remedies no longer exist. This view, which is difficult to support, is that the nineteenth century statutes were codifying Acts of Parliament that integrated both systems of rules into one. This may account for some decisions that cannot be explained by reference to law or equity but by reference to a set of new principles.

Prior to the introduction of the **Judicature Acts** the courts at law and equity applied separate rules in determining disputes. The most significant feature of this division was the refusal of the courts of law to recognise equitable rights and interests as sufficient to entitle the holder to relief at law. Unsuccessful attempts were made by beneficiaries in actions in debt brought in the common law courts to recover monies from their trustees. Before 1873/75 the correct procedure in these cases was for the beneficiaries to bring actions for account in the Court of Chancery.

In order to rectify the injustice of the separate courts system the **Judicature Acts 1873/75** were passed. **Section 25(11)** (now the **Senior Courts Act 1981, s 49**) enacted that in all matters 'of conflict or variance between the rules of law and equity with reference to the same matter, the rules of equity shall prevail'. There was nothing in the Act to indicate that this provision attempted to codify law and equity and create a new body of rules which did not owe its origin to the principles that existed before 1873. Thus, it is arguable that the Acts merely fused the administration of law and equity.

However there are occasions when the court may award damages (a common law remedy) for breach of an equitable obligation. This conclusion, in itself, is not of major significance but what is significant is the reasoning in the court to the effect that the remedy was available irrespective of the old jurisdiction that was involved. This was the approach of the Court of Appeal in *Seager v Copydex Ltd* (1967). The claim was in respect of breach of confidence in marketing a carpet grip belonging to the claimants. Despite the nature of the equitable claim the court awarded damages. It is arguable that this remedy was available under the **Chancery Amendment Act 1858 (Lord Cairns Act)**. But Lord Denning acted on the assumption that the **Judicature Acts** permitted remedies available in one court but not the other irrespective of the jurisdiction concerned. In *Re Pryce* (1917), the issue was whether the court would award damages at the instance of a third party volunteer for breach of a voluntary covenant to create a trust. Eve J reasoned that since damages may not be awarded at law, likewise damages would not be awarded in equity. If Eve J is correct this would mean that the **Judicature Acts** have altered the substantive law by depriving a claimant covenantee from enforcing a voluntary covenant at law. But where valuable consideration has been provided by the claimant, even though the transaction has not been reduced in the form required by law, the claim may be upheld in equity, see *Walsh v Lonsdale* (1882). Likewise, an equitable assignment for valuable consideration but does not comply with the provisions of **s 136** of the **Law of Property Act 1925**, may be enforceable in the same way as under the pre-1873 Act, see *Brandt's Sons & Co v Dunlop Rubber Ltd* (1905).

The better view is that although the two systems operate closely they are not fused. In appropriate cases it is still necessary to consider the origin of the jurisdiction underlying the claim or defence. In *MCC Proceeds v Lehman Brothers International* (1998), the issue was whether an equitable owner was capable of suing for conversion. The claim in conversion had its origins at law. It was decided that only the legal owner was capable of bringing such action. The court highlighted the distinctions between legal and equitable interests and decided that the **Judicature Acts** had not modified this rule. The Act introduced procedural improvements in the administration of law and equity. In *Swindle v Harrison* (1997), the court decided that common law damages was not available for breach of fiduciary duties.

However Lord Browne Wilkinson took a different view in the House of Lords decision *Tinsley v Milligan* (1994). The issue here was whether an equitable interest in real property may be asserted despite the existence of an element of illegality in contributing to the purchase of the property. The court allowed the equitable owner to succeed in her claim. Lord Browne Wilkinson said that the effect of fusion resulted in a single rule as to when an equitable owner may be entitled to enforce her interest acquired by an illegal transaction.

There have been many occasions in contemporary society requiring the rules of equity to be developed to meet the needs of society. This task has been achieved within the framework of equitable principles. In the event of a stranger to a trust knowingly receiving trust property for his own benefit in breach of trust the court may impose a personal liability on the defendant. The rationale as well as the specific elements of liability are the subjects of judicial and academic controversy. The remedy available is restitutionary. With regard to a stranger dishonestly assisting another in the commission of a fraudulent breach of trust, much of the law has been clarified by the Privy Council decision in *Royal Brunei Airlines v Tan* (1995). A further development of the law regarding rights of ownership of the family home has been achieved by the introduction of the remedial constructive trust in *Stack v Dowden* (2007) and *Jones v Kernott* (2011). With regard to the process of tracing in equity the requirement that the claimant establishes the existence of a fiduciary relationship relates back to the pre-**Judicature Acts**. Although today this may be considered to be an anachronism the courts have declared that it remains an integral requirement and cannot be modified except by statute, see *Westdeutsche Landesbank v Islington Borough Council* (1996).

In conclusion there is sufficient evidence to contend that the principles of law and equity have not been fused by the **Judicature Acts**. In contemporary society the principles of law and equity are not static and although the policy attributes its origin to pre-**Judicature** rules the details of such development may not be partial to either system.

QUESTION 39

'... in the field of equity, the length of the Chancellor's foot has been measured or is capable of measurement. This does not mean that equity is past childbearing; simply that its progeny must be legitimate – by precedent out of principle.' Per Bagnall J in *Cowcher v Cowcher* (1972).

▶ Evaluate this statement.

How to Read this Question

This essay question makes reference to the 'Chancellor's foot'. This is an expression that was used before the **Judicature Acts 1873/75** to describe the expansive power of equity in creating new rights and remedies. The question raises the issue as to whether in the post-**Judicature** period equity is still capable of development, albeit within limits.

How to Answer this Question

In answering this question it is necessary to indicate how creative the rules of equity were in the pre-**Judicature** period to such an extent that a commentator (John Selden) stated that the rules of equity varied with the length of the Chancellor's foot. The **Judicature Acts** were passed to fuse the administration of law and equity. However, it is necessary to demonstrate that, within limits, the rules of equity are still capable of development or refinement. The justification for acting within broad equitable principles achieves an element of certainty in the law which is desirable.

Up for Debate

The theme of this essay question has been the subject of some judicial and academic debate. An instructive article which sheds some light on the subject is A Mason, 'The place of equity and equitable remedies in the contemporary common law world' (1994) 110 LQR 238.

Answer Structure

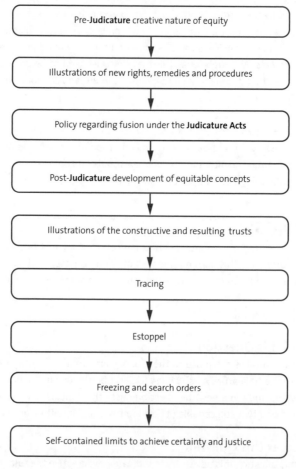

Pre-**Judicature** creative nature of equity

Illustrations of new rights, remedies and procedures

Policy regarding fusion under the **Judicature Acts**

Post-**Judicature** development of equitable concepts

Illustrations of the constructive and resulting trusts

Tracing

Estoppel

Freezing and search orders

Self-contained limits to achieve certainty and justice

This diagram highlights some of the main features in the structured development of equity.

ANSWER

The expression 'equity' has a variety of meanings that vary with the context in which it is used. First, it refers to the collection of rules created initially by the Lord Chancellor and subsequently by the Court of Chancery prior to the enactment of the **Judicature Acts 1873/75**. These rules were based on grounds of conscience, fairness and justice. The intervention by the Court of Chancery sought to deal with the proven limitations of the common law. Major contributions of equity in this context include the trust, partnerships, protection of the mortgagor against the mortgagee, the administration of estates of deceased persons, protection of vulnerable persons such as infants and those suffering from mental disability, bankruptcy law to mention a few. Second, the term refers to the equitable interest in property, i.e. a right of ownership not recognised by the common law before the **Judicature Acts**. Third, the expression refers to 'mere equities'. This is a procedural right which is ancillary to some right of property such as the right to have a document rectified or a right to have a transaction set aside for undue influence. The contribution of equity to the enrichment of the law may be summarised as the exclusive jurisdiction (creating new rights such as trusts), concurrent jurisdiction (creating new remedies such as injunctions, specific performance etc.) and the auxiliary jurisdiction (creating new procedures such as the subpoena, discoveries, interrogatories etc.). Referring to the question, the reference to 'equity' includes these three meanings. The reference to the 'Chancellor's foot' is an expression used by a commentator, Selden, to describe the unabashed approach of the Court of Chancery to judge each case according to the tenets of justice, conscience and fairness without regard to binding precedent. This approach, before the **Judicature** period, resulted in a great deal of uncertainty as to the equitable rulings and, in a broader sense, injustice to some litigants.

The reference in the question to 'childbearing' refers to the notion that post-**Judicature** equity is still capable of being developed or refined but by a systematic method in the context of overriding equitable principles. Some of these developments have been made in the context of the constructive trust, resulting trust, tracing, estoppel and special interim injunctions (freezing and search orders) to name a few.

Equity's creativity may be demonstrated in the field of the constructive trust. In the context of proprietary rights in the family home, the courts have moved away from the presumptions of resulting trust and advancement to the realistic principles of the resulting and constructive trust, see *Pettitt v Pettitt* (1970), *Gissing v Gissing* (1971) and *Lloyds Bank v Rossett* (1990) before finally settling on the remedial constructive trust principles laid down in *Stack v Dowden* (2007) and *Jones v Kernott* (2011). Prior to this journey the courts had advocated an unrestricted 'new model' constructive trust illustrated by *Eves v Eves* (1975) which had the undesirable effect of creating a great deal of volatility in this area.

Another area of development is with regard to the liability of a third party to the beneficiary for knowingly receiving trust property for his own benefit and dishonestly assisting another in a fraudulent scheme. The courts had frequently stated that the status of this liability is to account 'as a constructive trustee' but the better view is that the language of the constructive trust is misleading because liability is personal, not proprietary, see *Paragon Finance v Thakerar* (1991) and *Sinclair Investments v Versailles* (2011).

The resulting trust has also been a field for development by equity. The courts were justified in introducing the resulting trust to enhance the status of an unsecured lender to that of a beneficiary where a loan was made to promote a specific purpose. The funds did not become the general property of the recipient, see *Barclays Bank v Quistclose* (1970). Although the reasoning of Lord Wilberforce has been criticised the imposition of the trust has been welcomed in this context, see *Carreras Rothmans Ltd v Freeman Matthews Ltd* (1984) and *Re EVTR* (1987). On a different point, where the claimant transfers property with the intention of putting the property out of reach of his creditors, but subsequently repents and wishes to 'turn the clock back' and recover his property, was originally frustrated by the courts. The court originally applied the maxim, 'he who comes to equity must come with clean hands' and prevented the claimant from adducing evidence of his equitable interest, see *Tinker v Tinker* (1970). A significant development in this context is *Tinsley v Milligan* (1993), where the House of Lords decided that there is no inflexible rule to the effect that evidence of a fraudulent or unlawful purpose for a transfer of property is sufficient to prevent an equitable owner from recovering his property, if he does not rely on this purpose to support his claim.

The process of tracing in equity into a mixed fund held at a bank in which two or more innocent claimants are interested has been the source of some development. In this case the harsh and arbitrary principle in *Clayton's Case* (1816), may be avoided. The courts have recognised that the status of the claimants are in *pari passu* and they ought to share the loss proportionately rather than the winner takes all, see *Barlow Clowes v Vaughan* (1992) and *Commerzbank Aktiengesellschaft v IMB Morgan* (2004).

In the field of proprietary estoppel the modern approach is to broaden its scope and focus on the defendant's unconscionability rather than strict, rigid rules. In *Cobbe v Yeoman's Row Management Ltd* (2008), the House of Lords decided that a proprietary estoppel claim required clarity as to the terms of the representation and expectation of the interest in the property in question. In *Thorner v Major* (2009), the House of Lords decided that the test may be applied more flexibly in a domestic context.

In the latter part of the twentieth century the courts developed new forms of interim injunctions that may be regarded as formidable weapons in the litigation armoury. One of these was originally called the 'Mareva' injunction but which is now known as a freezing injunction. This type of injunction was designed to prevent a defendant from removing assets from the jurisdiction of the British courts (or dissipating assets within the jurisdiction) which, if not prohibited, may have the effect of defeating the whole purpose of litigation, see *Mareva Compania Naviera SA v International Bulkcarriers SA* (1975). During the same period the court developed another interim injunction originally called an 'Anton Piller' order, but now known as a 'search' order. The underlying principles were originally laid down in *Anton Piller KG v Manufacturing Processes Ltd* (1976), and are currently in statutory form in **s 7** of the **Civil Procedure Act 1997**.

In conclusion, in support of the statement by Bagnall J, the developments in equity noted above were all effected within the ambit of traditional equitable principles, as opposed to an unbridled, diverse collection of principles created by the courts.

QUESTION 40

What factors may the court take into consideration in deciding whether to exercise its discretion concerning an order for specific performance?

How to Read this Question

This essay question requires you to outline the circumstances when a defendant may successfully raise a defence to a claim for specific performance.

How to Answer this Question

In answering this question it is necessary to describe the nature of an order for specific performance and indicate that all equitable remedies are discretionary. It is at this stage that you may outline some of the occasions when the court refused to make an order for specific performance.

Up for Debate

This is a standard question that focuses on the limits to the order of specific performance and has been highlighted by C Harpum, 'Set-off, specific performance and relief against forfeiture' (1985) 44 CLJ 204.

Answer Structure

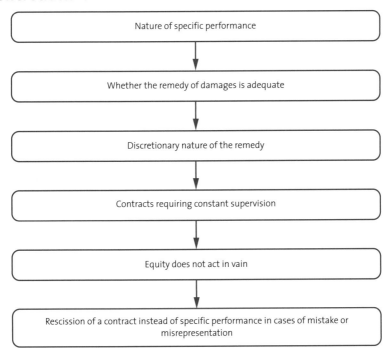

This diagram lists some of the factors that are considered before ordering specific performance.

ANSWER

The remedy of specific performance is an order of the court requiring the defendant to perform his part of the contract. It is an illustration of the concurrent jurisdiction of equity that was developed prior to the **Judicature Acts 1873/75**. The remedy operates *'in personam'*, i.e. against the defendant personally and will be a contempt of court if the defendant refuses to comply with the order without lawful excuse.

The remedy, like all equitable remedies, is discretionary in nature but there are some settled grounds on which the court will refuse to grant the order. The courts will take many factors into account when considering whether or not to grant a decree, including laches, the conduct of the claimant and the question of hardship to the defendant. In *Patel v Ali* (1984), it was held that, in considering the issue of hardship to the defendant, the court could take into account events which had occurred after the contract had been entered into, although this would be rare. In this case there was an unforeseen change in the defendant's circumstances subsequent to date of the contract for the sale of a house. The defendant, a young married woman with three young children contracted bone cancer resulting in amputation of her leg subsequent to date of contract. The defendant became dependent on assistance from family and friends living in the neighbourhood of the house contracted to be sold. The High Court decided that it would have inflicted hardship amounting to injustice on the defendant to order specific performance of the contract since that would have the effect of asking her to do what she had never bargained for, namely, to complete the sale after more than four years and after all the unforeseeable changes that had taken place during that period. Moreover, after the long period of delay (for which neither party was to blame) it would have been just and fair to leave the claimants to their remedy in damages. The court said that it could, in the exercise of its discretion in a proper case, refuse specific performance of such a contract on the ground of hardship suffered by the defendant subsequent to the date of the contract, even if the hardship was not caused by the claimant and did not relate to the subject matter of the contract. The court may also take into account the hardship that would be suffered by a third party in deciding whether to grant the decree of specific performance, see *Thames Guaranty Ltd v Campbell* (1984).

The discretionary nature of the remedy of specific performance was considered by the Court of Appeal in *Quadrant Visual Communications v Hutchinson Telephone (UK)* (1993), where the claimant did not come to court with 'clean hands' having failed to disclose to the defendant a material fact before entering the contract for which he was seeking specific performance.

If the claimant has defaulted in some way, for example, if he has failed to perform his part of the contract by the time specified, then the defendant may use the fact of the claimant's default in his defence. Except in specific circumstances, equity will not consider time to be of the essence of a contract. The exceptions have been clearly set out by the court in *British and Commonwealth Holdings v Quadrex Holdings* (1989), as occasions where the contract expressly so stipulate; or the circumstances of contract indicate that time is of the essence or where notice to complete has been given by the claimant.

In particular cases, such as those involving contracts which require supervision, other considerations may be relevant. It seems that the courts will view as one of degree the question of whether or not a contract requires continuous supervision. Even if continuous supervision of a contract should prove to be necessary, specific performance could still be granted provided that it is quite clear what the defendant is required to do. Thus, in *Beswick v Beswick* (1968), all the Law Lords thought it unimportant that the obligation under the contract was a continuing one. In *Co-Operative Insurance Society Ltd v Argyll Stores (Holdings) Ltd* (1997), the House of Lords reversed the Court of Appeal's decision and decided that the defendant would not be compelled to keep its supermarket open pursuant to a 'keep open' clause in the lease. One reason for this was because the court would not order specific performance of a contract requiring constant supervision.

It was obvious that the difficulties which the court would encounter in supervising performance would prevent it from enforcing contracts for personal services, see *Wolverhampton and Walsall Railway Co v London and North Western Railway* (1873). In addition, it was thought to be contrary to public policy to compel the parties to continue a working relationship where one of them was unwilling to do so. To grant an order for specific performance in such circumstances could be tantamount to turning the contracts of employment into contracts of slavery, see *Francesco v Barnum* (1890). In *Lumley v Wagner* (1852), the court refused to grant specific performance of a contract to sing at a theatre. Not all contracts for personal services present such difficulties. In *Hill v CA Parsons Ltd* (1971), an employee was dismissed after having refused to join the trade union at his place of employment where a closed shop was in operation. The court granted an interim injunction restraining the termination of his employment on the grounds that the **Industrial Relations Act 1971** (since repealed) would have come into force within a few weeks and would have given the employee protection in any event. Furthermore, the employer and employee retained mutual confidence in each other. Lord Denning noted that the decision in fact had the effect of granting specific performance of a contract of employment. In *Erskine McDonald Ltd v Eyles* (1921), the court decided that a breach of a copyright agreement offering the defendant, an authoress, a publishing contract to write her next three books subject to certain royalty terms, was specifically enforceable. In breach of this agreement the defendant attempted to sell her manuscripts to a rival publisher. The court decided that such agreements were not contracts to render personal services, but contracts to sell the products of the labour or industry of the contracting party.

As a general principle, specific performance will not be granted where it would be futile or impossible as 'equity does nothing in vain'. Thus, specific performance will not be ordered of a partnership agreement which is not for a fixed term as the partnership could be terminated anyway at will, see *Hercy v Birch* (1804).

Both mistake and misrepresentation may give one party the right to rescind the contract. They may also be used as a 'defence' to an action for specific performance as it seems that the court may be more willing to refuse a decree of specific performance than to grant rescission, see *Denny v Hancock* (1870).

QUESTION 41

'The decision whether or not a (search order) should be granted requires a balance to be struck between the plaintiff's need that the remedies allowed by the civil law for the breach of his rights should be attainable and the requirements of justice that a defendant should not be deprived of his property without being heard.' Per Scott J in *Columbia Pictures Incorporation v Robinson* (1986).

▶ Consider what safeguards exist to prevent abuse by a claimant in granting a search order.

How to Read this Question

This essay question requires you to identify and evaluate the pre-conditions before granting a search order

How to Answer this Question

It is necessary first to define a search order, second, to state the general rule in *Entinck v Carrington* and, third, to identify the relevant conditions that need to be satisfied before granting the order by reference to decided cases.

Up for Debate

It has been argued that the granting of a search order initially had been too often readily issued but the courts have subsequently changed its approach and applied strict requirements to avoid oppression, see M Dockray and H Laddie 'Piller problems' (1990) 106 LQR 601.

Applying the law

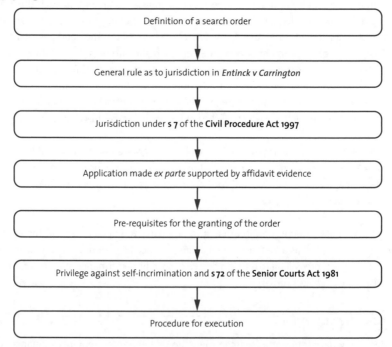

```
Definition of a search order
        ↓
General rule as to jurisdiction in Entinck v Carrington
        ↓
Jurisdiction under s 7 of the Civil Procedure Act 1997
        ↓
Application made ex parte supported by affidavit evidence
        ↓
Pre-requisites for the granting of the order
        ↓
Privilege against self-incrimination and s 72 of the Senior Courts Act 1981
        ↓
Procedure for execution
```

This diagram charts the main events in the history of the search order.

ANSWER

The 'search order' was originally called an Anton Piller order, a derivative from the case that is closely associated with the order namely, *Anton Piller v Manufacturing Processes Ltd* (1976). A search order is a form of mandatory interim injunction created to reduce the risks that, pending trial, the defendant does not dispose of any articles, including documents, that may be relevant to the claimant's action. More precisely it is an order, secured *ex parte*, authorising certain named persons to enter the defendant's premises for the purpose of inspecting, photographing and removing the objects specified in the order.

As far back as the eighteenth century the courts affirmed the constitutional right of the citizen to protect his property from official interference. This was achieved in *Entinck v Carrington* (1765). It was decided that the Secretary of State had no power at common law to issue general warrants for the arrest of those suspected of publishing seditious libels. Equally, at common law, the warrants may not authorise the search for, and seizure of, documents in the possession of the defendant. It was against this background that the courts in the twentieth century found a legal route to grant such orders. Initially this route involved a fiction that the defendant had consented to such search, see *Bhimji v Chatwani* (1991). It was in effect a search warrant in disguise. In *Anton Piller v Manufacturing Processes Ltd* the practice of granting such an order was approved by the Court of Appeal and in *Rank Film Distributors v Video Information Centre* (1982) the same was endorsed by the House of Lords. Today the practice has been endorsed in statutory form in **s 7** of the **Civil Procedure Act 1997**.

In *Anton Piller*, the Court of Appeal laid down the following pre-requisites for the granting of the order. These are:

❖ the claimant must have a strong prima facie case, the order may not be used as a fishing expedition;

❖ the claimant must show actual or potential damage of a very serious nature;

❖ there is clear evidence that the defendant has incriminating documents or things and that there is a real possibility of these documents or things being destroyed before an *inter partes* application could be made;

❖ the inspection on behalf of the claimant must do no real harm to the defendant or his case;

❖ the court will need to be satisfied that the claimant has the capacity to pay for any damages that may be ordered against him when the merits of the case are ultimately determined.

The application is made *ex parte* and supported by affidavit evidence with a form of the order attached. The court may reject, accept or amend the form in its discretion. Certain safeguards exist in the execution of the order. These were laid down by the court in *Universal Thermosensors Ltd v Hibben* (1992), and are now included in CPR 25. These are:

❖ that the order be served and supervised by a solicitor from a different firm from that acting for the claimant;

❖ that the solicitor supervising the search should be experienced and knowledgeable about the workings of search orders;

❖ that the supervising solicitor should explain in ordinary language the meaning and effect of the order to the defendant and his right to seek legal advice if done immediately;

❖ that the solicitor should prepare a written report on the execution of the order;

❖ that a copy of the report should be served on the defendant and that the report should be presented to the court at an *inter partes* hearing;

❖ that the orders should be served on weekdays during office hours in order to give the defendants the opportunity to obtain legal advice;

❖ that the party serving the order should include a woman if it is likely that a woman might be alone at the premises.

In the *Columbia Pictures* case, the court ruled that the claimant, having obtained the search order, should not act oppressively or abuse its power in the execution of the order. An order that allows the claimant's solicitors to take and retain all relevant documentary material and correspondence cannot be justified. The order is required to be proportionate. Once the claimant's solicitors have satisfied themselves what material exists and have had an opportunity to take copies thereof, the material ought to be returned to the owner, and should only be retained for a relatively short period for such purpose. It is inappropriate for seized material, the ownership of which is in dispute, such as alleged pirate tapes, to be retained by the claimant's solicitor pending trial. As soon as a solicitor for the defendant is on the record, the claimant's solicitor ought to deliver the material to the defendant's solicitor on his undertaking to keep it in safe custody and produce it, if required, in court.

Where these safeguards have been breached by either the claimant or his solicitor, the court may set aside the order. In the event of the order not being set aside, the court can award exemplary damages and the solicitor may be liable for contempt of court.

The effectiveness of the search order has been restricted by the application of the defendant's privilege against self-incrimination. The privilege is to the effect that no person is required to answer any question or produce a document in court proceedings where the information would incriminate him as to offences in contravention of the criminal law. In *Rank Film Distributors Ltd v Video Information Centre* (1982), the court upheld the defendant's claim to the privilege against self-incrimination in a case that involved breach of copyright. The standard form informs the defendant of this privilege. It should be noted that s 72 of the **Senior Courts Act 1981** restricts the privilege in cases involving passing off and/or cases relating to the infringement of intellectual property rights, see *Coca Cola Co v Gilbey* (1995). However, where the case falls outside the ambit of s 72, the defendant can rely on the privilege against self-incrimination. This would appear to be clear from the case of *Tate Access Floors Inc v Boswell* (1991), where the court stated that, in civil proceedings involving an allegation which could give rise to a criminal charge of conspiracy, the court could not make a search order since this would infringe the defendant's privilege against self-incrimination.

The court's jurisdiction to issue search orders was extended to occasions after judgment had been obtained where there was a risk of justice being thwarted by a defendant who was intent upon rendering any judgment nugatory, see *Distributori Automaci Italia v Holford General Trading* (1985).

In conclusion it is evident that today the courts are mindful of the draconian nature of search orders and will endeavour to ensure that the guidelines are followed and that such orders will not be granted, except in appropriate cases.

12 Pick and Mix Questions

It is sound examination technique to analyse the question and reflect on whether there are any additional substantial or incidental issues that need to be included in your examination answer. This selection of 'pick and mix' questions contains multiple issues for your benefit.

QUESTION 42

Alex and Bernard are trustees under the will of Klondyke, who died in 2012. Under the terms of the trust, the trustees are to hold various items of furniture, some family heirlooms and cash in Klondyke's deposit account on trust for Perky for life, thence absolutely for such of his children then living. In 2013, Alex approached James, a stockbroker, to seek his advice on the investment of the money, and although James was only recently authorised by the Stock Exchange, he confidently recommended several investments. Alex paid over half the trust monies to James in order to carry out the recommended investment policy after telling Bernard that this was 'purely a matter of form'. James invested the money as agreed but, due to his inexperience of high tech stocks, all the investments made a substantial loss. In response to James's further requests, Alex paid over the rest of the monies, this time failing to consult Bernard. Due to good fortune, the second batch of investments on old fashioned 'blue-chips' made a substantial profit and the eventual sum repaid to the trust was far in excess of the original sums invested. Meanwhile, Perky has persuaded both trustees to sell the furniture and family heirlooms and to purchase a sports car for him with the proceeds of the former and to donate the rest to charity.

In 2014, Perky dies and his two living children become aware of how the trust has been administered. Have they any cause for complaint and, if so, what are their remedies?

How to Read this Question

This problem question requires you to deal with a combination of issues. It is clear that trust duties are imposed on Alex and Bernard. Identify the possible breaches of trust by the trustees. Consider the liability of each or both trustees. Are there any grounds for relief? May the beneficiaries trace their assets in the hands of third parties?

How to Answer this Question

In answering this question you are required to deal with the trustees' duty to exercise reasonable care in appointing an agent, James, and reviewing his conduct. The appointment is required to be in writing which is absent in this question. Assuming Alex is liable for breach of trust would Bernard, the co-trustee, also be liable? Trustees are jointly and severally liable for breach of trust. May Bernard claim a contribution from Alex? Consider the measure of loss to the trust. Has there been a breach of trust when Perky persuades the trustees to sell the furniture and use the funds for Perky's personal benefit? In addition the beneficiaries may be entitled to trace their funds in the sports car and heirlooms in the hands of the purchasers.

Up for Debate

Questions on breach of trust vary enormously. It is necessary to focus not only on the breach by trustees but also to consider the reliefs and defences, if any, that are available to the trustees. The nature of the loss to the trust as well as the available remedies are all treated as a package. A useful article that deals with the loss to the trust is D Capper, 'Compensation for breach of trust' (1997) 61 Conv 14.

Answer Structure

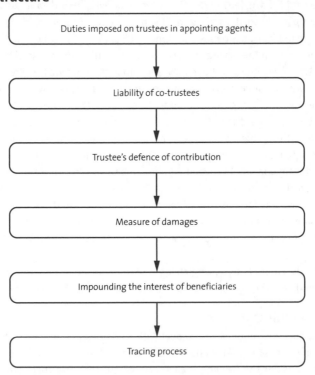

```
┌─────────────────────────────────────────────┐
│  Duties imposed on trustees in appointing agents  │
└─────────────────────────────────────────────┘
                      │
                      ▼
┌─────────────────────────────────────────────┐
│           Liability of co-trustees             │
└─────────────────────────────────────────────┘
                      │
                      ▼
┌─────────────────────────────────────────────┐
│       Trustee's defence of contribution        │
└─────────────────────────────────────────────┘
                      │
                      ▼
┌─────────────────────────────────────────────┐
│             Measure of damages                 │
└─────────────────────────────────────────────┘
                      │
                      ▼
┌─────────────────────────────────────────────┐
│     Impounding the interest of beneficiaries    │
└─────────────────────────────────────────────┘
                      │
                      ▼
┌─────────────────────────────────────────────┐
│              Tracing process                   │
└─────────────────────────────────────────────┘
```

This diagram depicts the main issues in answering the question.

ANSWER

On the face of it, one might think that Perky's children had little to complain about. As the problem makes clear, the sum held by the trust at Perky's death was 'far in excess' of the original sums and the investment policy seems to have been successful.

However, the essential nature of liability for breach of trust is that it is restitutionary: it should restore to the trust fund all the loss causally linked to any breach of trust and it matters not that certain activities of the trustees have brought considerable gains to the trust (*Dimes v Scott* (1828); *Bartlett v Barclays Bank Trust Co (No 2)* (1980)). Likewise, where investment powers are in question, the possibility of a breach is measured against the duty of care laid down in **s1** of the **Trustee Act 2000** namely, that a trustee 'must exercise such care and skill as is reasonable in the circumstances', having regard to any special knowledge or experience that the trustee has, or holds himself out as having, and with regard to any special knowledge and skill acquired by the trustee acting in the course of business. As under the law before the **2000 Act**, it is likely that fulfilment of the trustee's duty in regard to investments is not to be measured in terms of absolute results, be they gains or losses (see, also, *Nestlé v National Westminster Bank* (1993)), but in terms of the care exercised on reaching the gain or loss. Seen in this light, this problem raises a number of issues concerning the trustees' potential liability for breach of trust. In particular, it is necessary to determine, first, whether there have been any breaches of trust which have caused loss to the trust fund; second, who has caused these breaches and who is responsible in law for them; third, whether the trustees may raise any defences in an action by the beneficiaries; and, fourth, whether there are any other remedies the beneficiaries might pursue if the action for breach of trust proves insufficient to meet their claims.

The first matter to examine is whether Alex or Bernard, or both, can be said to have committed a breach of trust when the initial investments recommended and effected by James result in a substantial loss. There is no breach of trust simply because investments make a loss or only a little profit. That risk is in the nature of investment (*Nestlé v National Westminster Bank* (1993)). However, there are a number of reasons why Alex and Bernard might be liable. It will be remembered that Alex is the 'active' trustee in this matter and it is he who initiates these events. So, focusing on his position, it is clear that when exercising investment powers, he must meet the duty of care specified in **s1** of the **Trustee Act 2000**. This is to take reasonable care in all the circumstances (taking account of any particular skills he has or professes). The exact scope of this duty remains to be elucidated by the courts, but because Alex is not, and does not purport to be, an investment professional (who, after the Act may owe higher duties), his duty may well equate to the old common law standard of having to take such care as an ordinary prudent man of business would exercise when considering making an investment for the benefit of others (*Learoyd v Whitely* (1887)).

Moreover, in exercising this power, it is perfectly in order for Alex to employ an agent (**s11** of the **Trustee Act 2000**), provided that, because this is an asset management function (that is, investment), such delegation is either in writing or evidenced in writing (**s15** of the **Trustee Act 2000**).

Applying this law to our case, it appears that Alex is in breach of trust because even if he believed that James was a suitable person to act in this capacity (that is, assuming that Alex has discharged his duty of care with respect to the appointment: query James's inexperience), the appointment is not in writing or evidenced in writing. In consequence, all loss caused by the breach can be recovered from Alex and possibly from Bernard (see below) (*Target Holdings Ltd v Redferns* (1995); *Swindle v Harrison* (1997)). Note, however, that Alex (and possibly Bernard) is liable because of his failure to properly appoint. He is not liable because James has made a poor choice of investment because, even if such a poor choice amounted to a breach of trust, s 23 of the **Trustee Act 2000** makes it clear that a trustee is only liable for the acts of agents (such as James) if the appointment was effective (as in our case) or if the trustee failed in his duty to review the actions of the agent (of which in our case there is no evidence).

Assuming then that Alex has committed a breach of trust, what is the position of Bernard? Clearly, Bernard is not vicariously liable for Alex's actions (see s 23 of the **Trustee Act 2000**), but it may well be that Bernard has failed in his own duties to supervise the trust properly by failing to question Alex about his proposed dealings (*Styles v Guy* (1849)). A so-called 'passive' trustee cannot escape liability for breach of trust if that passivity itself amounts to a neglect of duty breaching the duty of care of the **Trustee Act 2000**. This could be the case in respect of the first amount of money paid to James and, if so, Alex and Bernard are jointly and severally liable to the beneficiaries. It seems unlikely that Bernard can be held responsible for the second payment of money to James unless he was so inattentive of the trust's affairs so as to fail in his duty. There is no evidence to support this and consequently Bernard should be able to claim a contribution from Alex under the **Civil Liability (Contribution) Act 1978**.

This brings us to the measure of loss. As is made clear, the second transaction actually makes a profit for the trust and, without doubt, this profit must be held for the beneficiaries, whether deriving from a breach of trust or not (*Vyse v Foster* (1874)). The real issue is whether the trustees will be able to set off the gains made by the second transaction against the losses made in the first (*Dimes v Scott* (1828)). The general principle from *Dimes* is that this is not permitted unless the 'two' transactions are so interdependent that one follows inextricably from the other (*Bartlett v Barclays Bank Trust Co (No 2)* (1980)). That limited exception is unlikely to apply here, leaving Alex (and possibly Bernard) liable to compensate for the loss caused to the beneficiaries by the breach in respect of the first investment (there being no loss with respect to the breach over the second set of investments).

It is also clear that a breach of trust is committed when Perky persuades the trustees to sell the furniture and heirlooms and to use the money for his personal benefit and for donations to charity. Such instigation of a breach of trust by the beneficiary will not only prevent Perky claiming against the trustees for any loss arising out of these breaches (*Life Association of Scotland v Siddal* (1861)), it may also result in his interest being confiscated to indemnify the trustees in so far as they are required to make restitution to the trust estate (*Chillingworth v Chambers* (1896) and s 62 of the **Trustee Act 1925**). In this connection, it is quite possible (even likely) that Perky is aware that his request amounts to a breach of trust (so satisfying *Re Somerset* (1894)) and his chances of avoiding the impounding of his interest are slim. However, any loss not covered from the use of Perky's interest will have to be met by the two trustees and it is unlikely in the circumstances of this case that they will have a defence under s 61 of the **Trustee Act 1925**.

Finally, if the personal actions against the trustees fail to recover the full loss to the trust estate, there is the possibility that the beneficiaries could trace the funds from the sale of the furniture to Perky's sports car (Perky not being a bona fide purchaser for value) and possibly also trace the heirlooms to the person now possessing them. Note, however, this may well prove impossible if the current possessor is a purchaser in good faith *(Re Diplock* (1948)).

QUESTION 43

George, a wealthy banker, comes to you for advice about a number of financial arrangements he wishes to make for his family and others. He has already drawn up a trust deed which appoints Abbott and Hardy as his executors and trustees and charges them with distributing:

(a) a reasonable amount of the money from my account at the Bounty Bank, within three years of my death, between such of my employees as my wife shall determine, the remainder to be divided equally between my children; and

(b) the residue of my estate to the inhabitants of my old village of Stanbrooke in such proportions as my trustees shall in their discretion determine.

During your discussions with George, it transpires that he has several bank accounts at the Bounty Bank and that his employees number over 5,000. Furthermore, your own researches reveal that the village of Stanbrooke now forms part of Greater London and is now officially called the London Borough of Stanbrooke.

▶ **He seeks your advice on all of his proposals.**

How to Read this Question

This problem question raises a number of interesting issues on aspects of certainties of subject matter and objects, construction of George's intention as to whether he wishes to create a power of appointment or discretionary trust and which is preferable.

How to Answer this Question

This question requires you to evaluate the various proposals put forward by George in the light of the three certainties required to establish a valid trust. In particular, this problem raises preliminary questions about certainty of subject matter and calls for a distinction to be drawn between trusts and powers, as this will define the nature of the trustees' duties. Finally, as George intends to make a number of class gifts – that is, gifts to a group of people who are not named individually but defined by reference to a shared characteristic – it is necessary to consider whether the objects of his trusts or powers satisfy the requirement for certainty of objects.

Up for Debate

The broad nature of discretionary trusts and its popularity as a tax avoidance tool requires thorough study. An article that explores the ramifications of the *Baden* principle in depth is Y Gribch, 'Baden: awakening the conceptually moribund trust' (1974) 37 MLR 643.

Answer Structure

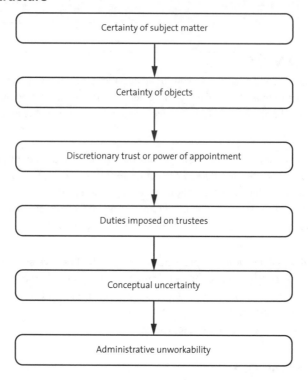

```
┌─────────────────────────────────────────────┐
│           Certainty of subject matter         │
└─────────────────────────────────────────────┘
                       │
                       ▼
┌─────────────────────────────────────────────┐
│              Certainty of objects             │
└─────────────────────────────────────────────┘
                       │
                       ▼
┌─────────────────────────────────────────────┐
│     Discretionary trust or power of appointment │
└─────────────────────────────────────────────┘
                       │
                       ▼
┌─────────────────────────────────────────────┐
│            Duties imposed on trustees         │
└─────────────────────────────────────────────┘
                       │
                       ▼
┌─────────────────────────────────────────────┐
│             Conceptual uncertainty            │
└─────────────────────────────────────────────┘
                       │
                       ▼
┌─────────────────────────────────────────────┐
│           Administrative unworkability        │
└─────────────────────────────────────────────┘
```

This diagram identifies some of the relevant points in answering this question.

ANSWER

(a) Reasonable Amount of Money from George's Account at the Bounty Bank, etc.

It is clear that George intends to transfer the money in his 'account' to his executors and trustees for them to hold at the direction of his wife. The first point must be to advise George that there is a danger that his disposition will be void for uncertainty of subject matter, irrespective of whether it is a trust or a power. There are two problems in this regard. On the one hand, the property held to his wife's direction is said to be 'a reasonable amount' of money standing in a bank account. This is indeterminate and it is unclear over what proportion of the money George's wife may exercise her discretion.

There is apparent uncertainty of subject matter. In *Re Golay* (1965), a trust of 'reasonable income' was held to be certain (reasonableness being an objective limitation that could be decided by the court), but the best advice would be to warn George not to rely on the court adopting a similarly generous construction of his will. He should be specific about the amount given to his wife's discretion. Likewise, and in any event, there is manifest uncertainty of subject matter, given that George has not identified from which of his accounts at the Bounty Bank the money is to be drawn (see, by analogy, *Boyce v Boyce* (1849)). This should be cured by a more accurate description of the specific source of the subject matter of the proposed trust/power, perhaps by use of an account number.

George should also be advised that this disposition could be construed in two ways, each investing his wife with different responsibilities and having fundamentally different consequences for his employees. First, this could be a non-exhaustive discretionary trust in favour of his employees, with a fixed trust in equal shares for his daughters of that amount of money which remains undistributed. Second, this could be a power of appointment given to his wife – probably as a non-fiduciary – with a fixed trust in default of appointment for his daughters in equal shares. The matter is not academic because, if the first construction is adopted, George's wife will be under a duty to distribute at least some money amongst the class of employees, who can then be regarded as beneficiaries under a trust able to compel her to do so. If, on the other hand, the second construction is adopted, George's wife will have a mere power to distribute among the employees, which she may or may not exercise as she chooses. The employees would be merely objects of the power with no enforceable claim to the property, with the daughters being regarded as the beneficiaries in default under the fixed trust.

Clearly, for both George's wife and the employees, resolution of this issue is important. The disposition itself gives little away, although leaving the 'remainder' to his daughters does suggest an intention to benefit at least some of his employees and hence a duty to distribute (a discretionary trust) might be implied. Conversely, it is rare to see the power of discretion under a discretionary trust being given to someone who is not a trustee (the wife), and it might be thought that the reference to George's daughters is intended to be a gift over in default of appointment, thus indicating a power (*Mettoy Pension Trustees Ltd v Evans* (1990)). To avoid this confusion, George should be advised to indicate clearly both the nature of his wife's duties and the rights of his employees. However, in at least one respect, it does not matter whether this is a discretionary trust or power because, since *McPhail v Doulton* (1971), the test for certainty of objects for discretionary trusts and powers has been the same. Moreover, it is likely that it *is* possible to say with certainty whether any given person is, or is not, an 'employee', and thus the class of beneficiaries or objects (as the case may be) is certain. This would be so whether Stamp LJ's, Sachs LJ's or Megaw LJ's analysis of the 'is or is not' test put forward in *Re Baden (No 2)* (1973), is accepted as correct, for there appear to be no evidential problems such as would trouble Stamp LJ. Finally, if this disposition is construed to be a discretionary trust, George should not fear that his disposition will be void for 'administrative unworkability'. There is nothing here to compare with the trust in *R v District Auditor ex p West Yorkshire MC* (1986), as the class of 5,000 does not seem too disparate or large to prevent his wife making a rational selection. Likewise, if this is a power, there is no 'capriciousness' here within the meaning given by Templeman J in *Re Manisty* (1974).

(b) The Residue of his Estate to the Inhabitants of my Old Village of Stanbrooke, etc.

This is clearly an attempt to establish a discretionary trust in favour of a class of beneficiaries defined by reference to a geographical condition. The intention is clear from the words used by George (that is, the trustees *shall* distribute), and the subject matter is certain. Any difficulty that there may be arises from doubts as to the certainty of the objects of the intended discretionary trust. There are three issues here, the first of which may be resolved by construction of George's disposition.

The first potential difficulty arises from the fact that the 'village' of Stanbrooke apparently is no more, having been subsumed by the London Borough of the same name. However, although this appears to raise questions concerning the certainty of the objects of the class, it will not be fatal to the validity of George's discretionary trust. For example, it may be possible to identify the old village and, in any event, there is no reason why, on a benevolent construction of the terms of the trust, the London Borough should not be taken to be the relevant geographical limitation. The matter is really one of ascertainability of the class rather than of certainty proper. However, the second difficulty is more pressing: whether, under the *McPhail* test of certainty of objects for discretionary trusts, it is possible to say with certainty whether any given person is, or is not, an 'inhabitant' of Stanbrooke. Much depends on whether the description 'inhabitant' is conceptually certain (compare Sachs LJ in *Re Baden (No 2)*), for there is unlikely to be any evidential difficulties once the class is geographically defined. In this sense, Stamp LJ's interpretation in *Baden* will not cause difficulties. Thus, if 'inhabitant' can be said to be certain – perhaps construed to mean 'resident' – George's discretionary trust will be valid. This is the most likely result, given the court's preference for validity rather than invalidity. Note, also, that in *R v District Auditor ex p West Yorkshire MC* (1986), a discretionary trust for 'inhabitants' did not fail the 'is or is not' test of certainty. Finally, there is always the danger that a court would decide that a class defined geographically was 'administratively unworkable' in the same way that the court in *West Yorkshire* went on to hold the discretionary trust void even though it had passed the 'is or is not' test. In that case, there were some 2.5 million potential beneficiaries and it must be a question of degree in each case whether the trustees can exercise their responsibilities under the trust in the light of the size and composition of the class. If there is a danger of this in our case – and to some extent it will depend on the geographical construction given to the trust – George would be best to define his class with greater precision so as not to overburden his trustees.

QUESTION 44

Mark, who has recently died, made a will in 2013 in which he made the following dispositions:

(a) my houses in Southwark and Suffolk on trust for my daughters, Amanda and Barbara, for their lifetimes and thence in equal shares between such of my other kinsfolk now living as may be resident in the London Borough of Southwark, save only that no person of the Protestant faith shall be entitled to any portion;

(b) the residue of my estate to Charles and David upon trust for such charitable or phil-
    anthropic objects as my trustees shall select.

▶ Consider the validity of the above dispositions.

How to Read this Question

This two part problem question requires you to deal with the tests for certainty of objects in respect of a private, fixed trust and the test of exclusivity in respect of public charitable trusts

How to Answer this Question

In answering this question you are required to deal with principles of certainty of objects in respect of fixed trusts. In this case it is the expression 'kinsfolk' that may cause some difficulty as well as the religious bar. The second part of the question raises issues concerning the validity of charitable trusts, in particular the test for certainty of objects.

Up for Debate

The notion of the imposition of a religious bar as a means of identifying the beneficiaries does not appear to be void on public policy grounds. Such clauses may be immoral but it appears that they are valid, see *Re Lysaght* (1966).

Answer Structure

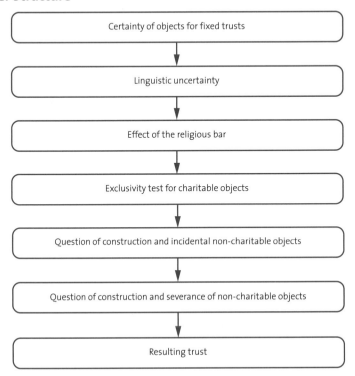

This diagram collects the main issues relevant to the problem.

ANSWER

(a) The Houses in Southwark and Suffolk

It is clear from the wording of the first disposition in Mark's will that a trust is intended. Although use of the word 'trust' does not always impose a trust in law (*Tito v Waddell (No 2)* (1977)), there is nothing here to suggest otherwise. Likewise, the subject matter of the trust is certain, always assuming Mark did own houses in Southwark and Suffolk. The problem is, then, one of certainty of objects. Clearly, there is no difficulty with the life interests given to Mark's daughters, who are both named. The disposition will operate under the **Trusts of Land and Appointment of Trustees Act 1996**, with Amanda and Barbara being given the rights to possession, etc., established by that statute. The problem arises with the class of persons entitled to the reversionary interests, being 'my kinsfolk now living as may be resident in the London borough of Southwark' and then subject to an exclusion against any person of the Protestant religion.

First, it is necessary to determine the nature of the trust affecting the two houses for this will help determine whether there is certainty of objects of the reversionary class. The houses are given in equal shares to the 'kinsfolk', etc., and thus Mark has fixed in advance the share of each person within the class. The trustees have no discretion to apportion the trust property among the class but must divide it up equally. This is a fixed trust and because the court must be able to execute the trust in default of the trustees and divide the property equally, the test of certainty of the objects is the 'complete list' test laid down in *IRC v Broadway Cottages Trust* (1955). It must be possible to draw up a complete list of all Thomas's 'kinsfolk' who currently reside in the borough of Southwark.

This may prove difficult, not because of the residence restriction, for that should be easy enough to determine, but because 'kinsfolk' is an imprecise concept. It will only be possible to draw up a list of kinsfolk if we know what 'kinsfolk' actually means. Such inherent uncertainty in the concept used by Mark to define his class may prove fatal unless the court is prepared to redefine the concept for the trustees in the same way that the Court of Appeal redefined 'relatives' in *Re Baden (No 2)* (1973). This should not be ruled out since a court of equity will generally prefer validity to invalidity, especially if the trustees' duties are not otherwise difficult to perform evidentially. Finally, even if the court adopts a benevolent attitude to the fixed trust, there is still the requirement that no person may have a share if he or she is 'of the Protestant religion'. Clearly, the point is that 'not being a Protestant' is to be a condition precedent for entry to the class of beneficiaries. Consequently, the scope of the condition precedent must also be certain because, otherwise, it will be impossible to determine who has been excluded. The test of certainty for conditions precedent is that it must be possible to say with certainty whether one person would or would not fulfil the condition (*Re Allen* (1958) and *Re Barlow* (1979)). As is clear from *Re Tuck* (1978), a condition precedent related to religion can be regarded as certain under this test although, in that case, a third person was given the task of deciding who fell within the religious condition. Subject then to it being possible to define what qualifies a person as 'a Protestant', the condition precedent will be valid. If the fixed trust for the class fails, a resulting trust for the residuary beneficiaries will arise.

(b) Residue to Charles and David upon Trust ...

The first question in issue is whether this gift of the residue of the estate is charitable. In the problem, the will transfers 'The residue of the estate to Charles and David upon trust for such charitable or philanthropic objects'. This raises the question as to whether the test for charitable objects is satisfied.

Charitable trusts, like private trusts, are subject to a test of certainty of objects. A charitable trust is subject to a unique test for certainty of objects, namely, whether the objects are exclusively charitable. This is affirmed in **s1(1)(a)** of the **Charities Act 2011**. In other words, if the trust funds may be used solely for charitable purposes the test will be satisfied. Indeed, it is unnecessary for the settlor or testator to specify the charitable objects which are intended to acquire the trust property: provided that the trust instrument manifests a clear intention to devote the funds for 'charitable purposes', the test will be satisfied.

Referring back to the problem, the question in turn concerns the construction of the expression 'or'. If this conjunction is used disjunctively, as is the norm, it would follow that the test for certainty of charitable objects will not be satisfied as otherwise philanthropic objects that are not charitable would, in theory, be entitled to benefit. In *Chichester Diocesan Fund v Simpson* (1944), a testator directed his executor to apply the residue of his estate 'for such charitable or benevolent objects' as they may select. The executors assumed that the clause created a valid charitable gift and distributed most of the funds to charitable bodies. The court decided that the clause did not create charitable gifts and therefore the gifts were void. A similar result was reached in *Attorney General of the Bahamas v Royal Trust* (1986). The effect will be that a resulting trust for the testator's residuary estate will arise. There is a possibility that the court may, on construction, decide that the non-charitable purposes are merely incidental to the main charitable purposes: see *Verge v Somerville* (1924). However, there is very little evidence on the facts of the problem that may support this contention. Likewise, the doctrine of severance may be too remote a possibility in order to rescue the charitable gift. Severance may be adopted if part of the funds have been devoted for charitable purposes and the remainder (or part) disposable for non-charitable purposes; see *Salisbury v Denton* (1857). In this problem there is very little evidence to support the contention that Mark, the testator, intended a division of the £5,000 for the different purposes. Alternatively, the legacy will be valid if the word 'or' is construed conjunctively in the sense that only philanthropic objects that are charitable are entitled to benefit. Again, one would be hard pressed to convince a court of such construction. The court will look at all the circumstances of the case, including the entire will and evidence that exists outside the will, to ascertain the intention of the testator.

The consequence is that the trust of the residuary estate will fail as a charity and the executors will be required to hold the same on resulting trust for the testator's next of kin.

QUESTION 45

Alfred transfers £50,000 to trustees, Joe and Jerry 'upon trusts to distribute all or such part of the income as they in their absolute discretion shall think fit for the maintenance and training of my housekeeper's daughter, Mary, until she graduates from university or reaches the age of 25, whichever happens first'. Mary, aged 24, has recently graduated from Brickfield University.

▶ Advise Joe and Jerry.

In a separate settlement Alfred transfers a valuable painting to William to hold on trust for the beneficiaries, Harold and Matilda absolutely. William decides to sell the painting at a 'knockdown' price to Jerry in return for an 'introduction fee' of £5,000. Shortly afterwards Jerry advertises the painting for sale and succeeds in selling it to a very wealthy businessman. William has now disappeared and Harold and Matilda seek your advice as to what claims, if any, they may pursue.

How to Read this Question

This two part question concerns the nature of determinable interests and the possibility of a resulting trust for the settlor, Alfred. The second part of the question involves a breach of trust by William and Jerry's liability to account to the beneficiaries, Harold and Matilda.

How to Answer this Question

You are required to answer this question by affirming that Alfred has created a discretionary trust of the income from the trust fund for Mary determinable on the occurrence of the specified events. It is a question of construction to ascertain which event determines the trust and triggers the resulting trust for Alfred. In the second part William may be liable for breaches of trust but since he has disappeared may escape a claim. In any event it may be possible that Jerry has intermeddled with trust property and may be accountable to the beneficiaries on an equitable claim of knowingly receiving trust property for his own use.

Up for Debate

The rationale of the equitable claim against Jerry has been the subject of judicial and academic controversy. Is liability restitutionary or based on fault? If the latter then what type of fault is involved? See S Gardner, 'Knowing assistance and knowing receipt: taking stock' (1996) 112 LQR 56.

Applying the law

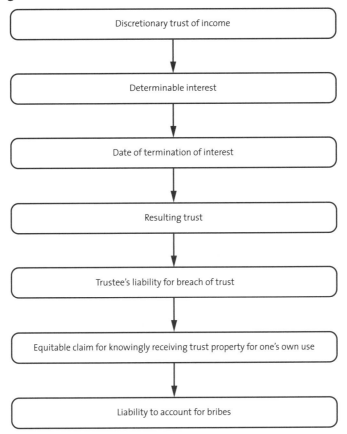

This diagram identifies the main points that are relevant to the question.

ANSWER

(i) The issue in this problem is whether Mary's beneficial interest terminates when she graduates from Brickfield University or, alternatively, whether her interest continues. If Mary's interest terminates an automatic resulting trust will arise in favour of the transferor as a default mechanism.

The transferor, Alfred, stipulated two alternative events that will trigger a termination of Mary's interest – attaining the age of 25 and graduating from University and added 'whichever happens first'. Mary has recently graduated from Brickfield University. This is the earlier event. What effect will this have in respect of the trust? It is a question of construction for the courts to decide whether this event amounts a determining event. One solution is that a resulting trust arises. The graduation from Brickfield University is a determinable condition that may signal the end of Mary's interest in the trust. This solution was adopted in *Re Abbott* (1900), where funds were raised for the benefit of two impecunious ladies. On the death of the last surviving beneficiary, creating a surplus of funds, the court decided that a resulting trust for the contributors had arisen.

Alternatively, the court may, on construction, decide that the ultimate intention of the transferor was to benefit Mary 'out and out' and education may be treated as the motive for the gift. This was the approach adopted in *Re Andrews* (1905) and *Re Osoba* (1979). There was a similarity in both of these cases in that the transfer on trust was for the education of the beneficiary and they were still capable of enjoying the benefit from the trust. In *Osoba* the court interpreted 'education' liberally and did not restrict it to formal education. In addition, the beneficiaries were still capable of benefiting from the trust. If this approach is adopted in respect of the facts of this problem it would be possible for Mary to remain a beneficiary and enjoy the income from the property until at least she attains the age of 25. On attaining that age, which is precise and does not create any room for construction, Mary's interest will terminate and a resulting trust will be set up for the transferor, Alfred.

(ii) The second element of the problem raises a number of issues, although now it is a question of whether the liability of Jerry (if any) lies in knowing receipt or dishonest assistance. It seems clear from the facts of the problem that the painting was 'sold' to Jerry for his own personal use. This seems to be a case of knowing receipt, being a case whether the stranger has received trust property for his own use (*AGIP (Africa) Ltd v Jackson* (1991)). As such, if Jerry is to be fixed with liability to account, and thereby be required to satisfy the claims of Harold and Matilda out of his own resources, it is clear that he must have acted with some degree of knowledge. This requires an understanding that the actions of William were in breach of trust (*Westdeutsche v Islington LBC* (1996)), expressed in *Akindele* (2000), as to whether it would be 'unconscionable' for Jerry to retain the benefit. Initially, of course, Jerry will claim that he is a bona fide purchaser for value of the painting and, in consequence, is not liable to account to the beneficiaries or be subject to claim involving tracing (*Re Diplock* (1948)). However, as the facts indicate, Jerry purchases the property for 'a knockdown price' and gives William an 'introduction fee'. Although one must not speculate unduly, the clear inference here is that Jerry is not bona fides. Of course, mere suspicion on his part that William is engaged in a breach of trust may not be sufficient to establish Jerry's liability; he must have 'knowledge' of the relevant facts and act 'unconscionably'. Unfortunately, what this means in practice is uncertain. The logic of the situation suggests that simple negligence (that is, any of the five categories of knowledge in *Baden Delvaux* (1983)) should suffice and this is supported by *dicta* in several cases (*International Sales Ltd v Marcus* (1982); *Belmont Finance Corporation v Williams Furniture (No 2)* (1980); *AGIP (Africa) Ltd v Jackson* (1991); *Box v Barclays* (1998)). However, other authorities have moved away from such an approach and have placed more emphasis on the 'want of probity' or deliberate fault of the stranger (that is, intention or recklessness). The case for restricting liability in this fashion is strongly argued in *Re Montague* (1987), and a spate of cases involving the alleged liability of professional financial advisers has tended to confirm this view (*Cowan de Groot Properties v Eagle Trust plc* (1992); *Polly Peck International plc v Nadir (No 2)* (1992)). In these so-called 'commercial' cases, the powerful nature of the constructive trust was emphasised and there were fears that commercial transactions would be hampered if mere negligence could trigger the personal liability of the stranger, especially as the stranger might well be liable in any event for breach of contract. As yet the matter is unclear and the decision in *Akindele*, that it is better to think in terms of unconscionability, may not prove any more helpful. In our case, while there is no doubt that Jerry was negligent, there is also evidence to suggest that he was, at best, reckless and, at worst, that he conspired with William to defeat the rights of the beneficiaries, all for personal gain. In such circumstances, there is a good chance that he would be held liable to account for knowing receipt. Likewise, if William was available, he would have been liable for breach of trust in selling the property at below the market value and accountable for the 'introduction fee' as having derived a profit from his position as trustee (*Williams v Barton* (1927); *Box v Barclays* (1998)). Further, if this was a bribe, William would be accountable for allowing his interests to conflict with his duties in accordance with the principle laid down in *Sinclair v Versailles* (2011). This significant case refused to follow the constructive trust route laid down in *Attorney General for Hong Kong v Reid* (1994).

Index